Nevada's Changing Wildlife Habitat

Nevada's Changing Wildlife Habitat

AN ECOLOGICAL HISTORY

George E. Gruell
with Sherman Swanson

University of Nevada Press
RENO AND LAS VEGAS

University of Nevada Press, Reno, Nevada 89557 USA
Copyright © 2012 by University of Nevada Press
All rights reserved
Manufactured in the United States of America
Design by Kathleen Szawiola

Library of Congress Cataloging-in-Publication Data
Gruell, George E.
Nevada's changing wildlife habitat : an ecological history / George E. Gruell
with Sherman Swanson.
p. cm.
Includes bibliographical references and index.
ISBN 978-0-87417-871-5 (hardcover : alk. paper) — ISBN 978-0-87417-878-4 (ebook)
1. Habitat (Ecology)—Nevada—History. 2. Natural history—Nevada. 3. Desert ecology—
Nevada—History. 4. Nature—Effect of human beings on—Nevada—History.
5. Human ecology—Nevada—History. 6. Landscape changes—Nevada—History.
7. Ecological disturbances—Nevada—History. 8. Nevada—Environmental conditions.
I. Swanson, Sherman 1952–   II. Title.
QH105.N3G78 2012
577.09793—dc23   2011039282

The paper used in this book is a recycled stock made from 30 percent post-consumer waste
materials, certified by FSC, and meets the requirements of American National Standard for
Information Sciences—Permanence of Paper for Printed Library Materials, ANSI/NISO
Z39.48-1992 (R2002). Binding materials were selected for strength and durability.

FIRST PRINTING
21 20 19 18 17 16 15 14 13 12
5 4 3 2 1

Contents

Illustrations

LONG
VALLEY

Sheldon
Wildlife
Refuge

PINE FOREST
RANGE

Owyhee River
East Fork

Jarbidge River

Mountain City

Bull Run Mtns

Bruneau River

Goose
Creek

Quinn River

Owyhee River
South Fork

Wildhorse
Reservoir

JARBIDGE MTNS

SANTA ROSA
RANGE

TUSCARORA MTNS

INDEPENDENCE VALLEY
INDEPENDENCE MNTS

N. Fk. Humboldt

Marys River

THOUSAND
SPRINGS
VALLEY

JACKSON MTNS

Black Rock Desert

Humboldt River

Winnemucca

BOULDER
VALLEY

Carlin

Elko

Wells

INDEPENDENCE
VALLEY

GRASS VALLEY

HUMBOLDT RANGE

Battle
Mountain

SHOSHONE RANGE

Reese River

Huntington Ck.

Huntington Valley

RUBY MTNS

RUBY VALLEY

EAST
HUMBOLDT
RANGE

GOSHUTE
VALLEY

Pyramid
Lake

Winnemucca
Lake

Lovelock

WEST HUMBOLDT
RANGE

CORTEZ MTNS

GRASS
VALLEY

ROBERTS
MTNS

Ruby Lake

ANTELOPE
VALLEY

Humboldt
Sink

STILLWATER RANGE

CLAN ALPINE MTNS

ANTELOPE VALLEY

SIMPSON PARK MTNS

ANTELOPE VALLEY

DIAMOND VALLEY

DIAMOND MTNS

LONG
VALLEY

PAH RAH
RANGE

Stillwater
Marsh

DESTOYA MTNS

SHOSHONE MTNS

Austin

KOBEH
VALLEY

Eureka

EGAN RANGE

Ely

STEPTOE VALLEY

SCHELL CREEK RANGE

SPRING
VALLEY

LONG
VALLEY

Truckee
River

Reno

Fallon

Lahontan Res.

WHITE PINE MTNS

CARSON
RANGE

Virginia City

Carson City

Genoa

Carson
River

Walker
Lake

TOIYABE RANGE

BIG SMOKY VALLEY

TOQUIMA RANGE

MONITOR RANGE

MONITOR VALLEY

ANTELOPE RANGE

SNAKE RANGE

SWEETWATER
MTNS

Tonopah

Pioche

S I E R R A   N E V A D A

Meadow Valley Wash

DEATH VALLEY

Lake
Mead

N

Pahrump

Las Vegas

0 10 20 30 40 50 60 mi

Preface

The hiker who spends a day enjoying Nevada's high mountains is not likely to see the mountain lion that is watching him. The motorist traveling a lonely highway through one of Nevada's sprawling valleys glimpses movement amidst the high-desert vegetation and then spots a coyote trying to catch a mouse before it can dive into a burrow. A driver stirring a dust trail on a dirt road notices an antelope keeping pace alongside. Experienced in the ways of antelope, the driver knows the animal might turn and dart in front of the vehicle at any moment.

We seldom consider that the landscapes we see today were once inhabited by animals that became extinct long ago. Boys on mountain bikes in the Pine Nut Range east of Gardnerville-Minden spot some large bones that are later identified as those of a prehistoric wooly mammoth. The floor of a chilly limestone cave in northeastern Nevada yields bone fragments of a saber-toothed tiger, a prehistoric bison (buffalo), and a camel. Tracks preserved in sandstone show that a giant ground sloth once crossed the land now occupied by the Nevada State Prison.

This book examines ecological evidence of changes in plants and animals from the Pleistocene ice ages to modern times. What wildlife species occupied Nevada before settlers arrived? What kind of vegetation supported these wildlife communities? How have the habitats changed over time, and how do these changes affect wildlife and humans today?

The book focuses on the "cold desert" region of Nevada as distinguished from the "hot desert" to the south. The cold desert is situated within the Great Basin, a physiographic region roughly between the Sierra Nevada of California and the Wasatch Mountains of Utah that is cut off from external drainage to the Pacific Ocean. The landscape is characterized by a basin and range topography made up of north–south-trending mountain ranges, many to above eleven thousand feet in elevation. The intervening valleys are arid, with some receiving less than four inches of precipitation in an average year. The mountainous areas are relatively moist, with some high-elevation sites receiving up to forty inches of precipitation annually on average. Although averages are useful statistics, seasonal variations and changes from one year to the next may be more important. Plants may grow as much as six times more in wet years than in dry years.

The area that constitutes Nevada today was acquired by the United States in 1848 through the Mexican-American War and the resulting Treaty of Guadalupe. Less than 20 percent of the land has since passed into state or private ownership. Management of the balance is largely the responsibility of the Bureau of Land Management in the U.S. Department of the Interior and the Forest Service in the U.S. Department of Agriculture. Many of the more productive wildlife summer ranges are situated on lands managed by the Forest Service.

Nevadans are regularly exposed to widely differing opinions about the condition of our vast public lands and how they should be managed. Wildlife-related issues are particularly hot-button items. Some environmental activists call for removing all types of livestock, which they argue are fundamentally destructive of soils and vegetation. Conversely, ranchers assert that livestock have a positive influence by stimulating plant growth and reducing wildfires. The controversy has wide-ranging implications, particularly for sage grouse and mule deer. Wildlife preservation groups routinely petition the U.S. Fish and Wildlife Service to list the greater sage grouse as an endangered species, claiming it is in jeopardy of becoming extinct. The long-term decline of mule deer is a concern of sportsmen and the Nevada Department of Wildlife.

Some activists object to the cutting of pinyon-juniper woodlands and use of prescribed fire to enhance productivity or resilience, arguing that ecosystems need protection from disturbance in order to heal. Environmental writer Dan Dagget has pointed out that this message is so familiar that most of us do not realize that it is an assumption rather than proven fact.[1] The missing element that might help us reach consensus on appropriate management is a sound understanding of landscape changes that have occurred since the Pleistocene, particularly over the past 150 years.

Our discussion begins in part I with the prehistoric western Great Basin, covering the period from the end of the last major ice age through the pre-Columbian era. The evidence that researchers are accumulating presents a surprisingly dynamic environment profoundly affected by changing climate and the activities of native people. Human influences on the land changed dramatically after the arrival of the Spanish conquistadores along with their European diseases and horses. Next we consider the native peoples, their lifestyles, and their effects on the landscape before they were marginalized and displaced by European Americans in the mid-1800s.

Part II chronicles ecological evidence of what historic landscapes were like. Periodically disturbed by fire, many landscapes were moving through early stages of plant succession. Wildlife species preferring early succession grasses and forbs were widely distributed. Reduction and loss of these plants following European settlement had a major influence on wildlife populations.

The postsettlement period, discussed in part III, considers the influence on vegetation of climate, woodcutting, livestock grazing, and changes in fire occurrence. Scientific evidence has demonstrated that plant growth is strongly linked to extreme weather events occurring at irregular intervals. We discuss the impacts of the removal of large volumes of pinyon, juniper, and other conifers in areas of western and central Nevada during silver-mining operations. We then move on to the mining boom and the associated increase in livestock grazing, which significantly altered vegetation and led to remarkable changes. Federal legislation that moderated the impacts of livestock grazing resulted in further unintended vegetation changes.

Once the historical background has been set, we revisit the role of fire on vegetation. Removal of grassy fuels by livestock virtually eliminated fire during the initial stage of Euro-American settlement. Later reductions in grazing caused fuels to build up, which along with the introduction of nonnative annual grasses and other weeds dramatically changed fire dynamics. The result has been wildfires that have burned millions of acres, particularly during the past dozen years. Some of these fires have been detrimental and others beneficial, depending on management and site potential.

Part IV addresses the remarkable changes in plant communities and wildlife that resulted from livestock grazing and the absence or marked reduction of fire disturbance. Changes include an enormous increase in woody shrubs and trees, and marked decline and loss of herbaceous plants. Dramatic changes in wildlife populations took place in concert with the transformation of wildlife habitat. Indiscriminate "hunting" was also a factor. Some animals became extinct; others became scarce or rare; still others responded favorably to the habitat changes.

The concluding chapter addresses current land management practices and options for sustaining plant communities critical to wildlife.

Appendixes 1 and 2, respectively, summarize the changes in vegetation, fire regimes, and wildlife over the period we consider in this book; and list common and scientific names of plants found in the cold desert discussed in this book.

Acknowledgments

Preparation of this book turned out to be an engrossing and demanding endeavor. Its publication would not have been possible without the steadfast support of forest ecologist Stephen F. Arno, U.S. Forest Service (retired). Steve provided seemingly endless inputs during the preparation and reviews of the draft manuscript.

A debt of gratitude is extended to Bob Stewart, Bureau of Land Management (retired), whose writing skills and knowledge of Nevada history made the initial draft more readable for general audiences. We thank James Brown, U.S. Forest Service research forester (retired); Eugene Hattori, Nevada State Museum curator of anthropology; the late Dave Mathis, Nevada Agricultural Department; Kent McAdoo, natural resource specialist, University of Nevada Cooperative Extension; Jenny Wilson, ranger, U.S. Forest Service, Carson Ranger District; and Alma Winward, U.S. Forest Service range ecologist (retired), for their review of chapter drafts and suggestions leading to substantial improvements.

Special thanks are extended to Amy Shannon, life sciences librarian at the University of Nevada, Reno, who skillfully located some of the more obscure references. Toni Mendive of the Northeast Nevada Museum was particularly helpful in locating historical documents. Bob Olson, U.S. Forest Service (retired), contributed pertinent documents from his wide-ranging natural resource collection for which we are grateful.

We are indebted to Dave Atkins, Doug Crocker, Cherrie Howell, Karen Kumiega, Ed Monnig, Tom Montoya, José Norega, Dave Palmer, Nancy Prall, Cheryl Probert, Bob Sommer, John Speck, Robin Tausch, Jeff Ulrich, and Steve Williams, all of the U.S. Forest Service; Keith Barker, Ken Ditwiler, Jim Genola (retired), Sandy Gregory, Fred Parry (retired), Ty Peterson, and Jim Yoakum (retired), all of the Bureau of Land Management; John Christopherson, Mike Dondero, and Rich Harvey, of the Nevada Division of Forestry; Larry Gilbertson, Mike Cox, Jim Jeffers (retired), Donald King (retired), Merlin McColm (retired), and Tony Wasley, of the Nevada Department of Wildlife; Charlie Clements and James Young (retired) of the Agricultural Research Service; and Jim Hulse (retired), Don Klebenow (retired), Paul Starrs, and John

Swanson, all of the University of Nevada, Reno, for sharing their knowledge and experience with us.

We are particularly grateful to Margaret Dalrymple, acquisitions editor at the University of Nevada Press, who saw the potential of this book and shepherded it through the review processes leading to publication.

Initial funding for research was provided by the Renewable Extension Act and University of Nevada Cooperative Extension.

I

Climate Changes and Consequences

The Pleistocene and Holocene Epochs
Prehuman Context

For most of the past two million years the prehistoric landscapes of the Great Basin were in the grip of the Pleistocene "Ice Age."[1] Through these millennia, vegetation responded to glacial and interglacial cycles of frigid and warm periods, and a variety of large mammals roamed the landscape (appendix 1 summarizes these events).

Paleoenvironmental studies have expanded our understanding of the late Pleistocene epoch in recent years. Core samples containing pollen from ponds, bogs, and lakes, and from sediments deposited in caves have allowed scientists to develop a virtually continuous sequential record of the plants of the region, many of which can be identified to genus or species. Studies of fossilized plant materials preserved in wood rat den middens have advanced our knowledge of climate and allowed the determination of vegetation trends going back tens of thousands of years.[2] Studies of growth rings using living and dead trees provide a definitive record of growing conditions.[3]

The Pleistocene vegetation of the Panamint Range bordering Death Valley, reflecting colder conditions 30,000–11,000 years ago, contrasts sharply with the vegetation we see in what is now one of the hottest and driest places on earth. Today's vegetation is largely creosote bush and white bursage. The vegetation 20,000 years ago was dominated by shadscale, Joshua trees, Utah juniper, and Whipple yucca. In the latter stages of the Pleistocene, Joshua trees grew at elevations down to 1,400 feet; today they are found no lower than about 4,000 feet.[4] To the northeast, in the Snake Range, pollen samples from a cave spanning 40,000 years indicate that bristlecone pine was a predominant plant both in the mountains and in the lowlands through the late stages of the Pleistocene. Pinyon pine and juniper woodlands and desert species now cover most of the lower-elevation late glacial sites that once supported bristlecone pine, which now grows 3,000 feet higher.[5] Pleistocene pollen samples from Hidden Cave in northwestern Nevada indicate that yellow pines grew at much lower elevations than today. Saltbushes, such an important vegetal component today, were at best rare during the latter stages of the Pleistocene.[6]

In northwestern Nevada, wood rat middens as much as 30,000 years old provide evidence of the plants that characterized Pleistocene vegetation. Juniper woodland covered much of the area at intermediate elevations. Whitebark pine and limber pine, now absent, grew as low as 4,530 feet in the Virginia Mountains near Reno. During this cooler period, curlleaf mountain-mahogany occurred 2,625 feet lower than it does today.[7] Studies in northern Nevada suggest that the vegetation was of an alpine and subalpine character during the late glacial period. Along the Snake River Plains–Great Basin divide, subalpine coniferous forests including subalpine fir, whitebark pine, and lodgepole pines predominated. These species grow at much higher elevations today.

During the last full glacial episode, the Wisconsin, mountain glaciers were present in sixteen of Nevada's mountain ranges—the most impressive being in Lamoille and Rattlesnake canyons on the western slope of the Ruby Mountains southeast of Elko. Calculations derived from Late Pleistocene vegetation and glaciers suggest the annual mean temperature was 9°F–13°F lower than today. Glaciers were already waning when pluvial lakes (shallow runoff lakes) in the valleys were hitting their high-water mark some 14,200 years ago.[8] The largest of these, Lake Lahontan, covered 8,665 square miles in western and northwestern Nevada and had a shoreline approximately 10,000 miles long. Pyramid and Walker lakes remain as remnants of this once vast freshwater body. Lake expansion from melting of the glaciers occurred under a warmer, wetter climate. Rapid wasting of glaciers, shrinking of Lake Lahontan and other shallower lakes, and catastrophic flooding accompanied postglacial conditions, marking the onset of the warmer Holocene epoch about 10,000 years ago.

The interglacial Holocene epoch, which continues today, has featured periods of distinctly different climates. Fluctuating climates have resulted in elevation and latitudinal shifts in vegetation, falling and rising lake levels, and buildup and melting of glaciers.

The climate in the Early Holocene, 10,000–7,500 years ago, was initially moist. During this period the Ruby Marsh was a freshwater lake deeper than today.[9] A warming period in the latter stages of the epoch saw an upward elevational shift in many plants, conversion of sagebrush communities to desert shrub, a northward movement of pinyon woodlands, and a significant reduction in lake levels or their complete desiccation.

The Middle Holocene, 7,500–3,500 years ago, has been characterized as very warm, although studies of this interval show unrelenting variability within a more arid period. July temperatures 4,500 years ago were likely 3.5°F warmer than they have been during the past few centuries. Reflecting these warmer temperatures, local tree lines in the White Mountains of eastern California and eastern Nevada's Snake Range were about five hundred feet higher than they are today.[10] Warm, dry conditions are likewise indicated at Lake Tahoe by the presence of conifer stumps submerged thirteen feet or more beneath the natural rim, having rooted there about 4,300 years ago.[11] Pyramid Lake was at a low level, and Walker Lake went dry.[12]

The later Holocene featured a much cooler and wetter climate with erratic periods of increased precipitation and decreased temperature. Mountain glaciers expanded in the Northern Hemisphere. Cooler, wetter weather, especially in the winter, allowed the pinyon and juniper trees that had earlier moved north to expand at middle and low elevations during the latter stages of the Holocene. Upper tree lines descended in elevation, and Lake Tahoe apparently spilled continuously.[13] Today's high-water mark is fifteen feet higher owing to a dam constructed in 1909–13.

This cooler and wetter climate was followed by drought beginning some 2,600 years ago and ending around AD 400. Studies covering this period suggest a dramatic decline in precipitation and an associated decline in vegetation cover. This reduction significantly increased hillside erosion, growth of alluvial fans, and alluvial deposition in channels and valley bottoms over most of the upland drainages in the central Great Basin.[14] The lack of rainfall resulted in the drying of precipitation-dependent pluvial lakes, a decrease in woodlands, and an increase in desert shrubs. Charcoal deposits and the pollen record suggest that fire was an important driver in those changes.

The major shift to warmer temperatures after the Pleistocene created new open niches in the bottom of Great Basin valleys as plant communities moved upslope. Polyploidy (having multiple sets of chromosomes) helped shadscale to evolve rapidly and move into new habitats.[15] The rapid and imperfect adaptation of desert shrub species and the plants occupying the dry end of the big sagebrush zone is likely the reason these zones are today so vulnerable to invasion by exotic annuals. In contrast, mountain big sagebrush communities have been adapting to change on the mountain for a longer time, moving around in response to changing climate.

The climate continued to fluctuate from warmer to cooler between AD 400 and 1350. During the following 500 years, known as the Little Ice Age, climatic conditions contrasted sharply with those of the previous 950 years. Lake levels and tree lines rose. The vegetation that developed during this cooler period dominated the landscape of Sierra Nevada and basin and range ecosystems when the first Europeans arrived.

A variety of prehistoric animals flourished across Nevada's landscapes during the latter stages of the Pleistocene more than 10,000 years ago.[16] Sabertooth cats, cheetahs, and American lions crept through grass that would have come to a human's waist. Like the dire wolves hunting in packs across the valleys, these predators sought herds of camels, horses, and other large herbivores. Tracks preserved in sandstone show that a lumbering ground sloth once frequented the location of the Nevada State Prison in the Carson Valley. Mammoths foraged on riparian vegetation in the shallows of Lake Lahontan north of the Jackson Mountains in Humboldt County.

The end of the Pleistocene in North America saw an episode of extinction that was astonishing in its breadth. By 10,000 years ago almost all the large mammals were gone—as were several smaller species adapted to moister conditions. Thirty-five genera of mammals and nineteen genera of birds died out within a remarkably brief period.[17] Humans may well have witnessed these late Pleistocene extinctions, and along with climate change may have been partly responsible for them.

Bones and teeth deposited in pluvial lake sediments, caves, and rock shelters record the presence of a variety of small mammals and birds that frequented the Great Basin during the latter stages of the Pleistocene and through the Holocene. Virtually all of these species have persisted to modern times.

The pika was present throughout the Great Basin at the end of the Pleistocene, ranging in Nevada from the Jarbidge Mountains to the Snake Range. Apparently unable to adapt to the relatively arid Middle Holocene climate, pikas had become extinct at low elevations on most of Nevada's mountains by 7,000 years ago. In the Toquima Range of central Nevada, the lowermost modern pika population is found at an elevation of 8,700 feet. That location is some 1,100 feet above the Gatecliff Shelter, where excavations produced fifty-eight pika specimens—only three of which had been deposited in the past 5,100 years. This dramatic change seems to record the movement to higher elevations where temperatures are more suited to pika habitat requirements.[18]

Pygmy rabbits offer further evidence of changes in animal populations coincident with long-term climate change. Typically found today in dense stands of sagebrush in deep, friable soils, these diminutive rabbits were much more widely distributed during the late Pleistocene when sagebrush dominated much of the landscape. Pygmy rabbits declined in abundance throughout much of the Great Basin sagebrush steppe about 7,000 years ago.

Scattered evidence that climate changes adversely affected other animals during the Middle Holocene is indicated by the decrease in jackrabbit numbers after 7,200 years ago at Connley Caves in southeastern Oregon, and at Danger Cave on the Utah–Nevada border after 6,500 years ago.[19]

Connley Caves also provides evidence that large mammals were adversely affected by climatic change. Twenty-four of twenty-five elk specimens discovered there were deposited between 11,000 and 7,200 years ago. Elk specimens from Last Supper Cave in northwestern Nevada appeared to be between 2,000 and 6,000 years old. Elk are unknown historically in northwestern Nevada and southeastern Oregon. These records, complemented by data from other locations, suggest that elk were once thinly scattered across the northern Great Basin. Bison apparently followed a similar distribution pattern. Grayson noted that "many large mammal collections from Holocene-age deposits in the northern half of the Great Basin contain small numbers of bison, suggesting that these animals were widespread, though apparently nowhere abundant, in this region during the past 10,000 years."[20] Their prehistoric presence in northern Nevada was confirmed in the 1960s when Bill Wright Jr. discovered a well-preserved skull in Secret Valley. These large herbivores disappeared long before European exploration of the Great Basin began.

Bighorn sheep, pronghorn, and mule deer are also represented in Holocene deposits. Bone fragments of bighorn sheep make up the great majority of large mammal materials from this period, suggesting rather high prehistoric populations. Pronghorn materials suggest that they were widely distributed, while mule deer bone fragments are routinely uncommon in prehistoric Great Basin faunas.[21]

Paleoenvironmental research has thus demonstrated profound changes in the region's plant and animal populations over the millennia as the climate varied among warm, wet, dry, and cool periods. The effects of early humans on these populations are still hotly debated, and evidence is very sparse and inconclusive. Various mammals could have played the role of keystone species by having wide-ranging effects on their ecosystems. These include the large herbivore species as well as the predators that presumably kept them moving and regulated their populations. Humans, who first entered the landscape about when the Pleistocene ended and expanded in numbers as they developed survival technologies for the new land, could have played that role as well.[22]

2

The First People
Hunters and Gatherers

Archaeological evidence suggests that the Great Basin was among the first areas of North America to be inhabited by humans.[1] Their artifacts indicate a hunting and gathering way of life involving seasonal migration between valleys and mountains to take advantage of changing resource availability. Wherever they lived, prehistoric peoples utilized a wide array of resources.[2] Marshes appear to have been especially attractive because edible plants and animals were easily found there. As the climate changed, the people adjusted to available food resources, migrated to other regions, or absorbed other peoples' cultures. Before Europeans arrived, Native Americans had no domesticated animals other than dogs and grew no crops other than the corn cultivated by the Frémont culture near Baker, Nevada, and patches of tobacco. They depended almost entirely on the wild products they could collect for food, shelter, and clothing.

Among the earliest settlement patterns in Nevada—dating back at least 4,000 years in the Reese River valley of central Nevada—was "the piñon-juniper winter village and the summer gathering camp" described by D. H. Thomas.[3] These pinyon winter villages were located above the frost pocket between the sagebrush flats and the pinyon-juniper belt. Anthropologists believe that the inhabitants returned to the same ridge year after year, but not to the same campsite. In the spring, when pinyon nut caches had generally been exhausted, the people moved to the valley floor in search of grass shoots, early-ripening tubers, and other riparian crops. Summer encampments were generally along the tributaries of the Reese River.[4]

In Nevada's Toquima Range and in the White Mountains of eastern California, prehistoric Native Americans frequented the alpine zone during the summer.[5] More than fifty hunting blinds, cairns (human-made rock piles), and associated animal drivelines have been found on Mount Jefferson, the highest mountain in the Toquima Range; all were located along the rimrock. Diagnostic artifacts associated with these hunting features imply an early use of the alpine area from roughly 4,000 years ago to approximately AD 800.

Diaries and reports of early travelers and oral interviews of tribal elders by anthropologists have created a basic understanding of the influence of Native Americans on their environment. This body of information indicates little change in the pattern of life from that of their ancestors, although innovations such as the atlatl, the use of bows rather than spears only, and better spear and arrowhead designs quickly spread from clan to clan and tribe to tribe. Historically, the Great Basin people comprised four tribes: the Washoe, Northern Paiute, Western Shoshone, and Southern Paiute.

The earliest scholarly study of the former ways of the Western Shoshone comes from 1934 interviews of a few old Indians who, as children, actually observed native life when it was relatively unaffected by civilization. One of these elders identified the location of approximately twenty-five summer camps between Austin and the upper Reese River valley. Sixteen camps on the east slope of the Toiyabes have also been identified. Historically, larger groups were concentrated in the more productive localities along the Humboldt and Reese rivers and in Ruby Valley. Because of its fertility and productive marshes, Ruby Valley had an exceptionally dense Indian population. To the south and east, Long, Butte, Independence, and Goshute valleys supported sparse populations living in small encampments at the few springs and streams. Families and family clusters commonly foraged in relatively small groups from the spring through the fall.[6] Elderly informants identified a wide variety of plants, mammals, reptiles, fish, and insects used as foods, with plants making up the greater portion of the diet. Rabbit skins (which need no tanning) and baskets, rather than tanned leathers and pottery, were among the technological innovations that sustained their nomadic lifestyle.

In early June 1826, Hudson's Bay Company trapping brigade leader Peter Skene Ogden exchanged trade items for roots dug by Indians along the Meadow Creek tributary of the Bruneau River.[7] In the spring of 1831 Ogden's successor, John Work, likewise traded with the Indians for roots on Jack Creek in the Independence Mountains.[8] Annual digging of roots on Jack Creek apparently continued into the late 1800s. R. M. Woodward, who came to the Jack Creek locality with his parents in 1876, recalled that "sometimes you would see 50–100 Indians digging on the hillsides. They would spread it on their blankets to dry for the winter use. When they left their ponies would be loaded down."[9] Early European travelers who witnessed such tuber digging coined the name

"Digger Indians" for this group. Clearly, the various roots and tubers provided a particularly important food source.

A variety of other plant materials were also gathered for food, some of the more important being pine nuts, fruits of shrubs, and the seeds of sunflowers, rye grass, and wild mustard. Anthropologist Warren d'Azevedo noted that "the remarkable retention of names for specific plants and information about their use on the part of older Washoe people in the mid-twentieth century attests to the focal importance of vegetation in the diet of Indians."[10] The cattail-eaters of the Stillwater Marsh subsisted on a wide variety of wetland foods, the most important of which were cattail, hardstem bulrush, common three-square, and sago pondweed.[11] On September 18, 1854, O. B. Huntington observed Indians at the Stillwater Marsh "thrashing the bayonette grass for its seeds that were pounded into flour."[12] In Spring Valley, Captain J. H. Simpson of the Corps of Geographical Engineers, who explored a wagon route from Camp Floyd, Utah, to Genoa, Nevada, in 1859, "noticed the women carrying on their backs monstrous willow baskets filled with a sort of carrot root, which they dig in the marsh, and the cacti, both of which they use for food."[13] In the uplands the people gathered seeds of several native sunflowers during the summer and early fall, along with the seeds of basin wildrye and Indian ricegrass. One of the more noteworthy descriptions of harvesting grass seeds is that of Virginia City newspaper writer Dan DeQuille, whose party in 1860 came upon an area of some thirty acres in the Stillwater Mountains where "the Piute woman had gathered seeds of the bunch grass."[14]

Pine nuts were an important source of food in regions south of the Humboldt River. Because pine nuts did not occur in sufficient quantities in the Battle Mountain region, local people sometimes traveled south to the vicinity of Austin to gather them. But pine nuts were not a dependable food source because yearly crops varied—a phenomenon familiar to pine nut enthusiasts today. Crop failures routinely followed years with deficient precipitation. When pine nuts were locally scarce, families would travel to outlying mountain ranges in search of better harvests. The Sulphur Springs and Roberts mountains were a prime source of pine nuts for local inhabitants. Pine nuts harvested some distance from the winter camp were cached.[15] W. J. Hoffman, attached to the Wheeler Geographical Survey, came on several such caches in the Monitor Valley of central Nevada in 1871. He reported that "a number of stones are collected, each of them from one-half to one cubic foot in bulk, which are arranged in the shape of a circle having a diameter of from 2 to 4 feet. When fruit is abundant (which happens but once in three years in respective localities), it is collected and piled into this circle, covered over with sticks and leaves, and finally a layer of earth, so as to secure them from rodents and birds."[16]

Annual harvests of pine nuts and other foods were critical for winter survival. In an 1860s conversation with an Indian friend, Dan DeQuille learned how Indians coped with imminent starvation before Euro-American contact: "Juan could still remember a time, when he was a little boy, when they were obliged to live almost wholly on white sage. . . . [I]n former times when there was a failure of the pine-nut crop and no game could be found, the whole tribe was obliged to subsist on white sage which was cooked and made into a soup."[17]

The annual cycle of food gathering included year-round hunting of small mammals. Virtually every animal that the environment offered was hunted to a greater or lesser degree. Anthropologist Omer Stewart's 1936 interview of Northern Paiute Tusi Nick, then eighty-six years of age, records the deep-rooted understanding of these food sources that elderly Indians retained. "His knowledge of birds and mammals, manifested by identifying and naming them from pictures, was astonishing," Stewart noted.[18]

Black-tailed jackrabbits, white-tailed jackrabbits, and cottontail rabbits supplied the most important meat products for Indians of the Great Basin. Black-tailed jackrabbits were taken in communal drives during the fall and early winter under the direction of a rabbit-drive boss. Beaters drove the rabbits, sometimes for miles, toward nets three feet high and two hundred feet or more in length that had been strung vertically on sagebrush across their path. Another method of capture was the fire surround, in which brush and grass surrounding an area a mile or more in diameter were ignited, forming a continuous ring that burned toward the center. The flames constrained the rabbits within an ever-decreasing circle where the Indians dispatched them with sticks.[19]

The white-tailed jackrabbit, generally found in grassy habitats, was preferred over the black-tailed jackrabbit because it was larger, had better fur, and was more edible. The Battle Mountain Western Shoshone traveled in excess of seventy straight-line miles southeast to Grass Valley to hunt them when furs were good.[20] The Western Shoshone living in Ruby Valley held drives for locally abundant white-tails. They dried the flesh for winter use and saved the skins to manufacture blankets and clothing.

Anthropologists' interviews with Indian elders and the reports of early visitors to the area indicate that ground squirrels, bushy-tailed wood rats, and yellow-bellied marmots were routinely hunted as well. In May 1854 Lt. E. G. Beckwith, exploring a route for the Pacific Railroad along the forty-first parallel, came upon Indians in the Cortez Mountains "industriously employed in catch-ing small ground-squirrels or gophers [on] which they subsist to such a large extent. . . . They shoot them with blunt arrows, catch them in ingeniously con-trived 'figure-four traps' set at the mouth of their burrows, and dig them out of the earth with their hands."[21] Indians sometimes traveled long distances to areas where squirrels were plentiful. During his trip in the summer of 1860, Dan DeQuille met a party of seven youths on the east side of the Stillwater Moun-tains who were returning to their families at the Stillwater Marsh. "They had left the Cold Springs Mountains [Desatoya] at sundown, and had been traveling all night across the desert. They carried small water bottles . . . and were loaded with a species of mountain rat [Uinta ground squirrels], smoked and dried, packed in oblong hampers made of twisted ropes of grass. . . . After staying an hour, to rest and breakfast, they set up the cañon toward the summit of the mountains."[22]

Diverting streams to flood out small mammals was another common prac-tice in aboriginal times. In May 1859, in upper Huntington Valley, Captain Simpson witnessed this effective way of taking pocket gophers and squirrels. His party "pass[ed] places where the Indians have dammed up the rills to cause them to flood the habitations or holes of badgers, gophers, rats etc. and thus they secure them for their flesh and skins."[23] Yellow-bellied marmots, a favor-ite food, were hunted with bows and arrows and taken with the aid of dogs. Although not hunted intentionally, porcupine and badger were likewise taken with bows and arrows when encountered.

Howard Egan, an early pioneer, described an effective method of taking bushy-tailed wood rats employed by an old man he encountered. The Indian was carrying a large sheet-iron kettle nearly full of them: "They had been caught the night before by dead falls, as we call them, which consists of two sticks about three and a half or four inches long fastened together at their cen-ters by a string that will allow them to be spread apart. . . . One of these, with any convenient flat rock heavy enough to kill a rat, is one dead fall." Bushy-tailed wood rats and ground squirrels were also speared in their holes by a stick turned up slightly on the end and by digging with a spade-like stick.[24]

The people ate a variety of land and water birds, with grouse, quail, and waterfowl being preferred. The Surprise Valley Paiute captured sage grouse using a noose attached by string to a bent-over willow. After the bird walked into the noose, a trigger released the willow, which sprang upright, ensnaring the bird. Concealed hunters took grouse with a noose or by hitting them with a stick. Sage grouse were particularly vulnerable in the spring when the males were performing their strutting display to attract females. A hunter wearing an antelope disguise could get close enough to hit the displaying birds over the head with a short stick. Netting grouse as they were coming to water was a particularly effective method of capturing them. A net ten to fifteen feet across was stretched horizontally about a foot and a half above the ground. One side was pegged down and the other was supported at the corners with posts. When a large enough number of birds were under the net, the hunter pulled a string, releasing the corner posts and dropping the net over the birds.[25]

Techniques used for taking waterfowl included decoy hunting, snaring, netting, and driving. A canvasback duck decoy made of tule stems found at Lovelock Cave on the shores of the Humboldt Sink dated to two thousand years ago. Of the resident waterfowl, the favorite of the Northern Paiute "tule eaters" at Stillwater Marsh was by far the American coot (mud hen). An Indian informant told anthropologist Catherine Fowler that hunters took the birds during large drives in late August when the birds were in molt and had "no wing."[26] The Western Shoshone of Ruby Valley likewise drove flightless coots out of the water and killed them with clubs as they ran through the marsh grasses.

The permanent streams, marshes, and lakes of the area yielded fish obtained with variety of techniques. On streams, the Shoshone constructed barriers of stones or loosely woven willow weirs to force the fish into restricted areas where they were herded together and speared or thrown to shore.[27] Some of these traps were rather elaborate. In the vicinity of Battle Mountain in early August 1846, immigrant Edwin Bryant "discovered, on the bank of the river, a fish trap, ingeniously constructed of willows interwoven. It was about ten or twelve feet in length and shaped like the cornucopia."[28]

Rock dams constructed on rivers or large streams formed pools from which large numbers of fish could be taken by means of seines, dip nets, and baskets placed in notches in the dams. In January 1844 John C. Frémont "followed the river [East Walker] . . . and crossed it at a dam which the Indians made us to comprehend had been built to catch salmon trout."[29] Indian elders of the Elko group informed anthropologist Julian Steward that rock dams were located on the Humboldt River west of Elko, on lower Susie Creek, and on the south fork of the Humboldt River. Baskets of fish weighing up to two hundred pounds were removed every two to four days from these dams.[30]

Early surveyors and pioneers commonly used the term "salmon trout" when referring to large cutthroat trout. At Pyramid Lake, Frémont wrote, "Northern Paiute caught numbers of salmon-trout of extraordinary size about as large as the Columbia River salmon—generally from two to four feet in length."[31] Although Pacific salmon and Lahontan cutthroat trout were the most sought-after species in northeastern Nevada, the local people also took suckers, tui chub, dace, and other small fish. Early reports indicate that cutthroat trout were abundant in the Humboldt River. In August 1863 immigrant James Yager encountered friendly Shoshone Indians near Elko who traded cutthroat trout eighteen to twenty-four inches long for bread and old clothes.[32]

North of Elko, the Shoshone harvested salmon and steelhead trout in Snake River tributaries of the Columbia River during annual migrations of the fish from the Pacific Ocean. A band of Indians came every spring and fished in the Jack Creek tributary of the south fork of the Owyhee River. Indians also took salmon in the summer on the Bruneau River, drying and packing the fish away "like bales of hay."[33]

Warren d'Azevedo reported that the various lakes and streams in western Nevada provided the most predictable and consistent source of year-round food for the aboriginal and early historic Washoe. Lake Tahoe, a traditional fishery, was full of very large Lahontan cutthroat trout, which were removed from tributary streams during annual spawning runs. The cui-ui lakesucker provided a plentiful source of food for the Northern Paiute living on Pyramid Lake. The northern Washoe harvested the Lahontan mountainsuckers that spawned profusely in the Long Valley Creek tributary of Honey Lake in the spring and early summer.[34]

Insects with periodic emergences, particularly black Mormon crickets, were a source of food when they were plentiful. Women, children, and sometimes entire families drove the insects into trenches, as witnessed by Howard Egan in the Deep Creek area on the Utah–Nevada border in the 1860s. The Indians had dug trenches on a contour of the slope and brought in large bundles of wildrye grass, which they spread over the trenches. The crickets were herded through the grass and into the trenches. Egan described what followed next: "When all had been driven in the Indians set fire to the grass they had in their hands and scattered it along on the top of that they had over the trenches, causing a big blaze and smoke, which soon left the crickets powerless to crawl out. . . . I rode along the line and in some places the trenches were over half full of dead and legless crickets."[35]

Bighorn sheep, antelope, and mule deer were the only large mammals in the prehistoric Western Shoshone economy. Bighorn were regularly hunted by ambushing and with the assistance of dogs during the summer. In December, when the sheep were rutting, concealed hunters attracted them by thumping logs, making sounds like rams fighting, and shot them with bows and arrows. They were also intercepted by hunters hiding in rock blinds and stone cairns.

People of the Egan Canyon spent considerable time hunting to the north in the lofty Ruby Mountains. Individuals of the upper Humboldt River hunted sheep in the Ruby Mountains, Swales Mountain, and the Independence and Jarbidge mountains.[36]

Pronghorn antelope, commonly known simply as antelope (although they are not antelopes at all), were widely distributed, as described by elderly Indian informants and evidenced by the remnants of drive wings and corrals used in their capture. Drives in eastern Nevada took place in the northern and southern ends of Spring, Steptoe, Antelope, and White River valleys. To the west, drives occurred in the southern end of Diamond Valley, the northern extremities of Butte and Long valleys, and the Humboldt River valley near present-day Battle Mountain. Corrals were also located in the upper Humboldt River watershed, including the hills north and south of Elko, Huntington, and Ruby valleys, and on the west side of Spruce Mountain. The animals were pushed between the two wings of a V-shaped runway into a corral constructed of brush, stone, and poles. Drives usually took place in the spring, or occasionally in the fall before pine nut harvests, under the direction of a shaman who was believed to have supernatural powers.[37]

Mule deer were particularly scarce in the southern regions and thus were hunted only occasionally by the Western Shoshone. Hunting strategies included the surround, burning woodland, ambushing along migration routes, and snares. Most of the hunting was by individual men of exceptional ability who shot the deer with arrows from blinds or stalked and pursued them.[38] Isabel Kelly's interview of a man whose father had sole rights to a particular site reveals how these hunters took deer along migration routes: "My father had a place on a rock butte at the head of Buck canyon. He made a brush fence running down-hill from each side of the butte where he left an open place like a gateway. He hid in a hole about ten feet from the road, and as the deer came through the gate, he shot. He killed one every night."[39]

Communal deer hunts were generally rare or unimportant, although they had some significance among the Ruby Valley, Steptoe, Battle Mountain, and Little Smoky groups. Cooperative hunts were feasible in the fall, when deer descended from the mountains by fairly well marked trails, and in the spring, when the deer returned to the mountains on the same trails. Brush or tree branch wings formed in a V converged into a corral where the animals were shot with bows and arrows. During communal hunts covering a large area, men stationed at one-hundred-yard intervals would set fire to the brush and drive the deer into a great circle where they could be shot.[40]

The extensive body of knowledge accumulated about the Great Basin peoples provides a good picture of how Indians following a hunter-gatherer way of life subsisted in the relatively hostile environment of the western Great Basin. One can only speculate how much greater their influence might have been before the drastic population reductions that followed contact with Europeans.[41] Animals, birds, and fish were widely distributed and locally abundant when the first Euro-Americans came on the scene. Although they were successful at exploiting the natural resources of the area, Indians had limited potential to alter flora and fauna except with fire and at locations and times of animal concentration such as at water in droughts. Use of fire had the potential to alter certain landscapes, and indeed, there is ample evidence that it did just that.[42]

II

Presettlement

3

Fire

A Natural Disturbance
and Human Tool

Before Euro-Americans settled the interior West, fires ignited by native peoples and lightning played a major role in shaping the dominant vegetation.[1] The frequency of these fires depended on available fuel (dead and living vegetation), topography, sources of ignition, and weather.

The journals of the earliest explorers and other travelers in the region offer insight into the role of fire prior to settlement (around 1860).[2] Ethnographers who interviewed Indian elders in the 1930s also recorded information regarding how Indians used fire and fire's importance as a force on the landscape.[3] Physical evidence of historic fires and their frequency can be gleaned by studying (dating) fire scars on trees.[4] The age of trees and long-lived shrubs at a given location can provide clues to the date of a past fire. For example, char beneath a two-hundred-year-old pinyon pine is an indication that the site burned more than two hundred years ago.

Lightning certainly ignited many fires, just as it does today. Native Americans used fire for many reasons—to signal between bands, to enhance the production of grass seed, to immobilize crickets and grasshoppers, to drive animals, and to harass their enemies.[5] Undoubtedly, their campfires spread extensively over the land when they were left unattended or were fanned by a sudden wind. Stewart's extensive literature search revealed almost no evidence of indigenous people extinguishing their fires.[6]

Using fire to signal between bands is a common practice of native peoples worldwide. It was a particularly important means of communication in the wide expanses of the western Great Basin. While approaching Independence Valley in northeastern Nevada in 1829, for example, Peter Skene Ogden, leader of the Hudson's Bay Company's beaver-trapping brigade, wrote: "It is very evident that from the number of fires in all directions that we are discovered by the natives." As he continued west into the Santa Rosa Range, Ogden saw fires "in almost every direction in the mountains."[7] In upper Goshute Valley near the Utah border, immigrant Heinrich Lienhard wrote on August 26, 1846: "Although we had not seen any Indians, their fires were visible on the nearby hills and mountains."[8] The Indians continued to use signal fires following European settlement. While gathering cattle along the lower Humboldt River in 1862, Joseph Triplett noted "Indian signal fires on the top of every mountain."[9]

Immigrants traveling along the Humboldt River corridor routinely observed Indian signal fires but recorded little evidence of burned landscape. Much of their travel took place in the spring and early summer, though, when grassy fuels were still green and too moist to burn. As the season advanced, the probability of fire dwindled along travel corridors because livestock had grazed down the grassy fuels. This was not the situation prior to the appearance of great numbers of immigrants and their livestock. In 1845 Frémont described the valley as "a rich alluvium, beautifully covered with blue grass, herd grass, clover, and nutritious grasses; and its course is marked from the plain by a line of willow and cottonwood trees, serving for fuel. The Indians in the fall set fire to the grass and destroy all trees except in low grounds near the water."[10] Other early reports provide further evidence that burning of riparian vegetation was a geographically widespread practice. In late September 1776 in the vicinity of Utah Lake, Father Escalante "found the grass of the plains where we came recently burned over and others already burning. . . . [Indians] had put the fires everywhere."[11] In southeast Oregon in late October 1826, Peter Skene Ogden was forced to camp early in the day near Malheur Lake because the countryside had been extensively burned.[12] Similarly, at a camp at the Humboldt Sink below Lovelock on September 4, 1833, Rocky Mountain Fur Company clerk Zenas Leonard described the area as "low and swampy, producing an abundance of very fine grass . . . which was very acceptable to our horses. . . . [A] little before sunset, on taking a view of the surrounding waste with a spyglass, we discovered smoke rising from the grass in every direction."[13]

The earliest record of burned landscape in Nevada is in Ogden's journal entry of May 15, 1826, written in upper Goose Creek near today's Nevada–Utah border. His trappers had been to the headwaters of Goose Creek and found it "well lined with willows fine smooth water but no beaver, it is their opinion that the fire has driven them away as the Country last Fall [was] overrun by Fire." Two weeks later his brigade was apparently in the upper Jarbidge watershed, where his men reported "no appearance of Beaver, it is however their opinion this country was once well stocked in Beaver but the Fire has driven them off." Ogden likely would not have mentioned the burned landscapes had fire not interfered with trapping beaver. The trapping season was early winter and spring, when pelts had thick fur. Fuels did not readily burn at this time, so the probability of seeing active fires was unlikely.

English aristocrat Sir Richard Burton, one of the greatest British travelers of the nineteenth century and a keen observer, traveled across central Nevada by stagecoach in October 1860, when fuels were dry. Approaching the Simpson's Park stage station, Burton noted grassy slopes and "smokes upcurling in slow heavy masses." Concerned about the fire threat to haystacks at stage stations, he remarked, "The haystacks were exposed to fire at a time of the year when no more forage could be collected." From Immigrant Summit in the Toiyabe Range he wrote: "We sighted everywhere on the heights the fires of the natives. . . . Below us 'Reese's River' Valley might have served as a sketch in the African desert: a plain of saleratus [alkaline], here yellow with sand or hay, there black with fire."[14] In other words, fire had not burned alkaline areas, but it had burned many grassy areas. The vulnerability of this landscape to fire is reflected in newspaper accounts in the *Reese River Reveille* in the 1860s describing basin wildrye grass as being so thick and high along the Reese River that settlers lived in fear of range fires each fall.[15] The occurrence of fires at upper elevations in the Peavine area near the upper Reese River can be inferred from T. B. Heller's journal entry of February 8, 1864: "The mountains here were quite high and seemly much burned."[16] Old place-names in this region, since modified, suggest recurrent fire. Big Creek in the Toiyabe Range was once called "Big Smoky Creek." The Toquima Range was known as the "Smoky Range." Between these ranges lies the Big Smoky Valley.

Great Basin Indians sometimes used fire as a defensive tactic. On October 4–5, 1850, in the vicinity of Honey Lake, immigrant Goldsborough Bruff wrote: "As we proceeded, saw smoke ahead, and soon perceived that it spread across the trail, and was continued above; and caused by the Indians, burning the grass to prevent us from ascending the valley. . . . We continued to advance however, til we saw the flames. . . . In about ¼ of a mile we got ahead of it. The flames and smoke had hit the foothills, behind which the rascally savages were."[17]

Indians' use of fire for hunting animals is widely documented. Northern Paiute elders told anthropologist Isabel Kelly that the only means of taking deer wholesale in the Surprise Valley region of the northern Nevada–California state line was by *Kupi't*, their method of firing.[18] That it was practiced about the middle of August demonstrates a desire for fires when the grassy fuels were highly flammable. Anthropologist W. Z. Park reported that small herds of deer near Honey Lake were occasionally driven to a low hill and surrounded by several hunters. The brush around the hill was set on fire, forcing the deer to the top of the hill or to an opening in the fire circle where the hunters waited with bows and arrows.[19] The Shoshone of Ruby Valley also started fires in order to drive deer out of the brush.[20] The fires sometimes continued to burn for weeks with no attempt made to suppress them.

Indians used fire to take black-tailed jackrabbits as well when there was sufficient fuel. Howard Egan, at the invitation of the chief, accompanied a group of Indians on an eastern Nevada rabbit drive in the 1850s and later described the experience.

> We came to the place selected for the drive—a piece of sage and rabbit brush land about a mile in diameter. The party I was with stopped, when we saw a fire about a half mile to our right and soon another about the same distance to the left, and then we could see the smoke rising a mile ahead of us. My party soon had their torches at work and the drive was on. Working all around the circle and towards the center was a continuous ring of fire and smoke, which was gradually closing in and the rabbits were being crowed together thicker and thicker. The Indians, including children, took up sticks and started killing the rabbits that were so dazed by the fire, smoke and tumult that they simply could not run. . . . When the drive was over the field was a black, fire-swept, but still smoking patch of ground.[21]

Egan estimated that the number of rabbits taken could not have been packed in a large wagon bed.

Fires were quite active during drought years. Edwin Bryant, a particularly observant early immigrant who kept a detailed journal, recorded regional fire activity during the course of his westward journey. While passing through Utah's Wasatch Mountains in late July 1846, he saw wind-driven fires that burned with "great fury." Across the Salt Lake Valley to the south, "a fire was raging in the mountains all night, and spread down into the valley, consuming the brown vegetation." Below Pilot Peak on today's Utah–Nevada border, "the fires before noticed were still blazing brightly before us on the side of the mountain, but those who had lighted them, had given no other signal of their proximity." Indian signal fires and smoke continued as the party proceeded west. On August 12 in the Boulder Valley north of present-day Beowawe, Bryant wrote: "We entered another large and level Valley, which stretches to the north as far as the vision can penetrate through the smoky vapor. The day has been excessively hot, and the sky is of the color of copper, from the effects of the dense smoke with which the atmosphere of the valley is filled." The smoke prevailed until the party had passed Nightingale Hot Springs about two hundred miles farther west.[22] Immigrants Alonzo Delano and Bernard Reid reported dense smoke in the vicinity of Winnemucca on August 11 and September 1, 1849, suggesting the persistence of smoke at times in this region.[23] Fires burning in the Sierra Nevada may have been the origin of this smoke, which was carried up the Humboldt Valley by westerly winds.

Other journalists recorded fires along the immigrant trail in northeastern Nevada. In September 1841 John Bidwell "saw the form of a high mountain through the smoky atmosphere" in the upper Goshute Valley south of Goose Creek.[24] William Kilgore wrote of seeing Indian-set fires near Goose Creek on July 8, 1850—twenty-four years after Ogden's experience.[25] On July 8, 1864, James Yager wrote, "While we were on the mountains descending to Goose Creek we could see their fires on the opposite side of the creek, above & below bursting up fresh and along the road in many places we could see the same."[26]

Anthropologists' interviews with elderly Indians living in the Great Basin and Plateau region in the 1930s revealed that fifteen of the nineteen Nevada and neighboring groups of Shoshone and seven of the fourteen Northern Paiute groups had historically practiced burning to encourage growth of wild plants.[27] Washoe tribe members were unwilling to admit to using fire because they knew that whites were opposed to it.

The native peoples recognized the relationship between fire and increased growth of certain plants the following year.[28] For example, they burned patches of sandbar willows, favored for making a variety of baskets and cradleboards, so that the shoots would be tall and straight the following year. The Western Shoshone of Ruby Valley, who called themselves "rye grass eaters," more than likely burned patches of this grass, which grows profusely following fire. They also used fire to promote growth of mug-wort. In Diamond Valley fire was used to increase growth of lambs quarters, which broadcasts its seed when burned. On Magruder Mountain near Lida in southwestern Nevada, the landscape was burned in the fall to promote plant growth. Anthropologist James F. Downs concluded that burning to encourage the growth of plants was a widespread practice.[29]

One of the last Native Americans with personal knowledge of fire use was Albert Hooper (1902–80), a Shoshone who lived almost his entire life in Monitor Valley. In conversations with rancher Wayne Hage, Hooper often mentioned his people setting fire to the western slope of the Monitor Range as they left high-country camps in the fall—presumably to rejuvenate the plants on which they depended.[30]

Charred wood in coniferous forests and pinyon-juniper woodlands provides convincing physical evidence of historic fire. Fire frequency can be determined by examining the annual growth rings of a tree wounded by a fire, which leaves a fire scar. A composite sample of fire scars from trees in three studies of mixed conifer forest on the eastern slope of the Sierra Nevada showed an average interval between fires of about 10 years during the period 1593–1899.[31] In eastern Nevada's Snake Range (Great Basin National Park), fire-scarred sections from 103 ponderosa pines and limber pines growing at elevations between 7,757 and 10,596 feet on 1,569 acres in the Mill Creek locality suggested mean fire intervals of 11 and 19 years, respectively.[32] The longer intervals in the limber pine stand reflect the cool, moist conditions at higher elevations. Further analysis of these data by S. G. Kitchen suggested a mean fire interval of 22.9 years at lower and middle elevations.[33]

Fire history studies in pinyon-juniper woodlands are much less definitive because old pinyon (the primary recorder) was restricted to fire-safe ridges and rocky sites with little grass and few shrubs. These trees were seldom scarred by the fires that passed over wider, more flammable areas and consumed their neighbors. Where fuels were plentiful, pinyon hardly ever survived fires, and thus fire-scarred trees are virtually absent. Despite these limitations, pinyon pines growing in the Snake and Strawberry Creek drainages of the Snake Range, where grassy fuels were abundant, had enough fire scars to suggest that presettlement fire intervals on northerly aspects and canyon bottoms averaged roughly 15–20 years.[34] Southerly slopes burned less often because fuel was sparse there.

The most definitive insight into fire history in pinyon-juniper woodlands was developed in the Sweetwater Mountains north of Bridgeport, California, where fire-resistant Jeffrey pines are intermixed with pinyon and juniper.[35] Fire-scarred pinyon was confined to widely scattered 200–400-year-old trees growing on fuel-limited sites protected from fire by a scarcity of fuel. The few fire scars on these pinyon pines suggest that fires burned at intervals of more than 100 years. In contrast, the thick-barked fire-resistant Jeffrey pines growing on productive sites among the pinyons bore multiple fire scars. A composite sample of six trees in an area of less than 100 acres suggested a fire frequency of 8 years over the 208-year period 1687–1895. These results and tree ages over broad areas indicate that fire was a frequent visitor on sites where fuels were sufficient to allow burning. The frequent fires prevented the establishment of pinyon and juniper on these sites, unlike the bare, gravelly sites where fires were rare and pinyon and juniper could become established.

Figure 3.1. Jeffrey pine cross-section showing seven fire scars formed between 1734 and 1839. Photograph by George E. Gruell.

Thus, various sources of evidence suggest that historically, Nevada's landscapes burned most frequently where fuels (grass and shrubs) grew productively. With the exception of localized grassy areas, semiarid valleys apparently burned infrequently because grass was sparse and shrub cover was discontinuous. At higher elevations, the more productive mountain sagebrush communities burned frequently owing to an abundance of grassy fuels and ignitions by Native Americans and lightning.

Native Americans used fire as a tool for improving their environment and harvesting resources. In the following chapter we will view evidence of a mountain landscape in early growth stages with a high component of grasses and forbs—an ecosystem dependent on fire to sustain certain plants and animals.

4

Vegetation
A Sea of Sagebrush or Landscape of Great Variety

What was Nevada's cold desert vegetation like at the time Europeans entered the Great Basin? The answer is steeped in controversy. George Stewart's analysis of ecological data and historical records in northwestern Utah showed a predominance of perennial grass.[1] On the other hand, analysis of immigrants' journals and government surveys, although documenting the presence of grass in the mountains, led Thomas Vale to conclude that shrubs visually dominated the pristine vegetation of Nevada.[2] These divergent assessments could be explained by differences in the ecological potential of sites described in early records. The Utah study involved elevated valleys, foothills, and benchlands where favorable precipitation and soil provided potential for growth of grass. Vale's Nevada review is largely confined to primary travel routes in semiarid valleys.

SEMIARID VALLEYS

Government surveys commissioned during the westward movement indicate that shrubs predominated in Nevada's semiarid valleys. An 1854 Corps of Geographical Engineers report concludes: "The greater part of the surface of these valleys is merely sprinkled by several varieties of sombre artemisia [wild sage], presenting the aspect of a dreary waste. Though there are spots more thickly covered with this vegetation, yet the soil is seldom half covered with it, even for a few acres."[3]

Captain J. H. Simpson came to the same conclusion: "The most abundant plant in the Great Basin is the *artemisia*, or wild sage, and it is seen almost everywhere in the valleys and on the mountains."[4] Botanist Sereno Watson, a member of Clarence King's 1867–68 geological survey of the new territories, found sagebrush to be "by far the most prevalent of all species covering valleys and foothills in broad stretches farther than the eye can reach, the growth never so dense as to seriously obstruct the way but very uniform over large surfaces."[5]

There are a variety of *Artemisia* species (see appendix 2), each with different habitat requirements. Wyoming big sagebrush, which is adapted to moderately deep soils in drier environments, is likely the principal sagebrush referred to in the valley areas covered by Watson and others, although failure to recognize different taxa of sagebrush may be part of a larger failure to recognize that not all gray shrubs are sagebrush of any kind. Forty-four species and subspecies of rabbitbrush grace the Intermountain West along with various chenopods and other low-desert shrubs.

Several observers recorded variation in the growth habits of sagebrush. During his 1854 survey Lieutenant Beckwith crossed an area in Diamond Valley "covered with rank sagebrush from three to five feet high."[6] Likewise, Captain Simpson found sagebrush to be "quite rank in growth" in upper Huntington Valley. South of the Roberts Mountains in Kobeh Valley, he reported that "the sage we have daily to break through with our wagons [basin big sagebrush] ranges from 3 to 8 inches at butt."[7] Basin big sagebrush commonly reaches heights of eight or more feet but rarely lives longer than sixty years. It grows on very deep soils and often indicated good cropland to settlers.

Less productive sites produced black sagebrush or low sagebrush. These species occupy thin soils atop clay layers or shallow bedrock that restricts water percolation. Black sagebrush grows on soils derived from limestone. In upper Big Smoky Valley Simpson reported that the soil was "very thinly covered by Artemisia." In the Goshute Valley of eastern Nevada Beckwith found that "the road was dry and hard, and the Artemisia, which covered the whole face of the country, small." Bryant, also in the Goshute Valley, found only "wild sage, greasewood, and a few shrubs of small size, for the most part leafless." The latter were likely shadscale and other salt desert shrubs. Crossing lower Grass Valley, south of Winnemucca, Beckwith found "the soil of the valley... friable and dry, supporting only a small variety of artemisia."[8]

Recognizing site potential differences, Watson recorded the presence of salt desert shrubs on the somewhat less alkaline and drier portions of valleys where the potential for grass and forbs was low. Noting the presence of clay soils on the west side of lower Steptoe Valley near Schellbourne, Simpson concluded that it was a poor, arid valley and surmised it would be boggy in wet weather. Saltgrass bordered the stream, and greasewood 2–4 feet tall was growing where the party crossed. Lower Newark Valley typifies areas occupied by playa lakes where heavy salt concentrations precluded growth of vegetation.[9]

To the north, vegetation in the Humboldt River valley was consistent with that of the semiarid valleys in central and eastern Nevada. James Yager's detailed 1863 journal suggests that sagebrush with a grass understory predominated on both sides of the Humboldt River west of Humboldt Wells. Greasewood formed part of the shrub cover in several localities. In the vicinity of today's Elko, Bryant found "benches of low hills, covered with sage and greasewood, slop[ing] down to the fertile land." Downriver in Boulder Valley, Bryant reported that "sage, grease-wood, etc., cover the low hills and benches of the mountains, and grass and willows, the margin of the river."[10]

The historical accounts of semiarid valleys noted above suggest that sagebrush distribution and density varied with soil type and moisture. Different subspecies of big sagebrush dominated the better-drained areas, while in less productive settings big sagebrush was intermixed with salt desert shrubs and dwarf sagebrush species. Depending on the soil salinity and pH, greasewood grew on poorly drained areas of heavy clay soils in the lower valleys along with rabbitbrush, shadscale, and other salt desert shrubs growing where drainage improved a bit. Saltgrass meadows prevailed where surface moisture persisted throughout the year.

RIPARIAN ZONES

Valleys and saturated soil wetlands harbored an abundance of grass and grasslike plants (sedges, rushes, etc). In upper Steptoe Valley Simpson found "the grass in the vicinity of our camp, along the bottom of the creek, in the valley, and in the mountains," to be "exceedingly abundant." To the south, "a bottom of good grass (a great deal of it red-top), 2 or 3 miles wide, extends for a distance of 8 or 10 miles northwardly." Simpson described the riparian zone of the Reese River emanating from the Toiyabe Range as productive of luxuriant grass (basin wildrye) but in many places alkaline (alkali sacaton). "It is best and very abundant further up the stream, and extends as far as the eye can reach." Above the riparian zone the soils were "covered with the wild sage and greasewood." Grass Valley to the east of the Toiyabe Range was so heavily covered with grasses that parts of the valley were cut for hay in the early 1860s.[11]

The Humboldt River bottom was covered by various grass species including a coarse, heavily seeded species that was most likely basin wildrye. The very palatable Nebraska sedge dominated the moister areas. The productivity of these bottomlands impressed immigrants, particularly those in the vanguard of wagon trains, who saw the grass before it had been heavily grazed by livestock. Near the confluence of the Marys River and the Humboldt, William Kilgore reported that "the bottom here is four to six miles wide and grass plenty near the river."[12] At lower Boulder Valley in vicinity of Rock Creek, Yager wrote: "The valley & bottom here is about eight miles wide & covered with fine grass." Downstream in the Iron Point locality, Yager was impressed with grass abundance: "It resembled a large meadow ready for the scythe."[13]

Robert Ridgway, the ornithologist for the King survey, described the vegetation in the vicinity of today's Oreana: "At this place the valley of the Humboldt was, as usual, destitute of trees, the only woody vegetation near the river being the thick clumps of small willows on the points and around the sloughs. The greater portion of the valley consisted of meadows of saltgrass."[14]

The journals of other early visitors seem to confirm the absence of large trees and the presence of small willows along the course of the Humboldt River. Kilgore remarked that "on the whole length of this River, we have not Seen a tree or Stick of wood"—the likely effects of frequent fire as reported by Frémont. Near present-day Fallon on the lower Carson River Kilgore observed "some Cotton wood Timber and the only trees that we have seen for the last four hundred mile travel." In the fertile Truckee River bottomlands below today's Wadsworth, Bryant found "a growth of small willows, hawthorns, and a few tall cotton-wood trees. In the openings, wild peas and a variety of grasses and other herbage, grow with luxuriance." In the Truckee River Canyon Bryant passed a few tall cottonwood trees that skirted the river's margin. "These, with small willows, and a variety of diminutive shrubs and rank weeds, with an occasional opening of grass make up the vegetation of the valley." At Truckee Meadows (the Reno-Sparks Valley) Bryant saw a landscape covered by a luxuriant stand of grass, while clumps of small willows lined the margins of the sloughs and river.[15] Twenty-one years later Ridgway noted that the banks of the Truckee along the middle portion of the Truckee Meadows "were fringed with dense thickets of rather tall willows, growing about 15 feet high."[16] This growth disparity may have reflected disruption of Indian burning by the influx of settlers.

UPLANDS

Observations of vegetation at upper elevations suggest that grass was abundant on sites of good ecological potential. The sagebrush steppe dominates many areas overlooking the headwaters of the Humboldt River and other streams and rivers flowing from mountains. On the Goose Creek drainage, the perceptive James Yager found "the finest grass seen on this side of the Missouri." Between Goose Creek and Little Goose Creek there was an abundance of fine-bladed grass, but in the less productive Rock Springs Valley he encountered "nothing much but sagebrush and greasewood." In the upper Thousand Springs locality the party "got into a fine body of fine stemed [sic] & fine bladed grass . . . the largest body of number one grass that I ever saw." Yager crossed a bench "grown in sage brush & greasewood" before reaching Humboldt Wells. The mountainsides and benchlands along the way were covered by fine bunchgrass.[17]

Beckwith reported that the benchlands along the eastern slope of the Ruby Mountains were "finely covered with grass, but we occasionally passed fields of sage and thorny bushes, the latter covered with myriads of nesting caterpillars."[18] Sir Richard Burton was impressed with the grazing potential of these benchlands, which he judged to be of excellent quality.[19] In Immigrant Pass above Palisade Canyon, Edward Kern, who led a contingent of Captain Frémont's expedition in 1845, reported an abundance of bunchgrass of fine quality.[20]

Farther to the north, reports from the Cornucopia locality beginning in 1873 note the lack of sagebrush on the surrounding hills for use as fuel to mill ore. A reporter wrote that the surrounding hills were covered by bunchgrass and ryegrass, and a stock company was running "thousands" of cattle adjacent to Cornucopia. In 1875 S. Mayhugh noted the "almost total absence of sagebrush, with an abundance of water and grass."[21]

MOUNTAINS

South of the Humboldt River, juniper (called cedar by early observers) and pinyon pine were widely distributed and of variable density, with juniper the more frequently observed. According to Simpson, Moorman Ridge in the White Pine Mountains in eastern Nevada was "covered with cedars as far as the eye could reach." In the Sulphur Springs Range he encountered thick cedars, and in Garden Pass his men cut small pinyons that blocked the passage of their wagons. At Simpson Park Creek an abundance of pinyon was observed on the adjacent mountain.[22]

The pinyon-juniper woodland had a more open character in other localities. Ridgway found that a "thin wood of cedar and pinyon prevailed" on the lower west slopes of the Toiyabe Range in the vicinity of Austin. In Wright's Canyon of the West Humboldt Range he observed scattered small cedars on the lower slopes.[23]

Bunchgrass was commonly associated with pinyon-juniper stands. Simpson "encamped in good grass and abundant cedar timber" on Willow Creek south of Kobeh Valley.[24] At Hastings Pass (now Overland Pass) Beckwith "crossed its summit, which is covered by a fine growth of cedar, and an equally fine growth of grass"—likely bluebunch wheatgrass and Idaho fescue. Crossing the

Shoshone range west of Horse Mountain he encountered "no trees upon it, but a few scattered cedar-bushes and a luxuriant growth of bunch-grass."[25]

Bunchgrasses were intermixed with sagebrush or grew in continuous stands. This environment had high potential for growth of grass because it fell within the productive shrub steppe. Native grasses were mostly basin wildrye, bluebunch wheatgrass, Idaho fescue, Thurber's needlegrass, and bottlebrush squirreltail. On sandy soils Indian ricegrass or needle and thread grass would have been more common.

On the southerly slopes of the Cortez Mountains Beckwith reported grass to be "abundant among the sage in the hills about our camp." On the south end of the Sonoma Range he "passed easily over the mountain through luxuriant fields of grass and sage."[26] Geologist Israel Cook Russell was impressed with the bunchgrass "that frequently abounds in the mountains and sometimes grows luxuriantly beneath the sagebrush."[27]

In the later 1800s John Muir found the lower slopes of Wheeler Peak in the Snake Range "like those of the Troy range, only more evenly clad with grasses."[28] Flora Bender's immigrant party in 1863 "stopped at the edge of the mountains [Egan Range] where there was splendid bunch grass, and let the stock out to graze."[29] On McCarthy Creek, Simpson encamped "amid excellent and superabundant hill and bottom grass. . . . The grass extends up the hills of the We-a-bah [Diamond Mountains] as far as the eye can reach." Farther to the west in the Dry Creek watershed of the Simpson Park Range, Simpson reported plenty of grass in the canyons.[30] Flora Bender stopped in this locality and found a "good camping place, splendid spring, and good bunch grass in the mountains."[31] In ascending Immigrant Pass in the Toiyabe Range, Simpson found "the grass in the pass very abundant and of the finest character. This fine mountain bunch-grass fattens and strengthens our animals like oats." Having matured, grasses were more conspicuous during Simpson's return trip in July. "The grass in Reese River Valley, through the canons we have passed to-day, as well as everywhere on the mountains, very abundant; more so than when we passed before."[32]

Grass abundance was the focus of an article that appeared in the June 6, 1863, edition of the *Reese River Reveille*. "It's a joy to bovines and horseflesh to see the long, wavy grass which abounds in such profusion on the slopes and main ridges of the Reese River Mountains (Toiyabe Range) from Austin to Toiyabe Peak and the devil knows how much further south. Immense tracts may be seen literally covered knee deep in tender grass, looking for the world like young fields of grain."

The historical record offers little on shrubs and deciduous trees of mountainous regions because travel routes were largely confined to valleys and foothills. An exception is found in the reports of Robert Ridgway and Sereno Watson, who worked in the Pah Rah, West Humboldt, Toiyabe, Ruby, and East Humboldt ranges during the summers of 1867 and 1868. These meticulous scientists identified plants and described their growth characteristics in canyons and on mountain slopes. Their descriptions provide a sense of the successional status of plants key to wildlife. Watson described the occurrence of mountain mahogany on rocky ridges and dry mountain slopes. Aspen growing along stream banks and in the upper reaches of canyons was of small size. Fire-dependent snowbrush ceanothus was frequent at higher elevations. Deciduous shrubs including currant, serviceberry, snowberry, and chokecherry were common on productive mountain brush sites.[33]

Ridgway's observations were more specific. In Wright's Canyon on the western slope of the West Humboldt Range he saw a luxuriant growth of shrubbery bordering the stream comprising dogwood, wild rose, willows, patches of elderberry, thickets of chokecherry, and isolated small aspens. In Buena Vista Canyon on the east side of the range the plant cover was more extensive, vigorous, and varied, consisting "chiefly of a thick growth of buffalo-berry bushes, willows, and wild-rose briers in the lower portion of the cañon, and higher up of chokecherry and rose bushes, mixed with extensive copses of small aspens." In the Toiyabe Range near Austin he described weed-clad and grassy slopes with intervening canyons and principal ravines watered by brooks and rivulets "whose course was followed by shrubbery from their sources to the valley." At the heads of these canyons, extensive clones of small aspens and chokecherry bushes prevailed, while two thousand feet below, thrifty snowberry bushes dominated. "Correspondingly in altitude with the aspens, were scant groves of stunted mountain mahogany, growing upon the summits or ridges of the mountains."[34]

Ridgway spent the remainder of the 1868 field season in the Ruby and East Humboldt mountains, reporting differences in productivity between the limestone formations of the southern Ruby Mountains and the granitic formations to the north. Shrubs and herbaceous vegetation in the southern Rubies was mostly confined to the canyons, while the spurs and higher slopes supported juniper and pinyon. The shrubby vegetation along the streams and canyons consisted chiefly of chokecherry, snowberry, and serviceberry. At the higher elevations where the canyon sides became less abrupt, the gentle slopes were covered by meadow vegetation. To the north, the steeper and more rugged granite peaks were almost destitute of vegetation. "The cañons, however, supported a luxuriant growth of shrubs and other plants, with here and there small copses or groves of aspen and narrow-leafed cottonwood." Ridgway found the vegetation along the western slope of the adjoining East Humboldt Range "more extensive and vigorous with numerous cotton-woods and aspens constituting extensive groves." The lower slopes of Trout Creek near the town of Wells were covered by the usual sagebrush plants, "but the upper portion, next to the lower foothills of the mountains, was clothed with rye-grass meadows, interspersed with willow and aspen copses."[35]

Professor Charles Sargent was also in the field in 1868 on a hurried trip to study the trees and shrubs on Table Mountain in the Monitor Range of central Nevada, which receives less moisture than that of the Ruby and East Humboldt ranges to the north. Reflecting on his experience in the humid eastern forests, Sargent wrote: "The forests which clothe, with a scanty and stunted vegetation, the mountain slopes of Nevada are miserably poor in extent, productiveness, and especially in the number of species of which they are composed." Aspen and mountain mahogany were among the seven tree species he described. "The Aspen borders all the mountain streams above 8,000 feet elevation, but, rarely surpassing fifteen feet in height and a few inches in diameter. . . . Further east in the Wahsatch Mts. this species is sometimes seen with stems two feet through." Mountain mahogany was "common at 6,000 to 8,000 feet elevation, and next to the Juniper and the Nut Pine is the most common of Central Nevada trees." Narrow growth rings indicated the exceedingly slow development of mahogany. The largest specimen Sargent found on Prospect Mountain near Eureka was about twenty feet tall and seven feet, five inches in diameter three feet above ground level. It was conservatively estimated to be 890 years old.[36]

These historic accounts and observations give a sense of what vegetation was like on Nevada's landscapes before modern humans influenced the region. Reflecting differences in site potential and time since the last fire, this record suggests that plant communities were widely variable and differed greatly in composition from site to site. Sagebrush and salt desert shrubs dominated the lower semiarid valleys, while riparian zones in these valleys supported an abundance of grasses, sedges, and small willows. Their extent away from any channel was determined by the pattern of floodplain flooding and the elevation of the water table relative to the soil surface.

Reflecting both Indian burning and naturally occurring lightning fires, many upland communities were in early to mid-succession and supported an abundance of bunchgrasses and open to moderate canopies of sagebrushes and other woody species. The small size of willows and aspen in the mountains suggests that these fire-adapted plants were in early succession. Fire-sensitive mountain mahogany—and in many ranges pinyon and juniper of large size—was restricted to ridges and upper slopes where fuel discontinuity limited fire spread. An abundance of bunchgrass reflected frequent fire disturbance. As contemporary studies demonstrate, bunchgrasses often survived fire in areas where competition from woody plants had not diminished them. The surviving perennial grasses return quickly after fire, protecting soil from excess erosion and occupying the site as succession slowly progresses toward a peak in diversity before being reduced by a strong expression of shrubs or trees. The fate of wildlife is closely tied to changes in habitats and the march of plant succession.

5

Wildlife
Abundance and Scarcity

What kinds of wildlife did early landscape vegetation support? A reasonably good impression comes from examining historical accounts of early travelers and interpreting them with contemporary knowledge about species' habitat requirements. We would expect a close correlation between the structure of the historical vegetation and the terrestrial and avian wildlife.

At the time Western civilization was coming to the Great Basin, wildlife habitat reflected human and natural disturbances as well as plant succession and the prevailing climate over the previous decades and centuries. Reflecting the continued occurrence of wildland fire and the renewal it brought to plant life, much of the plant cover was in early phases of succession dominated by grasses and forbs, especially in places where fire would be expected more often.

Wildlife species that required grasses and forbs likewise dominated the landscape. Such habitats particularly favored bighorn sheep and pronghorn, but not mule deer. White-tailed jackrabbits were plentiful where grasses were abundant. Although uncommon in the mountains, large numbers of black-tailed jackrabbits occupied the major valleys. Beaver were abundant in the main stem of the Humboldt River downstream from today's Carlin but were relatively uncommon in the mountains. Game birds observed by early travelers included sharp-tailed grouse, sage grouse, mountain quail, and blue grouse. Black bears and wolverines frequented parts of today's Elko County. Wolverines were also present in the Snake Range of northeastern Nevada. Fish were locally abundant in waters draining into the remnants of prehistoric Lake Lahontan.

Bighorn sheep seem to have been the most common big game in the mountains of the Great Basin when Europeans arrived, just as they were in prehistoric times. The earliest written records of bighorn sightings provide evidence of their presence. In June 1831 hunters from John Work's Hudson's Bay Company beaver-trapping brigade saw "the tracks of some sheep in the

[Independence] Mountains but they appear[ed] to have been driven off by some . . . Indians." In the Santa Rosa Range, Work reported that "the best hunters of the party were out in the mountains, in quest of sheep, but without success."[1] Another account suggests that bighorns were numerous in some localities. On January 12, 1844, Frémont's party "saw herds of mountain sheep . . . at Pyramid Lake" and the next day after moving camp "saw several flocks of sheep, but did not succeed in killing any."[2] Around 1890 Rancher Owen Vaughn observed as many as thirty mountain sheep in one band in the Ruby Mountains. Other small bands could be observed in the course of a day's horseback ride.[3]

According to longtime Reno resident Dr. E. C. Secor, sheep were numerous in the Ruby Mountains in the 1870s. Bighorns were common in the mountains to the north at the end of the nineteenth century. Homesteader Hugh Martin recalled firing at a lone ram on Copper Mountain. At the sound of his rifle, "the surrounding slopes, which earlier appeared devoid of life, suddenly erupted with running sheep."[4]

Pronghorn were widely distributed, as evidenced by the distribution of Indian antelope traps and "antelope" place-names on contemporary maps (e.g., Antelope Valley, Little Antelope Summit). Contemporary reports indicate that there were fewer antelope in the central and eastern valleys than were present north of today's U.S. Highway 50, where the valleys were more productive. Sightings in the north were nonetheless variable, probably reflecting weather factors and disturbance by Indians. On May 25, 1831, John Work's hunters killed two antelope on the Marys River. He wrote: "Some of the people were out hunting. F. Payette & L. Kanotte killed each an antelope, these are the only Animals to be seen here, and they are so shy that it is difficult to kill any of them." The antelope were scarce in other areas as well. On the east fork of the Owyhee River, Work's party found "not an animal except a chance antelope to be seen"; and in the vicinity of today's Wildhorse Reservoir, "not an animal to be seen but Antelopes and but few of them and even these are so shy that it is difficult to approach them." He saw no antelope at all in Independence Valley or on the lower Little Humboldt River. The two pronghorn sighted in the Quinn River valley Work characterized as a novelty.[5]

In June 1829 Peter Skene Ogden's men sighted eight antelope and killed two in three days' hunting in the mountains adjacent to the Humboldt Sink. "As this is the season that animals resort to the rivers and as we have not seen one on its banks," he reported, "I may consequently conclude that they are very scarce, and woe to him that depends on them for support."[6]

The antelope Edwin Bryant saw in the droughty summer of 1846 were concentrated along the Humboldt River near present-day Elko. Two hunters in Bryant's party killed an antelope on August 9 that "was one of a drove about twenty." On their march the following day they saw "not less than three or four hundred antelopes, with which the valley seems to teem. They are extremely timid and wild, discovering us usually by the scent." At Immigrant Springs, a day's travel to the west, they sighted "a large number of antelopes as usual."[7] Ogden's journal entries for the spring of 1829 make no mention of antelope in this region.[8]

Ogden's company saw large groups of antelope elsewhere in northeastern Nevada. "This day the hunters killed an antelope, a large herd was seen but were very wild," he wrote of his crossing of the Montello Valley in late December 1828. A few days later his party observed numerous antelope tracks on Grouse Creek, just across today's Utah–Nevada border, but saw no animals.[9] Nearly twenty years later, Robert Bliss was in nearby Thousand Springs Valley with the Mormon Battalion. On a day in early October 1847 he observed "plenty of antelope" but noted "they are shy of us."[10]

Few pioneers were as familiar with the area between Salt Lake City and today's Ely, Nevada, as Howard Egan, the Mormon settler who established the central route across Nevada. Having befriended the local Indians, he was one of the few white people to witness an antelope drive. Egan accompanied Chief Whitehorse and his Indian friends to the north end of Antelope Valley, about twenty miles northwest of Deep Creek near the Utah–Nevada boundary. The old trap had been repaired, the weather was cold, and the Indians expected a good catch. The wings of the trap, constructed of uprooted sagebrush piled atop other shrubs, started about four miles apart and gradually converged. The corral at the head of the wings was about two hundred feet in diameter and strongly constructed of juniper posts. The Indians moved slowly toward the corral, hazing the animals as they went. "The catch was about twenty-five, mostly all bucks and does, there being only five or six yearlings in the bunch," Egan reported. His Indian friends told him "that the last drive, before this one at this place, was nearly twelve years ago and the old men never expected to see another at this place, for it would take many years to increase in sufficient numbers to make it pay to drive."[11]

Several years later, Captain Simpson was informed that antelope were frequently seen in Antelope Valley, but two of his men who went out ahead of the main party were unsuccessful in killing any. Simpson encountered many signs of antelope and saw a herd in northern Monitor Valley. His party saw "a number of antelope" in Smoky Valley as well.[12]

All the early reports indicate that mule deer were scarce in contrast to bighorn sheep and pronghorn, probably because of habitat limitations. White-tailed deer did not occur at all in Nevada. Mule deer are browsers and thus prefer certain woody plants to grasses. Their scarcity in northern Nevada is reflected in the experiences of Hudson's Bay Company trapping expeditions, whose records make no mention of deer either being sighted or killed. Ogden's annoyance with the scarcity of mule deer is reflected in his May 31, 1826, journal entry: "Hunters were in the Mountains in quest of Deer but did not see the track of one what a wretched country." He traversed the west side of the Independence and Bull Run mountains in late April and early May 1829, then crossed the Santa Rosa Range. Not a single animal was sighted during that time despite the best efforts of his experienced hunters.[13]

The scarcity of deer had a critical bearing on the trappers' survival. Fore-warned by Ogden's 1826 experience, John Work wrote from the Raft River, Idaho, before entering Nevada: "We have a long way to march through a country nearly destitute of Animals of any kind, and this is the last place where we are likely to find any buffaloe [bison]." To avoid the risk of starving, Work and his party killed bison on the Snake and Raft rivers and dried the meat. Later in the march, those who had not laid in an adequate supply were eventually forced to kill their horses for food. Work's party did not see any deer on the Marys River, on the north fork of the Humboldt, or in the Independence Mountains. In the Santa Rosa Range he lamented that "the best hunters were out but as usual did not see a single animal of any sort."[14]

Captain Simpson's journal of his travels in central Nevada in 1859 likewise does not mention deer.[15] Henry Eno, a resident of Hamilton, wrote on August 8, 1869: "There is but little game here some few deer."[16] Deer were so rare in central Nevada in the 1860s that a hunt usually attracted the attention of local newspapers.

At the turn of the century, Tasker Oddie, a future governor of Nevada, observed a number of deer tracks at the head of the Reese River in the Toiyabe Range but did not actually see a deer. "They stay hidden in the mountains and are very hard to get unless you take plenty of time to hunt them," he noted.[17]

Although seldom seen on summer ranges, deer did concentrate in some localities during the winter. On January 26, 1844, Frémont recorded their presence in the vicinity of Devil's Gate north of Bridgeport, California, noting that "from the fresh trails which occurred frequently during the morning, deer appeared to be remarkably numerous in the mountain." These animals summered in the Sierra Nevada.[18] In 1878 John Muir noted that the upper slope of Wheeler Peak in the Snake Range of eastern Nevada "was well marked with tracks of the mule deer."[19]

The historical literature contains one record of elk being sighted in Nevada. The Simpson party encountered a lone animal on July 20, 1859, in Stevenson's Canyon near Conner Summit southeast of Ely. A second animal was observed the following day in Red Canyon in the Snake Range east of Sacramento Pass.[20] John Work observed "tracks of elk, black tail deer, & sheep" in the Toana Mountains in May 1831.[21] Being indigenous to northwestern Utah, elk could have occasionally entered eastern Nevada. The early literature does not mention wild horses, which arrived only with Euro-Americans.

Of the small mammals, black-tailed and white-tailed jackrabbits exhibited striking differences in habitat requirements. Indians netted large numbers of black-tails in sagebrush- and rabbitbrush-dominated valleys. White-tailed jackrabbits were particularly numerous in grassy valleys. Homesteader Charles "Syd" Tremewan recalled times in the latter 1800s when white-tails were so numerous north of Elko that he had trouble with the rabbits eating his haystacks. If not protected, the bottom of the stack would be eaten away and the weight of the overhang would cause it to topple over. According to Tremewan, white-tails were essentially the only jackrabbit species found north of Elko. People traveling north of town around the turn of the century had something to talk about if they happened to run across a black-tailed jackrabbit.[22] George Nelson recalled a winter before the turn of the century when he trapped more than five hundred white-tails around haystacks at his grandfather's Gance Creek ranch in the southern Independence Mountains.[23]

The journals of Hudson's Bay Company trappers Peter Skene Ogden and his successor John Work provide a revealing picture of early beaver populations on the Humboldt River watershed and tributaries of the Snake River. Beaver were not indigenous to the interior drainages of eastern and central Nevada; nor were they found in the Walker, Carson, and Truckee rivers. Beaver-trapping success was generally poor on small mountain-fed streams, while large numbers were taken from the main stem of the Humboldt River and the south fork of the Owyhee River.

While trapping on lower Goose Creek in May 1826, Ogden's men took several dozen beaver during a period of stormy weather. Trapping success fell off, however, as they worked their way northwest into the Snake River watershed. Empty traps on Salmon Falls Creek suggested the absence of beaver. Indians confirmed that this drainage was entirely destitute of them. What was apparently the upper Jarbidge River yielded no beaver; nor were they found in Meadow Creek, a tributary of the Bruneau River. Poor trapping continued as the party worked tributaries of the east fork of the Owyhee River. Though trapping success was influenced to some extent by high water, only six beaver were taken from fifty traps on June 10. The higher-flowing Owyhee River produced forty-four animals—the best one-day catch of the season—and the trappers had a "joyous feast" to celebrate.[24]

Five years later, in May 1831, John Work found all of the low ground flooded along the Marys River. As he advanced up the river he noted that it was "well wooded with willows and appears admirably adapted for beaver yet few appeared to be in it." Trappers "who went farthest up the river" found "no better accounts of the appearance of beaver." This report was consistent with that of Indians who informed Work "that there are some small streams in the mountains where there are a few beaver." The party proceeded west, taking 18 beaver and a single otter in five days. Although the streams in the vicinity of today's Wildhorse Reservoir were well adapted for beaver, the trappers set traps in every direction but "complained that the marks of beaver were scarce." Only 12 were taken from 150 traps, even though, an insert in the journal states, "this valley is not known to have ever been hunted." On the north fork of the Humboldt, trappers "found only one solitary lodge and scarcely a mark of beaver either old or new." Unlike the ephemeral tracks of big game, easily destroyed by wind and rain, beaver sign is hard to miss. Crossing the watershed divide, the party encamped on a tributary of the south fork of the Owyhee River (Jack Creek), which Work described as "well wooded with poplar [aspen] and willows, yet in two places is a mark of beaver to be seen." Work's men took 85 beaver from the south fork and its tributaries.[25] When Ogden had worked these waters during late April and early May 1829, his men took a total of 245.[26]

Trapping success in the Humboldt River far exceeded that in the mountains. Ogden's men trapped the Humboldt from its confluence with the Little Humboldt upstream to the vicinity of today's Carlin in late November and December 1828. Despite extreme cold (which meant high-quality pelts), this region yielded 651 beaver, including more than a dozen procured from Indians. On December 9 the trappers were forced to suspend operations because of ice buildup. After wintering in Utah, Ogden commenced the spring hunt on April 10, 1829, about a mile below the confluence of the north fork of the Humboldt. Trappers dispatched to the north fork found "no beaver in it." When twenty traps set on the Humboldt yielded none either, Ogden pulled his camp and headed downstream, remarking: "Beaver are certainly scattered in this river." A contingent of trappers sent up the south fork of the Humboldt returned with fifty-seven pelts, and 30 more beaver were trapped below Elko.[27]

After an exploration sortie to the north, Ogden resumed trapping on the Humboldt a few miles above present-day Winnemucca. These waters proved highly productive. Between May 11 and June 5 the party took 541 beaver between the outlet of the Little Humboldt and the Humboldt Sink. Pleased with the results, Ogden remarked: "In no part of the country have I found beaver more abundant than in this river and I apprehend that we will not soon find another to equal it." The productivity of this region is evident in his observation: "I have already observed the Indians of this river destroy a great number of beaver, and I am correct in saying so for scarcely one have I seen but his shoes are made of beaver skin, and when I consider how numerous they are the number destroyed must be great." After losing nearly one hundred traps to beavers and Indians, the brigade was down to eighty-two. Having learned from Indians that eight days' travel would take them to a large river (the Truckee) devoid of beaver, the brigade turned for home.[28]

That the Humboldt and the south fork of the Owyhee produced many beavers while trapping success was generally poor in mountainous streams apparently reflected differences in carrying capacity. However, this does not explain the scarcity or absence of these animals in streams characterized as "admirably suited to beaver." Suggestions that the Rocky Mountain or American Fur Company had already trapped these waters are not substantiated in the Hudson's Bay Company journals or elsewhere in the literature. It is evident that beaver were susceptible to depredation by Indians, who killed them by breaking dams and destroying lodges for food and pelts. Mountain streams were also vulnerable to being overrun by fire. Though no doubt an exaggeration, Ogden estimated that at least 60,000 beaver had been killed by fire in southeastern Oregon during the extremely dry summer of 1827 when streamside vegetation and marshes dried up and burned.[29]

Fire certainly played a significant ecological role for the beaver. By setting vegetation back to initial succession, it influenced the structural integrity of dams built with young aspen on steep-gradient streams. These dams would have been susceptible to washout during high water.[30]

Government surveys in the second half of the 1800s provide snippets of information on avian wildlife. Ornithologists attached to government surveys collected birds and prepared skins that were placed in the Smithsonian Institution and other repositories. King survey ornithologist Robert Ridgway worked in western, central, and northern Nevada in 1867–68. W. J. Hoffman, attached to the 1871 Wheeler survey, traversed a portion of northern Nevada and the central and southern parts of the state. H. W. Henshaw made collections in the Carson City locality and regions to the north for the Corps of Engineers' survey of 1877–78.

Ridgway left a detailed account of his fieldwork, including camp locations, collection areas, and vegetation types comprising bird habitats. He recorded bird distribution as it related to vegetation in twelve distinct habitat types and identified 108 bird species in these habitats, including a few unique to Utah. Seven species were characteristic of aspen groves, 9 of pinyon-juniper, 9 of mountain meadows or parks, and 25 of wooded river valleys. At Pyramid Lake Ridgway collected "large numbers of the previously very rare eggs of several species of water-fowl breeding on islands."[31] The lake's Anaho Island continues to provide an important sanctuary immune from terrestrial predators other than rattlesnakes.

Game bird populations varied regionally across Nevada. Immigrants' journals indicate that sage grouse were common along the Humboldt River corridor during the 1840s and 1850s. In 1859 Simpson found "many signs of sage-hen" in the Kobeh Valley.[32] In the latter 1870s Henshaw reported that these birds were abundant east of the Sierra Nevada, a conclusion consistent with the experience of J. LeConte's University of California, Berkeley excursion party of 1870 near Fales Hot Springs east of the Sonora Junction, which found sage grouse to be "very abundant in the brush and trout in the streams, in this region."[33] Curiously, the 1826–31 Hudson's Bay Company journals covering what was to be in later years highly productive habitat in northern Nevada do not mention sage grouse at all. The hungry trappers would almost certainly have supplemented their meager food supply with sage grouse had these been common.

Ornithologists found sharp-tailed grouse closely associated with perennial grass and aspen. In September 1868 Ridgway collected a young female sharp-tail and found the species "very abundant" in ryegrass meadows of the East Humboldt Range near Wells.[34] Hoffman found them in moderate numbers in the Bull Run Mountains.[35] Henshaw reported an absence of sharp-tails in the latter 1870s in western Nevada, but to the north, near the Oregon border, found them present in large numbers.[36] Sharp-tails also occurred historically in eastern Nevada, as evidenced by Henry Eno's report of a few grouse and sage hens near Hamilton in 1869. "The grouse resemble prairie chickens," he wrote.[37]

Few historical accounts of blue grouse are available. This bird is a resident of coniferous forests, which for the most part are restricted to northerly slopes in mountainous regions of Nevada. Henshaw reported blue grouse on the eastern slope of the Sierra Nevada in the latter 1870s, and independent scientists and others reported them in various mountainous regions in the early 1900s.[38]

Fragmentary reports indicate that mountain quail were indigenous to several locations in Nevada. During the latter 1870s Henshaw found them to be "much more numerous within an area 25 miles outside Carson City than anywhere to the north." Post-1900 reports show widely scattered populations. California valley quail, common today in the valleys of western Nevada, were introduced by pioneers. According to Henshaw, "this quail is nowhere indigenous to the eastern slope [Sierra Nevada], as the high mountains offer a complete barrier to its extension."[39]

Despite its reputation as the driest state in the nation, Nevada has played host to a wide variety of migrating and nesting waterfowl. Primary areas of concentration included Pyramid Lake, Walker Lake, Humboldt Sink, Stillwater Marsh, Ruby Marsh, and Duckwater Marsh. In years of plentiful precipitation, many waterfowl occupied playa lakes. In May 1859 Captain Simpson observed numerous sandhill cranes, curlews, and other marsh birds in Diamond Valley.[40] Mountain streams also had their visitors. An immigrant party traveling down Bishop Creek north of Wells in 1849 reported: "Game is ours in plenty—sage hens, ducks, geese, and cranes are numerous."[41]

The widespread historical distribution of fish in Great Basin waters is well documented. The Lahontan cutthroat trout was found in all of the Lahontan drainage system of west-central Nevada; Pyramid, Tahoe, and Walker lakes; and the Humboldt, Truckee, Carson, and Walker rivers and their tributary lakes and streams.[42] Redband trout, an interior form of rainbow trout, are native to northern Nevada tributaries of the Snake River. Yellowstone cutthroat trout occur in the upper Snake River tributaries in extreme northeastern Nevada. Bonneville cutthroat trout occupy isolated eastern Nevada streams once connected to glacial Lake Bonneville in Utah.[43] Salmon came up the waters of the Columbia River system to spawn in the Owyhee, Bruneau, Jarbidge, and Salmon Falls drainages.

The Carson River supported trout in abundance. On August 14, 1849, immigrant Palmer C. Tiffany stopped and camped north of present-day Genoa and wrote: "We feasted this morning to our heart's content on some excellent salmon trout that were taken with hooks and lines last evening. . . . The largest we caught was 20 inches long, tho there are larger ones in the river."[44] Other anglers were not always so successful. In 1860 newspaper reporter Dan DeQuille fished on the Carson River eight miles below Fort Churchill for trout ranging in weight from one to five pounds—without success.[45]

The Reese River—named by Captain Simpson for John Reese—was known to Indians as Fish Creek. Simpson reported that "trout weighing two and a half pounds are found in it."[46] On August 26, 1859, L. A. Scott, a member of what was probably the first wagon train to Genoa, camped on the Reese River and "caught a mess of trout for supper, the largest weighing nearly three pounds."[47]

Immigrants' experiences indicate that the upper Humboldt River fishery was highly productive. On September 9, 1848, Henry Bigler "caught lots of trout . . . where the Humboldt River rises from springs near today's Wells, Nevada."[48] While encamped on Goose Creek on October 7, 1847, Robert Bliss' party had "a fine sport catching Trout to night; the streams are full of fish in this country."[49] On August 12, 1863, James Yager's party spent the evening near today's Elko Hot Springs catching fish with hook and line and a seine constructed from willow brush. They took a total of 140 trout, suckers, and other fish species, the largest trout being eighteen inches in length.[50] The *Elko Independent* of June 30, 1869, noted that boys were catching long stringers of cutthroat trout in Maggie and Susie creeks and on stretches of the Humboldt River near Carlin using grasshoppers for bait. "It was not unusual for fish to weigh 5–6 pounds and a recent catch went 8 pounds." Cutthroat of this size continued to be caught into the 1950s.

Few firsthand accounts of fishing for salmon in Nevada have surfaced. One of these is the experience of Eva Rizzi Smith documented in an October 31, 1945, interview when she was seventy-four years old. The salmon used to come up the Owyhee River in the spring to spawn and would continue up into the smaller streams. "They came up Jerritt Creek where my father's first ranch was located," she recalled. "I remember the people coming up from town to spear the salmon, it was great sport and easier to get them in the smaller streams."[51] In the mid-1950s rancher Steve Urriola related a corroborating fish story from Marsh Creek, which emanates from the Independence Mountains just north of Jerritt Canyon. He told Gruell of the time an elderly woman had stopped by on a warm summer day and asked if she could cross his property. She said she wanted to visit Marsh Creek and reminisce about the time when, as a young girl, she jumped into Marsh Creek and straddled a large salmon.

Colorful anecdotes from longtime residents of northern Elko County add flavor to the rich heritage of the land. Two such involve black bears, and three are about wolverines. Even though scientific evidence of the presence of these animals in the Bruneau and Jarbidge river basins is lacking, the fireside tales have the ring of truth. In a 1963 interview, Hugh Martin recalled the experience of an old Indian friend who had been badly injured by a female black bear.

The Indian was walking along a trail with his head down, not paying attention, when a female black bear swiped her powerful paw across his face, breaking his jaw. From time to time the Indian would present the Martin family with a salmon and be invited to dinner. Because the jaw had not knitted properly, the Indian had to hold it into place in order to chew.[52]

Another bear incident involved Antone Alives and Johnnie Failas while they were riding horseback in the Wickiup Creek drainage, a tributary of the Bruneau. They chanced upon a large black bear, and Failas came close to being badly mauled when he tried to rope the animal. He was saved by the skill of Alives, who managed to rope one of the bear's feet.[53]

The 1963 Martin interview included his recollection of trapping wolverine, which the locals called "skunk bear" or "man eaters." Around 1883, Hugh and his older brother trapped about a dozen of these animals, several of them in Martin Creek above the family homestead. Syd Tremewan told of John Weatherford (Rutherford) witnessing a wolverine dragging a lamb that it had killed. George Nelson recalled Mexican cowboys in the Bruneau country "offering a pretty good price if you could get them a wolverine hide, because they had their chaps made of it." One winter, Nelson took a shot at a wolverine in the Bruneau drainage and wounded the animal. After following a blood trail on horseback through deep snow, he set his dog on the track. The dog could throw a deer, yearling heifer, or steer by grabbing the nose or throat, but it was no match for a wolverine, even a wounded one. "That dog came back with his tail between his legs and he wouldn't get away from me," Nelson said.[54]

Early wildlife populations reflected the composition and structure of the vegetation that made up their habitat. Those that preferred herbaceous plants for food were well represented, having been habituated to these environments over millennia. Antelope and bighorn sheep were relatively common. Mule deer were scarce. Considerable numbers of white-tailed jackrabbits and sharp-tailed grouse frequented grassy areas. Yearly runs of Pacific salmon took place on waters flowing into the Snake River. Lahontan cutthroat trout and native suckers were abundant in many Great Basin rivers and streams. These habitats and their occupants were to undergo a dramatic change following Euro-American settlement. Probable reasons for the change include climatic extremes, woodcutting, livestock grazing, and altered fire regimes.

III

Postsettlement

6

Climate
Averages and Extremes

Along with Euro-American settlement came an unprecedented increase in Nevada's woody vegetation. The causes are widely debated. Some plant ecologists believe that the temperature increase of 0.6°F–1.1°F since 1900 has increased the growth of perennial forbs and woody plants.[1] Others have pointed out that the primary impacts of climate result from extreme events—a reflection of the fact the climate is inherently variable.[2] Semiarid regions such as Nevada are particularly erratic, being influenced by wide variations in climatic extremes much more than humid regions are. Thus, one might expect short-term changes in woody vegetation to be influenced more by extreme events than by climatic averages. In fact, extreme events are an essential aspect of the functioning of ecosystems.[3]

Plants in a particular region are adapted to a composite of weather conditions that includes the timing of frost and frost-free periods, temperature, humidity, precipitation, sunshine, and winds. Every farmer and gardener is aware that plants respond to the frequency and magnitude of extremes in these weather events.

Plant growth in the Great Basin can be six times greater in wet years than in dry years.[4] A year of high moisture can promote an abundance of sagebrush or pinyon pine seedlings. Two or more consecutive moist years may be needed for successful reproduction of perennials—one to produce more seeds than needed by ants and rodents, and then additional amounts of rainfall to promote germination and establishment. Extensive die-offs of desert shrubs occur during or following successive years of above average precipitation. During periods of drought, shallow-rooted perennial grasses may die because of insufficient moisture while deep-rooted shrubs survive.[5] Likewise, moisture-stressed pinyon becomes susceptible to being killed by insects when precipitation is deficient. These and other examples clearly show that plant growth is inextricably linked to large fluctuations in seasonal temperature and precipitation.

Ernst Anteves' classic 1930s study of tree growth in the Susanville region provides a snapshot of fluctuating weather patterns of the past.[6] Knowing that growth patterns are sensitive to the vicissitudes of precipitation and temperature, he used trees as an indicator of past weather and climate. The growth rings of trees are narrow in drought years and wide in wet years, when conditions for growth are optimum. Using growth rings of trees in a virgin forest just bordering the Great Basin, Anteves was able to determine the general growing conditions that occurred during a span of four hundred years. Contributing to his study were trees that became established during the beginning years of the Little Ice Age, which ended in the mid-1800s.

Anteves identified thirteen periods during which precipitation was extremely light. These included two long intervals of serious drought, one lasting some twenty-seven years, from 1621 to 1648, and the second lasting thirteen years during the birth of the nation, from 1776 to 1789. Anteves believed that conditions during these years were even more severe than the Dust Bowl years (1924–34) during which he was completing his study. The severe drought of 1776–89 was followed a dozen years later by the twelve wettest years of the four-hundred-year study.

Fluctuating periods of wetness and drought were influencing lake levels before Euro-American settlement. James Clyman, a fur trapper and contemporary of Jim Bridger, bore witness to that. Visiting Utah's Great Salt Lake on June 1, 1846, he "observed that this lake like all the rest of this wide spread Sterility has nearly wasted away one half of its surface since 1825 when I floated around it in my Bull Boate and we crossed a large Bay of this Lake with our horses which is now dry." The signs of drought he was observing in 1846 were widespread. Earlier, at the Humboldt Sink, Clyman had noted: "This entire region is now entirely dried up and has the most thirsty appearance of any place I have ever witnessed."[7]

Anteves also observed a pattern of drought and moisture abundance at Walker and Pyramid lakes from historical accounts he analyzed. Walker Lake was at a low level in 1861 when its surface stood at 4,060 feet above sea level. Fed by the Walker River and unimpeded by reservoir dams, the lake rose 17 feet in 1862 on being fed by meltwater from the abundant snowpack of 1861–62. Fluctuating lake levels were further indicated by dead trees standing under 4 or 5 feet of water at the northern end of the lake in 1882, trees that may have grown during the 1840s and 1850s and drowned during the rise in water in the 1860s. From Frémont's account and sketches Anteves determined that Pyramid Lake stood at about 3,860 feet above sea level in 1844. It was very low in 1862, and dead trees standing in the water testified to even lower levels previously. Pyramid Lake rose to 3,877 feet in 1867, rose an additional 10–15 feet in 1868, and reached its highest observed stand in 1869. During the latter two years it overflowed into Winnemucca Lake. Anteves concluded that in 1862, adjacent Winnemucca Lake "had been confined to the central part of its basin . . . and submerged dead cottonwood trees also showed that the lake had previously been much smaller, doubtless nearly or fully desiccated."[8] By 1882 the lake had risen more than 50 feet above the 1867 level.[9]

Anteves' analysis of meteorological records in western Nevada going back to 1870 indicated "large fluctuations" during the 1870s and 1880s; 1870 and 1871 were unusually droughty, and 1873 and 1875 were also dry. The winter of 1873–74 was cold and snowy; that of 1875–76 was rainy and snowy. The winter of 1879–80 was so severe that one-third of the livestock in Nevada perished. A few years after that tragic and disastrous winter, the summers of 1887–89 were increasingly dry, with 1889 being the driest in the history of the state until 1931. Extreme drought was abruptly broken by enormous precipitation in the winter of 1889–90, the most severe winter ever experienced in Nevada.[10]

Beginning in 1901, precipitation emanating from the Sierra Nevada was calculated by formal measurement of flows from the Truckee, Carson, and Walker rivers. On the whole, precipitation increased from the turn of the century to 1907—one of the heaviest winters on record. Then precipitation decreased in general through 1937. Anteves observed that "subnormal snow and rain from December 1930 to July 1931 combined with high summer temperatures caused an exceptionally severe drought, with disastrous effects on agriculture and stock raising. The year ranks as the driest in the history of the state up to that date."[11]

Anteves' analysis of northeastern Nevada meteorological records going back to 1870 indicated a fluctuating pattern like that of western Nevada. Other observations support this. Measurements at Elko, Halleck, and Wells showed a low minimum annual snowfall and rainfall in 1872, low maximums in 1876 and 1877, and low minimum precipitation in 1878 and 1879. Humboldt River flows suggest the water supply in most of the 1880s was quite good. In 1882 the river spilled from Humboldt Lake and flowed into the Carson Sink. Flows for irrigation were more than adequate in the period 1885–87, but in 1888 sections of the Humboldt River at Halleck were entirely dry. The deadly winter of 1889–90 was followed by spring flooding. Precipitation in the Humboldt River basin was apparently quite low in 1909, but the greatest flood on record followed in March 1910. Annual flow in the river was unusually high in 1914 and exceedingly low in 1915. Exceptional quantities of snow accumulated in the Ruby Mountains during the winter of 1916–17, followed by heavy and frequent rains in the spring and early summer. Subnormal moisture prevailed over the next three years. In 1923–24 the snow cover in the mountains was extremely light, and the precipitation recorded at the weather stations was the lowest on record. In 1925 precipitation was comparatively heavy, but because of exceptional melting in the early spring, the Humboldt was lower than it had been since 1889.[12]

This litany of statistics demonstrates the inconsistency of weather patterns in the western Great Basin. Wide fluctuations in temperature and precipitation continue. Extreme winters occurred in 1948–49 and particularly in 1951–52, which stands out as one of the most severe since Euro-American settlement. One of the driest years on record occurred in 1954, when stretches of the lower south fork of the Humboldt River went dry. The wet year of 1983–84 resulted in filling of pluvial lakes—lakes dependent on precipitation—including the Great Salt Lake, which reached a record level in 1984. That year, the Western Pacific Railroad had to haul in hundreds of trainloads of earth from northeastern Nevada to maintain dikes to keep the roadbed dry. Pluvial lakes of Nevada were dry in 1992, a consequence of drought. This trend was broken when heavy precipitation occurred in 1993, 1995, and 1996. The flood of record on the Truckee occurred early in 1997, and rainfall in 1998 was also above average. In a desert, most years receive below average precipitation; however, some years are extremely wet with 200 percent or more of average occurring. The decade 1999–2009 was droughty, excepting the moist years of 2005 and 2006.[13]

Plant ecologists have also identified factors other than climate that appear to have played a role in the unprecedented changes in western Great Basin vegetation. Carbon dioxide related to the burning of fossil fuels will likely cause further changes. Increased carbon dioxide acts as a fertilizer and tends to favor cool-season grasses over warm-season grasses, woody plants over herbaceous ones, and annuals over perennials. Carbon dioxide levels have been increasing since records have been kept and are now at their highest since 2.7 million years ago.[14]

Nevadans often say, "If you don't like the weather, wait a bit—it will change." The record supports that maxim. Nevada's climate is uncertain and uneven. There have been irregular periods of drought and wetness over the past several hundred years. Weather extremes can result in loss of plants or heightened reproduction, depending on the individual species and its physiological requirements. Variability in weather patterns appears to have been more important than climatic averages in influencing regeneration and growth of vegetation.

In the century and a half since silver was discovered on the Comstock, people have affected the land in many ways, particularly by woodcutting, livestock grazing, and influencing fire occurrence. In the following three chapters we will examine evidence of these impacts.

7

Woodcutting
Boomtowns before
Fossil Fuels

The arrival of Euro-American settlers, especially miners, brought a quick and dramatic change to Nevada's woodlands. Processing ore required heat. Miners and the local economy that supported them needed wood for infrastructure, cooking, and fuel. The trees for miles around mining camps began to fall under the onslaught of ax and saw. The thrifty Chinese even dug up tree roots in some localities.

The discovery of silver at Virginia City in 1859 attracted thousands of miners, and by 1864 hundreds of laborers were cutting and hauling pinyon and juniper to keep up with the demand for fuel for mills, hoisting works, and domestic use. Neighboring hills were soon stripped of their trees, and woodcutters ventured farther afield to meet requirements. Trains of loaded carts came daily from the outlying Palmyra district and El Dorado Canyon—the chief sources of the wood supply. Historian Eliot Lord wrote of the Comstock, "Cheap fuel was a pressing want of the mining district, and the neighboring hills were so scantly covered with trees that it was soon necessary to bring wood from the Sierra."[1] The eastern slope of the Sierra Nevada produced an abundant supply of pine and fir, great quantities of which were either sawed into square-cut timber for shoring mine shafts or used for fuel. Lumber consumption for building purposes and mining timbers was estimated to run twenty-five million board feet yearly. During the height of Comstock mining in 1867, mining commissioner J. Ross Browne estimated that 120,000 cords of wood were used annually.[2] By 1881 Virginia City's ore had played out, and the demand for wood faded away.

Woodcutting in Nevada's interior had begun in 1862 with the discovery of silver at Austin. Within a few years prospectors had located ore deposits containing silver, gold, and lead. The most productive of these were in the Aurora, Bodie, Austin, Eureka, Belmont, White Pine, and Pioche mining districts.[3] Enormous quantities of trees were taken from adjacent woodlands for domestic use and to fuel stamp mills and stoke furnaces. Eureka, the largest of these operations, had been cleared of trees for a distance of twenty miles by 1874. As mining continued and hauling distances increased, the mining companies began burning charcoal rather than cordwood for fuel. Charcoal was advantageous because it burned at a much higher temperature than wood, weighed one-third less, and had one-half the bulk. The conversion of wood into charcoal at Eureka and at other large districts allowed mines to meet fuel requirements that would have been prohibitive had fuels been constrained to cordwood.[4] Woodcutters produced the charcoal by partially burning pinyon in shallow earthen pits or in brick ovens. Charcoal production in the Eureka district was centered on the Mount Hope region, the outlying Diamond Mountains, and in the Fish Creek range. The Ward charcoal ovens south of Ely, still standing today, are vivid reminders of these early operations. The conversion of great quantities of trees into charcoal required hauling wood forty miles or more in some localities.

Mines outside the major mining districts were widely separated, and woodcutting intensity varied with the size of the operation. Much of the activity was at small camps that operated briefly. The litter and disturbed land at these ephemeral camps drew the attention of John Muir, who was appalled by the extent of the abandoned mining operations he saw in 1879. "Wander where you may throughout the length and breadth of this mountain-barred wilderness, you everywhere come upon these dead mining towns, with their tall chimney-stacks, standing forlorn amid broken walls and furnaces, and machinery half buried in sand."[5]

Mines with higher-grade ore deposits operated until the ore was exhausted, meanwhile consuming enormous quantities of wood that required cutting over considerable acreages. Others terminated operations prematurely because of processing difficulties, the high cost of pumping flooded shafts, or deficient financing. The Tybo Mining Company located in the Hot Creek range, having exhausted the local wood supply, built fifteen brick charcoal ovens five miles to the north to meet its fuel requirements. Mining operations were curtailed in 1879, shortly after the ovens were completed, because of technical difficulties in ore reduction.

The deforestation in various localities, while impressive, did not exhaust the pinyon-juniper woodlands of the western Great Basin. After exploring the mountain ranges of central and eastern Nevada during a considerable portion of the summers of 1876–78, Muir commented: "Many a square mile has already been denuded in supplying [fuel] demands, but so great is the area covered by it, no appreciable loss has as yet been sustained."[6] Even though some mining camps hauled in wood from up to fifty miles away, this did not translate into a one-hundred-mile-diameter circle devoid of trees. Trees easy to access because they were locally abundant, low on a mountain, close to a road, or of optimum size would have been taken first and hauled farther.

Pinyon pine burns hot because of its pitch content, but it makes poor lumber for construction. Woodcutters had to venture into the higher elevations to cut limber pine, Jeffrey pine, white fir, and subalpine fir for that purpose. The intensity of this cutting was particularly heavy in parts of the Toiyabe, Toquima, and White Pine ranges adjacent to the major central Nevada mining districts. In the mid-1860s five mills were supplying mines at Belmont. There were a dozen mills in the White Pine mining district. Even so, many high-elevation tree stands were spared because they were too far removed from the mines and mills.

The absence of pinyon and juniper in the mining districts of Elko and Humboldt counties forced companies to utilize alternative fuels. Sagebrush fueled furnaces at Tuscarora and Cornucopia. Aspen and mountain-mahogany drove the low-capacity Spring City smelter in the Santa Rosa Range. The Pequop, Toana, Ruby, Monitor, and Desatoya ranges had no operational mines, so trees were not cut for mining purposes there.

Within a span of just over two decades, woodcutting in support of mining had nearly ended in Nevada. When a new mining boom began in the treeless Tonopah-Goldfield area in the early 1900s, the demand for trees as fuel was minimal. Power needs were now met by electricity or coal brought in by railroads.

Many of the ranches that were established to provide meat for mining camps remained after the miners left. The ranchers cut durable juniper for fence posts, and juniper, pinyon, and mahogany supplied heating and cooking needs for ranch families and for communities adjacent to woodland.

8

Livestock Grazing

Herbivory and Range Depletion

Word of rich silver ore east of the Sierra Nevada spread through California like wildfire in 1860. Crowds of men packed their belongings and hiked over the high mountain passes in search of riches. When ore was discovered at Aurora, prospectors began to spread out across northern Nevada. Fresh meat was needed in large quantities to supply the miners and the merchants who provisioned them. Livestock operators began releasing cattle and sheep on ranges that had been little grazed by large mammals since the long moist periods of the Pleistocene. The new concentration of animals caused extreme soil disturbance and steady depletion of grasses and herbs that had stabilized watersheds for millennia. The degradation of this groundcover would have serious consequences.

Livestock grazing began in Nevada before the Comstock discovery. A party from Council Bluffs, Iowa, drove a small herd of cattle across northern Nevada to California in 1844.[1] In the coming years, large numbers of sheep from Texas and New Mexico passed through Nevada en route to California, where demand for meat was high.[2] Dick Wooton apparently followed the Humboldt River route in 1852 with a herd 9,000 sheep. The following year, Kit Carson and Lucien Maxwell came down the Humboldt route with a herd of 13,000 sheep, also bound for California. As the sheep population expanded in California, sheep owners began driving their animals east. Some 2–3 million sheep were driven east between 1865 and 1900. One of the first such operations was Major Kimball's thirty-five-man party who drove a herd of sheep across northern Washoe and Humboldt counties in 1864, bound for the Idaho gold fields.

The Nevada cattle industry had its beginning in 1858 when 1,500 head were driven over the Sierra Nevada and grazed in Carson Valley and the Truckee Meadows. After fattening, they were driven back and "quickly snapped up at the California mining districts."[3] Newspaper publisher Horace Greeley saw evidence of a cattle drive through central Nevada on his cross-country trip in 1859.[4] At Pine Creek his stage was delayed where "a drove of 1,000 head of cattle" had destroyed the bridge. Lewis "Longhorn" Bradley, a future governor of Nevada, introduced five hundred Texas longhorns into the Reese River valley in 1862, becoming the first significant livestock operator in central Nevada. A "goodly number of ranchers" had established operations in the valley by the end of 1863.[5] Significant cattle grazing in northern Nevada began during the drought of 1864, when Jack Southerland drove 20,000 head from his ranch in Tulare County, California, to this productive summer range.[6]

Nevada's cattle industry was in full swing by 1869 when thousands of longhorns were trailed up from Texas. By the end of the 1870s cattle ranches occupied virtually all of Nevada's valleys. Weather conditions at this time were highly favorable. Abundant rich native grass and adequate water allowed rapid increases in cattle numbers. Seizing the opportunity to expand their operations, some of the more industrious individuals began buying up land. Large ranches were formed in northern Nevada by leasing or purchasing blocks of Central Pacific Railroad lands. People could control enormous acreages of public domain land by purchasing relatively small tracts of nearby land along streams and around springs. Daniel Murphy was one of these enterprising individuals. In 1869 he was reputed to be one of the largest landowners in the world, owning sixty thousand acres in Elko and White Pine counties where he ran 20,000 head of cattle. John Sparks, in partnership with Jasper Harrell and James Tinnian, branded 14,000 calves in 1884. Their breeding herd was said to number 70,000.[7]

Sheep operations were well under way during the 1870s as available feed in the valleys and mountains allowed their numbers to expand. The combined stocking of cattle and sheep proved excessive, however, because the forage base could not sustain such concentrations of large herbivores. By the mid-1880s many areas had been overgrazed to the point of destruction. A December 3, 1886, *Carson City Appeal* article titled "Enough Cattle on the Range" noted that "there is enough horses, cattle and sheep to consume all the grass that grows.... Every year the fact is becoming more apparent that the ranges of the sagebrush country are deteriorating ... it will not be many years before the occupation of most of our stockmen will be gone unless they heed the signs of the times."

Nearly all of the early cattle operators ran their stock on the open range year-round without feeding supplemental hay during the winter months. This practice was to have severe consequences. Coming on the heels of extreme drought during the summer of 1889, the winter of 1889–90 proved to be devastating. Free-ranging cattle, denied the benefit of supplemental hay, perished in great numbers.[8] In the Truckee Meadows and Carson Valley, one-third of the livestock population was lost. One out of every four animals died in Humboldt County, and many ranchers lost half their herds in the Reese River country in central Nevada.

The reduced numbers of cattle on the ranges opened the door for the sheep industry to expand. Prominent sheepmen such as Patrick Flannigan, Henry Anderson, and John G. Taylor got their start in western Nevada. Flannigan grazed 40,000 sheep, 5,000 cattle, and 1,500 horses at the peak of his operation. Anderson ran thousands of sheep in the Sierra Nevada, as well as in Washoe, Eureka, Lander, and Elko counties.[9] Taylor earned the title "King of the Sheepmen" for the size of his operation. After suffering severe losses of sheep in the winter of 1889–90, his operation peaked after World War I with some 60,000 sheep and 10,000 head of cattle grazing on rangelands from Lovelock to Elko County and on into southern Idaho.[10]

In the early 1900s the Adams-McGill Company ran 40,000 sheep and 5,000 cattle in Spring Valley and adjacent ranges in eastern Nevada. In 1909, 137,480 sheep were permitted on the Reese River watershed under the jurisdiction of the Nevada National Forest (later the Toiyabe National Forest, and then combined with the Humboldt to become the Humboldt-Toiyabe National Forest). This region had previously been "open range" and had been heavily stocked since the late 1800s. In 1909 the Humboldt County tax assessor estimated the sheep population in the Santa Rosa Mountains at 180,000, having been augmented by unauthorized "tramp sheep" from the Humboldt National Forest lands to the east. Sheep ranging on the Ruby Mountains during the summer of 1905 numbered somewhere between 80,000 and 100,000.[11]

In 1908 an estimated 1.25 million sheep were crowded onto the best rangelands of northern Elko County according to records of inspectors in charge of dipping sheep under the direction of the Bureau of Animal Industry. Forest inspector G. C. Thompson believed that about 800,000 of them were grazing within the proposed U.S. Forest Service Bruneau addition, which was to become the northern Independence, Gold Creek, and Jarbidge ranger districts of the Humboldt National Forest. The sheep's extreme browsing of aspen was a particularly disturbing impact. After "destroying the forage of the early summer," Thompson explained, the sheep turned to aspen for sustenance. "In all the territory it was noted that all young seedlings had been killed that had been in reach of these stock."[12]

Although sheep numbers were reduced substantially, the depleted ranges continued to be subjected to excessive sheep grazing. In his September 1915 inspection of the Humboldt Division, C. N. Woods found "on many allotments practically no reproduction of aspen less than five or ten years of age." Snowberry, a palatable shrub, "was being killed out by over grazing on some sheep allotments where it grew in least abundance."[13]

At the turn of the century, wild horses (mustangs)—descendants of strays or animals turned out from immigrant wagon trains, mining towns, and ranches—were also making a significant impact on the soils and vegetation. Herds increased rapidly from the 1870s into the 1890s. The plentiful supply depressed prices, which in turn discouraged ranchers from gathering the horses up for sale. The public outcry over excessive horse numbers led to the passage of state legislation in 1897 permitting the removal of "unbranded wild" horses.[14]

Tom Bradstreet from Grand Rapids, Nebraska, was among the first to conduct a large roundup under the new law. He paid cowhands to gather animals from the Diamond A Desert east of the Bruneau River.[15] At the time, local ranchers estimated the population at around five thousand animals. Many were gathered and driven to the railroad at Elko some one hundred miles to the south, but the horse population continued to stay at a high level. Despite efforts to gather them, nearly one hundred thousand mustangs could be found on Nevada's ranges as late as 1910.[16]

Horses were a nuisance, but it was sheep that were stripping most of the forage off the range. The severe impacts of sheep grazing reached a breaking point with cattle operators as the twentieth century opened. Responding to their concerns, the U.S. Forest Service conducted surveys to inventory the quality of the best grazing lands and evaluate their worthiness for inclusion in the federal forest reserve system. In 1905 F. W. Reed concluded that the Ruby Mountains, one of the most important watersheds, "unless properly protected threaten in a few years to become practically ruined by the overgrazing by sheep." To the north, inspections of the Bruneau River region by R. B. Wilson (1906) and G. C. Thompson (1908) revealed that excessive grazing had greatly decreased the carrying capacity of the range. "Since the sheep have been coming in such tremendous numbers in the past five years," Wilson reported, "the cattlemen complain that they can not get their stock fat enough during the summer to winter out hence they are forced to bring in a greater number for feeding than their hay will allow."[17]

The impact of sheep grazing was particularly severe in the Santa Rosa Range. Land Examiner H. E. Woolley's 1910 report describes the effects as devastating and the watersheds as "really in a deplorable condition." Lacking the stabilizing effects of grass cover, many small meadows were being gullied by runoff from spring floods and were "fast disappearing." The condition of live-stock in the Santa Rosas was comparable to that of the Independence Mountains, where "neither the steers nor the wethers are in a marketable condition in the fall."[18]

Syd Tremewan, the first forest supervisor on the Humboldt National Forest, recalled conditions in the Independence Mountains before the land was placed in the forest reserve system. "There were so many [sheep] that the herders would run back and forth trying to beat one another to the better camp sites. This trampling and running around did more damage to the range than the feeding. The whole mountain from Foreman Creek south to Taylor Canyon was just a dust bed." He continued: "One fall in about 1905, Joe Pattani, Sr., sold his cattle to Barney Horn. . . . Those animals were so thin and weak that they had to be fed hay for several weeks at the ranch before they could be driven down to the railroad at Elko."[19]

Cattlemen were convinced that they would be forced out of business unless the government introduced some kind of control measures. A forest reserve system in which the federal government regulated grazing was widely recognized by stockmen and confirmed by the Forest Service's inspections as the only solution to the problem. The first of these federal reserves was established in the Ruby Mountains in 1906, followed by designation of the Humboldt, Santa Rosa, and Toiyabe forest reserves, which were given national forest status shortly thereafter.

The first order of business for Supervisor Tremewan was to reduce sheep numbers on the Humboldt National Forest. A meeting toward that end was held in Elko in March 1909. In attendance were all the stockmen who had been grazing lands under Forest Service jurisdiction. The ultimate objective was to determine which of the operators would be given preference to graze sheep on the forest. Among them were large operators with base property (deeded land) in various counties of the state who had been grazing the public lands in question for a number of years. Others were "tramp outfits," itinerant operators who had swarmed onto prospective forest lands in 1908 in order to establish preference. Supervisor Tremewan recalled that they talked it over among themselves with a great deal of arguing. "One would say, 'I ran sheep in that country a certain year.' . . . 'I had my camp in there first,' and so on." At the end of two days of give and take, it was resolved that sheep running on the Humboldt Division would be reduced from 560,000 to 350,000 head. Operators who had no base property were banished from the Humboldt National Forest.[20] These operators moved to unreserved and unregulated public domain lands (later administered under the Taylor Grazing Act—Grazing Service and then Bureau of Land Management) outside national forests.

The inspection of public lands made in 1901 by Dr. David Griffiths confirmed the abuse of unregulated public lands since the latter part of the nineteenth century. His itinerary took him from Winnemucca to the Pine Forest range and on into Oregon. He reported that with the exception of the tough and persistent saltgrass, no open range in the sagebrush communities had any feed left. Everything edible had been cropped to the ground. "To say the southern portion of this region [Nevada] is overstocked would be putting the matter very mildly," reported Griffiths. In the Pine Forest Range he noted extreme soil impacts due to close pasturing of sheep. His dismay is clear in his comment, "Beautiful pure growths of sheep fescue were completely ruined."[21] According to zoologist Walter P. Taylor of the University of California, this range was stocked with ten thousand cattle and twenty-two thousand sheep in 1909.[22]

University of Nevada botanist P. B. Kennedy surveyed forage conditions in the Tuscarora Mountains and Lone Mountain region of Elko County in the summer of 1902. The area had been grazed exclusively by cattle from the latter 1800s until three years earlier, when sheep had been introduced. All the sagebrush–salt desert shrub communities at the lower elevations showed signs of overgrazing and trampling. "In the surrounding mountains many hundreds of cattle and horses were seen feeding on a luxuriant growth of grasses. . . . The cattle had done considerable trampling damage along the creeks and were . . . exceedingly destructive to serviceberry and chokecherry," which had been transformed to "many thousands of dry sticks four to seven feet high." Sheep grazing had not been extreme except around herders' camps. "There were miles of range country which at this season, were not touched by the sheep." However, fall grazing on shrubby vegetation had left its mark. Sheep had been primarily responsible "for the total destruction of numerous Indian currant, wild currant, and rose bushes."[23]

Grazing continued on public lands without supervision or restrictions into the 1930s. *The Western Range,* a 1936 comprehensive U.S. Forest Service report to Congress, concluded that the detrimental consequences for Nevada's plant communities of a half-century of overgrazing were enormous. Four levels were used to evaluate the degree of depletion rangelands had suffered. Northern Nevada was in the "material depletion" category (26–50 percent), while the vast majority of Nevada was in the "severe" category (51–75 percent).[24]

Responding to the need for management of public lands, Congress passed the Taylor Grazing Act of 1934. The Act affected land all across the West, including

71 percent of Nevada's landscape. The Taylor Act would have little effect on abusive grazing practices owing to a lack of serious commitment to develop and enforce grazing regulations. To keep the public domain lands from going to the Forest Service, Secretary of the Interior Harold Ickes had bargained away any opportunity for a strong agency. He promised ranchers no extensive bureaucracy and low fees tied to the cost of minimally administering a lease program. During World War II, even these regulations were all but ignored to allow maximum production of meat for the armed forces.[25]

In 1946 an executive reorganization combined the remnants of the Grazing Service with those of the General Land Office to create the Bureau of Land Management (BLM). The Grazing Service had been grossly underfunded because Congress could not agree about grazing fees. The House demanded an increase, but the Senate continued to refuse after years of scrutinizing the Grazing Service, with field hearings held throughout the West by Nevada senator Pat McCarran's Public Lands Committee.[26] No mission or mandate was specified for the BLM; the authorities and functions of the predecessor agencies remained in effect. In the early 1950s the BLM set a ten-year goal to bring grazing use into balance with the capacity of the range to produce forage.[27] Adjudication continued into the 1960s and 1970s, when rest rotation grazing was widely implemented to benefit the productivity of perennial plants. Unfortunately, it had mixed results in riparian areas and has become a wildfire liability during years of abundant herbage production. The effects of the National Environmental Policy Act (NEPA) of 1969 opened livestock grazing to more scientific scrutiny. NEPA requires environmental impact statements (EISs) analyzing the effects of land management alternatives. Continued inventory gave way to monitoring for allotment evaluations and multiple use decisions. The ultimate result of these measures has been significant reduction of the number of livestock grazing public rangelands.

Changing social values with respect to environmental protection and conservation of natural resources resulted in passage of the Federal Land Policy and Management Act of 1976, which gave the BLM a charter and brought about further scrutiny of livestock grazing practices and levels.[28] The act placed particular emphasis on wildlife and fish conservation values.

During the 1950s and 1960s efforts were made to rehabilitate deteriorated federal rangelands. Methods included plowing, disking, and seeding with introduced grasses; spraying sagebrush with the herbicide 2-4-D; and removing pinyon and juniper by dragging anchor chains across woodlands and cutting trees with chainsaws. Unfortunately, much of the chaining killed many valuable old trees because treatments were not restricted to areas where trees had encroached sagebrush. These projects brought about short-term increases in forage productivity, but rising fuel costs in the 1970s and shifting staff time to inventories and EISs halted plowing, disking, chaining, seeding, and spraying. Prescribed fire has since been utilized to increase forage production, but the scale of such burning has been minor. Without periodic treatment or naturally recurring fire, sagebrush and/or pinyon and juniper trees return. Woody plants increase while fuels accumulate.

Management on national forests took a turn from livestock production toward recreation with passage of the Multiple Use Sustained Yield Act of 1960. The Renewable Resources Planning Act (1974) and the National Forest Management Act (1976) signaled a changing national philosophy toward planning and recognition of wildlife, water, and environmental conservation values. A key element in this transition was preparation of livestock grazing allotment management plans that stipulated maintenance of desirable ecological conditions for wildlife and fish.

Livestock numbers on Forest Service allotments have been substantially reduced since an aggressive program was initiated in the early 1950s. Conversion of sheep allotments to cattle in the 1960s resulted in a marked change in the distribution of grazing animals. Delaying spring turnout until the range was ready to support them (range readiness) also promoted range improvement on uplands. Many sheep operations shifted to cattle, responding to a changing market for wool and mutton as well as sportsmen's pressure to restock native bighorn sheep. Today, fewer than twenty-five thousand sheep graze Nevada's national forest lands, a drastic reduction from the hundreds of thousands in the past. Cattle avoid the steep terrain formerly utilized by domestic sheep, preferring a more gentle topography. This has shifted the focus of grazing pressure toward riparian areas.

Rangeland management textbooks once taught that land near water should be sacrificed while managers focused on improving the bulk of the forage in the pasture. This held true until the 1980s, when biologists documented the large number of wildlife—and of course fish—that depend on riparian areas for some part or all of their lives. Afterward, riparian areas became the focus in Nevada and across the West.

"Overgrazed" riparian areas fueled the ongoing trend to reduce livestock numbers to attain utilization standards, yet reducing the numbers left the remaining stock concentrated in and near riparian areas. Cattle must drink, and they must have forage. Green riparian plants become the most palatable forage available after uplands have dried out. To avoid substantial stock reductions, exclosures were placed around places where cattle concentrated their use.

It soon became clear that plants and streams protected within exclosures fared much better than those outside the fence. Colonizing plants such as spike rush and brook grass growing on bare, moist sites close to the stream collected fine sediment. This allowed stabilizing plants such as Nebraska sedge and other sedges and willows to anchor stream banks against the forces of flowing water. Areas that had down-cut after historic severe grazing and then widened with the concentrated forces of floods large and small changed dramatically. Wide, shallow streams that formerly got too warm in the summer and too cold in the winter became narrower and deeper active channels with a new floodplain. The floodplain dispersed some of the flood energy, and the stable banks created deeper pools and cover for fish. As water spread across the expanding floodplain it recharged the aquifer. Clean, cool groundwater then flowed back into the stream during long dry periods, benefiting riparian vegetation and fish.

Exclosures are costly to build and maintain, however, and whole watersheds needed restoration. Building exclosures was clearly not *the* answer; nor was extensive fencing, as demonstrated by the Mahogany Creek tributary to Summit Lake where much of the watershed and part of the creek was fenced. Research across the Intermountain West began to show that changing or shortening the period of use for livestock allowed animals to graze and even increase their riparian forage base while riparian areas improved. Riparian plants thrived with periodic use and long periods for uninterrupted growth.[29]

Riparian pastures along with grazing systems or management plans developed for specific watersheds or allotments have been steadily replacing a simple utilization-based approach.[30] Stream survey data using methods first applied in Nevada in 1953 and systematically reapplied after 1977 showed considerable damage to stream habitats.[31] Follow-up surveys have shown considerable improvement in most places.[32] Continued application of "more good than bad practices" remains a focus for improving management along the many streams and seeps where riparian functions are lacking. The interagency Creeks and Community Team now offers Riparian Proper Functioning Condition Assessment and Riparian Grazing Management classes. Rangeland Monitoring and Range Management are also taught collaboratively by interagency teams led by the University of Nevada Cooperative Extension.

A major problem confronting Forest Service and BLM managers today is the proliferation of introduced annual weeds, particularly cheatgrass.[33] An aggressive annual, cheatgrass entered Nevada in the early 1900s, apparently as a contaminant in grain seed.[34] It spread rapidly across western and northern Nevada, being particularly troublesome in the drier regions with a history of heavy livestock grazing. By mid-century cheatgrass was growing abundantly across northern Nevada and had become the number one forage plant for cattle, especially over lower-elevation landscapes. The proliferation of annual and perennial weeds has gained the attention of citizens and agencies across Nevada who have collaboratively formed active cooperative weed management groups. A University of Nevada Cooperative Extension weeds management program identifies many aspects of the weed problem, and a state weed plan provides direction for weed management.[35] Today we recognize that weeds are distributed by virtually all forms of human movement as well as wind, water, livestock, and wildlife. Their proliferation is most noticeable in disturbed sites where there is a virtual absence of competition from native species, but invasive weeds may enter and dominate even undisturbed plant communities. Spraying with approved chemicals or pulling aggressive invasives such as perennial pepperweed (tall white top) and knapweeds is a yearly endeavor to combat their proliferation in problem areas. Reseeding with native or adapted perennials helps prevent reinvasion after spraying. In dry areas successful reseeding may require exotic perennials such as varieties of crested wheatgrass, which has proven remarkably successful after wildfire in sagebrush by mimicking the ecological function of native perennials. Despite such successes, the weed problem will not go away. Weeds will exact high costs whenever they are allowed to dominate native vegetation.

Beginning in the mid-1960s, dry cheatgrass (or red brome in the Mojave region), increasing amounts of perennial grasses, and extensive stands of decadent woody sagebrush and pinyon-juniper trees fueled a series of large, high-intensity wildfires. Fire size and acreage burned increased enormously in the mid-1980s and again in the middle and late 1990s. Continued large fire years raise concerns for the future viability of Nevada's plant communities.

9

Fire

A Changing Force on the Landscape

Settlement brought about profound changes in the way fires burned on the Nevada landscape. By the end of the 1800s towns and mining camps had sprung up throughout the region. Towns such as Winnemucca, Battle Mountain, Elko, and Wells provided railheads for shipping livestock to markets in San Francisco and Chicago. A network of roads served the towns, ranches, and mining camps. Cattle, sheep, and horses grazed freely on open rangelands, removing the grass that formerly allowed fires to spread.

Protective of their homes, property, and rangeland forage, settlers and government discouraged traditional Indian burning practices. Native American populations were greatly reduced by disease and competition with Euro-Americans, and in the end they were largely confined to reservations. By the end of the nineteenth century fire was no longer a factor shaping vegetation on the Nevada landscape.[1] Settlers had begun battling wildland fires as early as the 1860s. These fires were usually of low intensity and might not even spot (by burning embers) or spread across narrow dirt roads.

Fire occurrence in recent times contrasts sharply with the relatively insignificant fires of the late 1800s and early 1900s.[2] In 1901 range examiner David Griffiths saw no evidence of fire in the valleys between Winnemucca and the Pine Forest Range in Humboldt County, which he concluded was "due, no doubt, to there being on the whole less combustible material and consequently less probability of fire spreading . . . than in the pasture and forest lands of Montana and Wyoming." At higher elevations in the Pine Forest Range he noted burned patches of snowbrush ceanothus, which requires fire to produce seedlings and sprouts. Griffiths surmised that one of these fires "was willfully set for the purpose of facilitating the movement of bands of sheep."[3]

Range inspection reports from before the establishment of Humboldt National Forest likewise document small human-caused fires in the mountains. Cattlemen blamed the sheepherders, who in turn blamed the Indians for setting these fires. Addressing the Bruneau addition to Humboldt National Forest, R. B. Wilson wrote in 1906: "The fire situation is commensurate with the limited amount of timber. What few fires there are occur in the fall and are directly attributable to sheep herders.... They do this in a desire to increase the feed area."[4] Inspector George Thompson reported that burns "occur principally in small areas of from 5 to 10 acres, but in some cases run as high as 400 acres."[5] In the Santa Rosa Range H. E. Woolley encountered "numerous small areas in practically all of the canyons where herders started fires in order to clear trails through the chaparral."[6]

Fires deliberately set by sheepherders were virtually eliminated following the establishment of Humboldt National Forest. Annual reports from the forest supervisor to Region 4 headquarters in Ogden, Utah, describe wildfire as being of little consequence in the 1920s. The fires that did occur burned only a few acres before running out of fuel.[7]

Wildfire was likewise incidental in pinyon-juniper woodlands. Forest Service reports from the early 1900s show no record of major forest fires in the pinyon- and juniper–covered Snake Range. Rancher Wayne Gonder recalled that the largest fire after the turn of the century occurred around 1910 and burned between 30 and 50 acres. Fire prevention became a concern in 1939 after three fires broke out along Lehman Creek. The largest (85 acres), ignited by hot coals dumped into a garbage pit, swept through cheatgrass and nearly destroyed the campground. Having been off limits to grazing, the campground was reopened to sheep in the spring and fall in order to keep the grass down and eliminate "a dangerous hazard."[8]

Although woody fuels continued to increase in pinyon-juniper woodlands as tree groves encroached sagebrush and thickened during the 1940s and 1950s, high-intensity fires were not yet a problem. Low-intensity fires were easily extinguished, especially in areas where competition from trees had reduced understory fuels, earning pinyon-juniper the reputation of being an "asbestos type." That reputation was dispelled in July 1979 when the wind-driven, human-caused Shanty Town wildfire swept 8,000 acres in the southern Ruby Mountains. The 1981 Austin fire, covering nearly 6,000 acres north of Crow Creek, provided further evidence that pinyon-juniper had become susceptible to high-intensity fire when driven by strong winds. Ironically, in the earlier decades trees were decreasing the flammability of fuels by diminishing the understory even as total fuels increased. Eventually the fuel load became too great and the trees too close together. Today it is only a matter of time before large areas burn hot.

One of the first large wildfires in sagebrush-cheatgrass occurred in 1939 when several thousand acres burned on the western slope of the Santa Rosa Range near Orovada. That fire surprised the Civilian Conservation Corps men called out to fight it. A shift in the wind drove the fire over them, killing several. A year later wildfire swept 17,000 acres in the adjacent Paradise Hill–Paradise Valley locality—much of which was within the Little Humboldt River watershed administered by the BLM. This fire accounted for most of the 26,456 acres burned in this watershed during 1940–62.[9]

Fire activity increased during periods of high fire danger. In 1947, 10,000 acres burned on Frenchie Flat in Crescent Valley. A comparable acreage was scorched in the Cortez Mountains Mill Canyon fire of 1957, while that same year 20,000 acres were swept in the Mack and Welch creek drainages to the north.[10]

By the mid-1900s, after decades of intensive livestock grazing and negligible fire disturbance, sagebrush and other shrubs had proliferated and largely displaced native grasses. The increase in woody vegetation augmented the fuel available for fires. Sagebrush with high amounts of volatile oils burns much hotter and with much longer flame lengths than low bunchgrass does. Bunchgrass with spaces among the plants often requires high winds for fire to spread quickly. Also by the 1930s, highly combustible annual cheatgrass had become widely established in sagebrush ecosystems, further increasing the wildfire hazard.[11] Cheatgrass fuels dry earlier are finer, more easily ignited, and more continuous, enabling rapid fire expansion. Firefighters were able to contain most of these fires until a hot day in August 1964 when many lightning strikes touched off multiple fires that burned more than 300,000 acres of rangeland in the Tuscarora Mountains–Boulder Flat region of northern Nevada. Firefighters were not prepared for such a conflagration, and the Nevada National Guard had to be called out to provide food and field support for them.

The unprecedented number of wildfires in 1964 demonstrated the vulnerability of northern Nevada to high-intensity fires. Driven by high winds and fueled by dense sagebrush and a bumper crop of cheatgrass, the Tuscarora Mountains–Boulder Flat conflagration burned for five days, a striking portent of large wildfires to come. Millions of acres of sagebrush-grass have been swept by wildfire in the four decades since.

A government report recognized the impending conflagration, noting that "present equipment, personnel and organizations are capable of controlling most fires with minimum damage when fires occur within a reasonable distance of initial attack forces, and burning conditions are not extreme. . . .

The 1964 Elko County Fire Storm, when over 300,000 acres burned within the Humboldt Basin, clearly indicated what still may happen in a bad fire year."[12]

Following the 1964 fire season, state and federal agencies began developing a comprehensive fire suppression program. Specialized management teams and trained firefighters brought in from other regions handle wildfires now. Fire retardant dropped from air tankers and water dropped from helicopters form part of the initial attack. Ground operations include dispatch of large pumper trucks, bulldozers, and water tenders (tankers). Firefighters are airlifted to strategic locations by helicopter, and smoke jumpers parachute into remote areas. Contractors provide meals, field showers and toilet facilities, vehicle fuel and maintenance, and other support to highly trained class A firefighting teams. Nationwide lightning detection has improved the response time to fire starts, often allowing prepositioning of crews.

Despite the expenditure of hundreds of millions of dollars, however, acreage burned and fire severity have increased enormously since the 1970s. Extreme fire years are generally preceded by a year or two of high springtime moisture that produces an abundance of grass followed by a hot, dry summer with many dry lightning storms. A half million acres burned in 1974, 895,000 acres in 1985, and more than 800,000 acres in 1996. High temperatures, single-digit daytime relative humidity, and strong winds combined to set records for fire severity and acres burned in 1999, when large fires burned nearly continuously between mid-June and the end of September in north-central Nevada. By the end of the fire season, 113 fires of 300 acres or larger had blackened in excess of 1.6 million acres, mostly during a week in early August after lightning ignited many fires over a wide area of the Humboldt Basin. The largest of these was the 288,000 Dun Glen complex.[13]

Following active fire seasons in 2000 and 2001, averaging 650,000 acres burned each year, the fire weather moderated. Over the next three years the average annual acreage burned dropped to 48,000. Although there were short periods of extreme fire weather, there were few dry lightning storms. Only 17,548 acres burned during the cool summer of 2003, the fewest since 1982.[14]

Drought-breaking wet springs and consequent growth of fine fuel greater than anything seen in many years set the stage for the extreme wildfires of 2005 and 2006. Unusually warm temperatures, high winds, and dry lightning storms aggravated conditions in 2005 when 1.7 million acres burned. Daily maximum temperatures in Reno averaging 100°F during a ten-day period broke records in July 2005. Most of the acreage burned in 2005 was in Lincoln County, where intense dry lightning storms ignited highly flammable annual red brome (another exotic invader) and cheatgrass.[15] This large southern Nevada fire complex in the Mojave Desert burned plant communities that rarely burn.

The 2006 wildfires were concentrated in the mountain big sagebrush and bunchgrass communities of Elko County, where nearly a million acres burned.[16] An abundance of spring moisture produced a bumper crop of perennial bunchgrass that had cured by late June when afternoon highs reached 102°F. One hundred and twenty lightning fires were burning in grass and decadent sagebrush during June 22–27. Well above normal July temperatures produced explosive conditions, with wind-driven and erratic fire behavior that even veteran firefighters had not experienced. Between July 25 and August 3, 238,000 acres were scorched by the Winters fire west of the Independence Mountains. Large numbers of ignitions overwhelmed firefighting resources, but the multiple agencies involved managed to hold 90–95 percent of the fires to less than 300 acres within twenty-four hours. During the period August 6–20, 51 lightning fires were burning in Elko County, the largest being the 190,000-acre Charleston complex. From September 2 to 4, the Sheep and Amazon fires burned 250,000 acres. The Snow Canyon fire of September 20–24 swept across 22,000 acres of perennial grass and mountain shrub communities in the Independence Mountains. Driven by high winds throughout the first night, this fire carried through aspen stands on north-facing slopes where fuels are normally too moist to burn. In all likelihood, these fuels had not burned for well over one hundred years.

A total of 890,000 acres burned statewide in 2007, including the 221,000-acre Murphy fire, which originated in Idaho and swept southwest into upper elevations of the Humboldt-Toiyabe National Forest in Elko County. The 2008 and 2009 fire seasons were quite mild in comparison. Only 72,000 acres burned in 2008. Snowfall compacted the dead carry-over light fuels, making them far less of a threat to carry fire than in previous years. Thunderstorms brought sufficient moisture later in the season to stop large fire growth, even in areas of abundant fuels. In 2009 fuels were strongly affected by an abnormally cool and wet spring that resulted in a second green-up of grassy fuels—decreasing fire potential across the state. The storms brought numerous lightning strikes, but sufficient moisture prevented fire starts from becoming large fires. As a result, only 33,000 acres burned statewide.[17] The 2010 fire season was also quiet with a cool spring and summer and few lightning strikes. In retrospect, the number of acres burned per decade has steadily increased since the 1970s, with 1.5 million more acres burned each decade than in the previous decade.[18]

Increasingly severe wildfires are an outgrowth of rangeland deterioration, proliferation of annuals, accumulating woody fuel, and increased perennial grasses, or combinations of these. Most of the 6.5 million acres that have burned since 1999 consisted of degraded Wyoming sagebrush and low desert shrub communities invaded by cheatgrass and red brome. A century of heavy livestock grazing led to dominance by the more combustible cheatgrass, allowing wildfires to sweep through the major valleys and adjoining uplands during periods of extreme fire weather. Severe wildfires will continue to burn degraded rangelands so long as they are dominated by annual grasses. To reduce the frequency of these fires will require replacement of the annuals with seeded perennial grasses, a practice that has its challenges.[19]

The problem with our big fire years was not that too much acreage burned, but that where we had fire, we had too much of it. Instead of being a force that creates or maintains plant heterogeneity with mosaics of different-aged shrubs, our fires have created even-aged stands over wide areas that lack the diversity favored by many wildlife species. Seed dispersal from unburned margins becomes increasingly difficult as distances to the edge increase, and fewer unburned islands remain for seed dispersal. Extremely large fires increase the likelihood of weed invasion and water and wind erosion in areas prone to such problems.

After the Austin fire of 1981, despite heavy fuel buildup, Nevada pinyon-juniper woodlands had no large, high-intensity wildfires until 2006. The 7,600-acre Jackass fire on the Bridgeport Ranger District announced an end to this trend in July. This lightning-ignited, uncontrollable, high-intensity fire swept through dense tree crowns during extreme fire weather. The lack of large wildfires in this fuel type reflects a low incidence of multiple ignitions during extreme fire weather rather than any immunity to fire. Fire crews have so far been able to suppress most woodland fires before they burn out of control. In Nevada, it is only a matter of time before extensive areas of pinyon-juniper woodlands burn. All it will take is a coincidence of multiple ignitions and extreme fire weather. Meanwhile, millions of acres continue to accumulate fuel at roughly two hundred pounds of one-hour fuels per acre per year.[20] As woody fuels continue to accumulate and as trees extend their branches toward neighbors, the potential for fire spread becomes greater. Large fires in pinyon-juniper are increasingly becoming a *when,* not an *if,* question.

Plant recovery following fire has been linked to preburn vegetation and fire severity. Removal of overly dense sagebrush with an understory of cheatgrass has given rise to dominance of cheatgrass and other annuals in wide areas once occupied by Wyoming sagebrush and native grasses. Reestablishment of Wyoming sagebrush has been slow because few of these shrubs survive burning, seed longevity is generally less than a year, and seed dispersal is quite low. However, good recovery of residual native grasses has occurred after several growing seasons on cooler north-facing slopes and at higher elevations or on sandy soils where cheatgrass is not as competitive.

Fires often kill bitterbrush, an important early-winter forage for mule deer, although the shrubs killed tend to be old and lacking in vigor. On sites of low fire severity, bitterbrush has survived fire and produced seedlings. Reestablishment of bitterbrush communities following fire has been highly variable.

Mountain big sagebrush communities at higher elevations show good response to wildfire because their potential for recovery is better than that of Wyoming big sagebrush communities.[21] Cheatgrass is usually either absent or a minor part of the plant composition, being restricted to south-facing slopes or localized disturbed areas. Removal of sagebrush by fire often results in significant increases in native grasses and forbs that were already present in the preburn understory. Desirable shrubs such as wild rose, snowberry, and currant

Figure 9.1. Cheatgrass response to fire on a site that lacked native plants. Photograph by Sherman Swanson.

that require disturbance to stimulate reproduction have benefited from wildfire by sprouting from underground stems, dormant buds, and root crowns.

Most riparian plants, including willows and rhizomatous grasses and sedges, also respond favorably to fire by sprouting and then growing quickly. Studies at eighty streams across northern Nevada after the 1999–2001 fires showed that many riparian areas were in better condition a few years after fire than they had been up to several years before the fire.[22] This response seems to reflect continuing progress with livestock grazing management, short-term closure to grazing after fire, the resilience of riparian plants, and the increase in base flows after fire reduces transpiration loss.

Fire on Nevada's landscapes has changed monumentally since presettlement times, when it was common wherever sufficient fuel was present to burn and especially where Native Americans had an incentive to burn. After Euro-American settlement, cessation of Indian ignitions, and removal of fine fuels by livestock, fire became an infrequent disturbance agent. With the introduction of cheatgrass, the buildup of sagebrush and other shrubs, and the recovery of grasses with more conservative management late in the twentieth century, fire once again became a significant factor. Now it often causes damage to degraded plant communities while rejuvenating those that are more resilient.

The catalyst for our recent high-intensity wildfires has been the coincidence of fuel buildup and extreme fire weather. Woody evergreen sagebrush and pinyon-juniper trees compete with herbaceous perennials, especially bunchgrasses. Areas dominated by these woody plants burn with increasing intensity as they age, leaving wide-open niches for cheatgrass and other flammable weeds to colonize. Many of the perennial invasives are also highly flammable and can lead to more frequent fires.

The concern over our big fire years was magnified by the large size of the bigger fires and their unbalanced distribution across the region. Although the composite area burned has been significant, and cheatgrass has proliferated as a result, even more acreage at middle elevations and in mountainous regions has not burned. These landscapes include the more productive wildlife habitats, some of which have not had the benefit of fire disturbance for more than a century. Lacking disturbance, much of the plant cover has reached advanced age and is much less productive than it was in earlier stages of succession.

IV

Changes on the Landscape

10

Vegetation

Resilience and Succession
Meet Abuse and Decadence

The first European settlers began changing North American landscapes as soon as they arrived. The newcomers cut trees, and their Old World–style farms displaced oak-hickory forests and Indian cornfields east of the Mississippi River. In Missouri, oak parklands were cut and livestock closely grazed the expansive grasslands. Within a matter of decades, dense patches of saplings appeared and the landscape took on a brushy appearance. To the west, the prairies were converted to vast wheat and corn fields. In California, the rich, grassy San Joaquin Valley, home to tule elk, antelope, black-tailed deer, and grizzly bears, was put to the plow. Within a relatively short time, wildlife was displaced, water was diverted into irrigation, and livestock and orchards occupied the landscape.

Profound changes in vegetation also followed Euro-American settlement in Nevada. These changes largely resulted from livestock grazing, alteration of fire disturbance, and the introduction of Eurasian weeds. Woody shrubs and trees expanded and grew, cheatgrass exploded on the scene, and native herbaceous plants declined.

Basin wildrye grass has largely disappeared from many valley communities. A striking example comes from an analysis of early newspapers and interviews of pioneer stockmen by Hazeltine and colleagues. "In the Long Valley area of northwestern Nevada, W. B. Todhunter is said to have first wintered 10,000 to 12,000 head of cattle on nothing but ryegrass in 1871. This was done quite a few years into the 70s and 80s. Now [1965] the valley shows only scattered ryegrass plants and is predominately greasewood, rabbitbrush, shadscale and big sagebrush."[1]

When George Gruell visited Long Valley in late June 2008, he found the plant cover essentially the same as Hazeltine described it in 1965. Subsequent prescribed fire treatment of desert shrub communities north of the valley and on the nearby Sheldon National Wildlife Refuge had resulted in profuse growth of basin wildrye from rootstocks, providing examples of how these communities appeared before the era of extreme livestock grazing. Similar increases have been seen at the Gund Ranch, Marys River, and elsewhere.

Wyoming big sagebrush (the big sagebrush subspecies of semiarid valleys) is in low ecological condition. A marked increase in the sage cover coincided with and at least partially resulted in a depleted understory, which is now practically devoid of native plants.[2] The understory has literally been "frozen in time," showing little change over the past 50 years. In many localities, especially on fine soils, cheatgrass has filled the void created by displacement of the native bunchgrasses.

Early stockmen spoke of the abundance of grass and the sparseness of sagebrush on productive rangelands. Charles Demick of Alturas, California, who worked as a cowboy for the Miller and Lux Cattle Company, observed in 1895 that dry ryegrass areas in northern Washoe County "formerly looked like grain fields in the fall of the year. There were also large amounts of rice grass, other bunchgrasses, and only scattered areas of big sagebrush." During the initial stages of grazing, ryegrass in the valleys was grazed in the winter. One of the summer jobs of cowboys was to keep cattle away from this tall winter forage, which was valued because it could stand out in deep snows. Under this system it continued to thrive. Its demise followed intense spring and summer grazing.[3] The rapid spring growth of leaves and stems allows livestock to graze the outside repeatedly before tillers recover, shrinking the plants from the outside in.

Dan DeQuille's 1860 experience in the Stillwater Mountains provides a sense of what mountain big sagebrush–grass communities were like before the introduction of domestic livestock. The locality he described fits West Lee Canyon, which coincides with both DeQuille's travel route and his description of the topography: "After traveling some five miles up the canyon the trail went up a ridge to some comparatively level ground covering some thirty acres. Here, the Paiute women had gathered seeds of the bunch grass [wildrye grass]. Many tons of sheaves had been thickly strewn over the ground after the grass seeds had been thrashed. . . . Not only were the flats and the lower parts of the hills thus luxuriantly clothed in bunch grass and red-tops, but the tallest peaks were green to their very summits."[4]

When he visited West Lee Canyon in July 1998, Gruell found no ryegrass on the comparatively level ground where the Paiute woman had once harvested it in abundance. Sagebrush and a scattering of rabbitbrush dominated the area. The understory beneath the sagebrush, which now largely comprised Sandberg bluegrass and cheatgrass, indicated a long history of heavy grazing by mustangs, domestic sheep, and cattle. At upper elevations the dense bunchgrass reported by DeQuille had been displaced by sagebrush, a trend repeated across this and other mountain ranges of Nevada.

Another early traveler provided a glimpse of plant distribution in the mountains farther west. Dr. Henry H. O. Smeathman made observations in 1864 in the region east of Winnemucca Lake: "Leaving this range [Antelope Range] we passed through deserts of sagebrush and greasewood, destitute alike of vegetation and wildlife, thence over ranges clothed with the most luxuriant herbage, with fertile canons, numerous springs of excellent water, and rich alluvial bottoms. . . . Traveled through a series of elevated ranges, destitute of trees, even the scrubby cedar, but richly clothed from base to summit with herbage, particularly the bunch grass."[5] Luxuriant herbage no longer covers this area; nor are there rich alluvial bottoms. The long history of livestock grazing and plant succession without the influence of fire has made perennial grass sparse among the shrubs.

The reports of professionals corroborate the vegetation changes in upland sagebrush-grass communities. A repeat of P. B. Kennedy's turn-of-the-century survey in 1952 showed a deterioration of the plant cover in the Tuscarora Mountains and on the adjoining lowlands. Bluebunch wheatgrass was generally absent at lower elevations and formed less than 5 percent of its former density at middle elevations. On more productive sites at higher elevations, it approached 20 percent of the cover on southern and eastern slopes. Introduced annual weeds such as cheatgrass, pepperweed, and halogeton had increased to an extreme extent at lower elevations by 1952. Signs of watershed deterioration were evident. Stream channels had deepened and widened, and the old willows and aspens that once grew on their banks had toppled into the streambed. The lowered water table, a consequence of erosion, had dried out and favored meadow invasion by sagebrush.[6]

Soil Conservation Service and Forest Service personnel evaluated the condition of the upper Humboldt River watershed between 1962 and 1966.[7] A comparison of their detailed onsite examinations with historical accounts testifies to the historical abundance of native grass in Elko County. Sam Furnis, a cowboy who came to Elko in 1881, wrote of "waving grass in all directions from town. . . . Grass was so thick and high that the cattle first reaching it were lost to sight."[8] A March 16, 1870, editorial in the *Elko Daily Free Press* marveled at the condition of rangeland around Elko: "In the summer season we have rich bunchgrass covering every hillside with a luxuriant growth." The recollections of Hugh Martin, Syd Tremewan, and George Nelson are consistent with the reports of others. Grass was abundant when they were young men. Martin described the Bruneau River watershed as primarily grassland with little sagebrush. "Wildrye grew quite rank in all ravines and moist areas, often reaching above the backs of cattle." Hugh's father, Walt Martin, cut his winter hay by mowing the ridges. Bunchgrass covered the slopes of the Independence Mountains. Tremewan homesteaded on the Bruneau River in 1900, "a great grass country, where we were running 400 head of cattle and never thought of feeding them during the winter. The grass was a foot and a half high and waved in the wind all over the hills." George Nelson, who homesteaded on the Bruneau River and Mill Creek near Mountain City, described the grass as being "everywhere" in the latter 1800s. "You could drive four miles from Elko and turn the horses out wherever there was water."[9] Photos taken in the early twentieth century verify the dominance of native grasses on the mountain big sagebrush steppe of northern Nevada.

On completing the 5-year study of the upper Humboldt River basin and its history in 1966, range scientists concluded that most of the plant cover was in a deteriorated condition. "Approximately 80 percent is in the low forage production class, 15 percent in the medium, and only five percent in the fairly high."[10] The better forage species, including bluebunch wheatgrass, Thurber's needlegrass, Idaho fescue, and Nevada bluegrass, had been largely replaced by less valuable or inferior forage species such as Sandberg bluegrass, cheatgrass, lupine, balsamroot, big sagebrush, desert peach, and low Douglas rabbitbrush.

Range scientists found a fair semblance of the original plant cover in the fenced 15,000-acre Jenkins "25" Ranch St. John Field on the western slope of the Tuscarora Mountains. Close management of the livestock in this privately owned unit had paid dividends. The field was clothed with desirable grasses, including Idaho fescue, spikefescue, bluebunch wheatgrass, and Nevada bluegrass—species that had largely disappeared from adjacent private and public domain lands. The upper reaches of California Creek on Humboldt National Forest in the Independence Mountains constituted another area of good grass production.[11]

In the Reese River sub-basin to the south, the only extensive relic areas supporting native grasses were on the higher slopes and mountaintops in the Mount Lewis region of the Shoshone Range. Upper Humboldt study personnel concluded that "heavy overuse of the high, open uplands of the Shoshones, Toiyabes, the Galena Range, and the Cortez Mountains by sheep in the last twenty years of the Nineteenth Century and the first ten years of the Twentieth has almost eliminated the bluebunch wheatgrass–Nevada bluegrass understory."[12] The verdant ryegrass meadows that once skirted the Reese River had largely disappeared. In the early 1960s anthropologist David Hurst Thomas wrote that the absence of native grasses was apparent to even the most casual traveler in the Reese River and nearby central Nevada valleys.[13]

The upper Humboldt watershed report concluded that most of the low-condition forage class was in salt desert shrub bottomlands. "On much of the present acreage in the saline bottomlands, characterized by continuous heavy livestock use and a lack of a suitable range management program, rubber rabbitbrush and black greasewood have invaded these former grassland sites, following thinning of the grass cover and the resultant gullying and meadow desiccation."[14]

In 1953 George Banks, a pioneer Elko County cattleman, reminisced while viewing the deeply gullied saline bottom at the head of Susie Creek north of Carlin: "This gully was not here when I was a boy [late 1870s–early 1880s]. The sagebrush and rabbitbrush along the bottom used to be a meadow. Water ran on top of the ground, where the grasses used it and in turn held the soil in place." A photograph in the Humboldt River watershed report shows Mr. Banks standing on the edge of the now-degraded Susie Creek.[15]

Immigrant Madison Moorman's observation of August 10, 1850, suggests a far different appearance for upper Huntington Creek, west of the Ruby Mountains, than we see today. "Just at dusk we stopped and encamped on a little clear rivulet, a tributary of the South Fork of St. Mary River or Humboldt River, coursing its way to the north through a fertile little valley well set with grass."[16] In the mid-1960s this stream ran "intermittently in a deeply incised gully through a bottom land predominately covered by rabbitbrush, with little or no perennial grass understory."[17] It is in much the same condition today, except for a raised water table caused by beavers in some localities.

The Pah Rah Range landscape that Robert Ridgway described in 1867 and 1868 was vastly different from the one Gruell saw on April 19, 1999. Ridgway wrote: "From the south end of Pyramid Lake, a wide canyon [Rodero Creek] leads up into these mountains, and this was ascended on three occasions—twice in December and once in June. The slopes of this canyon were dotted with scattered cedar and pinyon groves and in many places were covered with bunchgrass meadows, while along the stream the fringe of shrubbery usual to the banks of streams in the Great Basin."[18] Gruell found that in the absence of fire, the bunchgrass meadows of 140 years ago have disappeared from this drainage and have been replaced by sagebrush with an understory mostly of

(a)

(b)

Figure 10.1. Photograph sequence showing changes in plant cover on southwesterly slope at headwaters of Swamp Creek, a tributary to the east fork of the Jarbidge River.
(a) August 19, 1919: Perennial grasses that have been closely grazed dominate. The dark shrubs at upper right are snowbrush ceanothus. Courtesy U.S. Forest Service.
(b) August 23, 1966: Sagebrush dominates the landscape; snowbrush ceanothus has been encroached by chokecherry and aspen. Photograph by George E. Gruell.

(c)

(d)

(c) September 12, 1977: Native grasses dominate the plant cover, having been rejuve-
nated by a prescribed fire in the spring of 1974. Unknown Forest Service photographer.
(d) June 15, 2010: Sagebrush once again dominates the landscape. Outside the perim-
eter of the prescribed fire, aspen and chokecherry encroachment of ceanothus continues. Photograph by George E. Gruell.

Sandberg bluegrass and cheatgrass. The fringe of shrubbery no longer exists. Instead dense, decadent willows and patches of chokecherry and aspen exceeding 30 feet in height choke the stream course. Swanson observed that the stream itself appears to have cut a steep-sided, V-shaped flood channel into a U-shaped valley bottom.

Changes in Great Basin woody vegetation have been widely documented in pinyon-juniper woodlands. Numerous studies have reported an enormous expansion of such woodlands. Sampling of stand age structure suggests that more than 90 percent of today's tree cover became established after 1860, a change coincidental with the introduction of livestock and cessation of fire.[19] Prehistoric expansions during the Holocene did not occur on that scale.

At the time of European contact, pinyon-juniper woodlands were restricted to steep, rocky southerly aspects and shallow soils lacking fuels where trees were protected from fire.[20] Sagebrush and grass occupied the more productive soils. Frequent burning prevented trees from growing or restricted them to small size. After a century or more without fire the tree cover has increased, especially on sites formerly occupied by sagebrush and grass. Functioning as protective "nurse plants," sagebrush provided optimal microsites for tree seedlings to become established. The expanded tree cover has significant impacts on soil resources, plant community structure and composition, forage quality and quantity, water and nutrient cycles, wildlife habitat, biodiversity, and fire severity and frequency.[21]

The decline is scarcely visible to those traveling on secondary roads through pinyon-juniper woodlands, but walking away from the road and through the tree cover gives a better perspective. Shrub remnants occupy the understory beneath tree canopies. Shrubs and herbs that persist in open spaces between trees are in a degraded condition because the tree roots reach out far beyond tree canopies and deplete the soil moisture. The tree canopy intercepts rain and snow, which then evaporates rather than reaching the soil or flows down the tree trunk, watering the tree but no other plants. Only precipitation greater than 13 inches is likely to replenish soil moisture. The more trees present, the more the amount needed increases.

The competition of pinyon and juniper with understory plants is evidenced where trees have been killed by insects. Densely spaced and weakened by soil moisture deficiencies during drought, these trees become vulnerable to attacks. On productive sites, openings in the tree canopy have been colonized by herbs and shrubs that regenerate from seeds blown in or that formerly lay dormant in the soil.

(a)

(b)

Figure 10.2. East slope of the Toquima Range viewed from Pine Creek Ranch in Monitor Valley. (a) 1902: Patchy pinyon-juniper grows in the distance, a consequence of past fire disturbance. Courtesy Nevada Historical Society, photograph by Tasker Oddie. (b) July 15, 1998: Pinyon pine has increased enormously. Photograph by George E. Gruell.

(a)

(b)

Figure 10.3. Photograph sequence showing changes in vegetation in the upper Mill Creek drainage, Snake Range. (a) Summer 1923: This scene was captioned "a mixed *closed stand* of ponderosa pine, white fir, aspen, pinyon pine, juniper, mahogany and willow [emphasis added]." Note pinyon pine seedlings on the grassy slope at upper right. Courtesy U.S. Forest Service. (b) August 10, 1966: George Gruell had to climb a tree to photograph the same spot. Note: Climbed tree in 1966. Repeat impossible in 2004.

Ridgway wrote that during the late 1800s curlleaf mountain-mahogany in the Toiyabe Range was confined to ridges or summits. Its growth form was stunted, and "groves" or stands were "scant."[22] Research and observation throughout the Great Basin confirm Ridgway's observations. The sparse distribution

Figure 10.4. Sagebrush die-off resulting from pinyon encroachment. Photograph by Sherman Swanson.

of stumps and old growth demonstrate that this fire-sensitive tree was formerly restricted to rocky ridges with discontinuous fuels where it was protected from fire.

Prolonged absence of fire resulted in unprecedented expansion of mountain mahogany trees on the landscape. Seeds from existing mature mountain mahogany were disseminated into nearby sagebrush-grass communities, and the young trees were no longer killed by fires. Tallies of annual growth rings suggest that the principal period of mountain mahogany regeneration took place between 1880 and 1940.[23] This is the period with the greatest livestock numbers and the fewest fires. The range of tree ages further suggests that as new mahogany trees reached seed-bearing age, the rate of regeneration increased dramatically.

Mountain mahogany stands today vary from scattered individuals to those that cover many acres. Most stands are now mature, declining in vigor, and periodically defoliated by the looper moth, which can lead to death of the trees. Canopies have closed, and the soil surface is covered by an accumulation of litter that has inhibited the growth of new trees. A study of mountain mahogany covering four states found no seedlings where litter exceeded one-quarter inch in depth. Seedlings died before their roots could reach moisture-bearing mineral soil.[24] Reproduction from seed has been restricted to canopy gaps and stand margins where the soil in microsites is bare of plants (bare soil).[25]

(a)

(b)

Mahogany is also found growing among conifers, with which it cannot compete. It has been displaced by pinyon in pinyon-juniper woodlands and by other pines or by firs at upper elevations. When mule deer numbers were at high levels during the mid-1900s, game managers were concerned about a marked reduction in the availability of mahogany leaders (new twigs), an important deer forage. The problem was that the mahogany had grown out of the reach of deer. Efforts to mechanically stimulate sprouting by pushing over the trees with bulldozers while leaving the roots intact in the soil met with little success. The resulting soil scarification did result in seedling germination, but intensive deer foraging limited successful reproduction.

Use of prescribed fire to promote mahogany reproduction has not been seriously considered because of the plant's sensitivity to fire. Reproductive response to fire treatment seems to vary with fuel loading and fire intensity. Stands of mahogany on fire-prone soils are vulnerable to the return of fire generally. A high-intensity wildfire can kill an entire stand, destroying much of the seed. Examples in recent years include the Hallelujah Junction vicinity north of Reno's Peavine Mountain, the Badger Mountain fire on the Sheldon Wildlife Refuge, and the Murphy and East Slide Rock Ridge fires in Elko County. High-intensity fire in mahogany kills not only expansion trees but also old legacy trees on rocky sites that had escaped fire for hundreds of years. Reproduction from seed following high-intensity fire is often sparse and often restricted to bare soil openings adjacent to trees that were not killed. This response was documented in a low-density stand on a north exposure at Dutch John Creek in the Santa Rosa Range where several mahoganies survived a 1994 wildfire. Observations in 1996 showed no evidence of seedlings, which would have been very small. Ten years after the fire, the site was well stocked with young mahogany.[26] Swanson, touring with the Cottonwood Ranch Holistic Management Team, noted similar postfire mahogany reproduction a few years after the wind-driven fire in 2000 that skirted the mid-elevation mahoganies.

FACING PAGE: **Figure 10.5.** Photograph sequence in the southern Ruby Mountains showing changes in curlleaf mountain-mahogany, pinyon pine, and other woody plants. (a) 1868: Mahoganies are mostly restricted to steep, rocky slopes where they were protected from fire. A lone mahogany persists on open slope at lower left. Adjacent aspen clone in an initial stage of growth shows evidence of a recent fire. Courtesy National Archives, Washington, D.C., photograph by Timothy O'Sullivan. (b) June 10, 2010: After 142 years, the herbaceous plants and shrubs on the far slope are losing out to mahogany and pinyon pine. The aspen clone is senescent. Photograph by Calib McAdoo.

(a)

(b)

Figure 10.6. Photograph sequence showing changes in curlleaf mountain-mahogany on slopes above Jarbidge mining camp. (a) 1910: Mahogany on the steep, rocky south-easterly slope at right is of low density and widely scattered. The slope at left supports low-density conifers, aspen, and deciduous shrubs. Courtesy U.S. Geological Survey Library, Denver, photograph by F. C. Schrader. (b) 1998: The mahogany at right has grown into dense stands, and conifers have thickened on the slopes at left. Photograph by George E. Gruell. Note: This was *the* Jarbidge mining camp and site of the town of Jarbidge.

Other examples demonstrate rapid establishment of mahogany seedlings following wildfire. An October 1975 wildfire completely destroyed the parent stand located near Mountain City north of Elko.[27] More than 4,000 seedlings per acre older than 3 years were tallied in 1982. Initial germination was apparently from viable seeds of the 1975 crop that had fallen to the ground or seed banks stored in the litter. This response was not an anomaly. In the spring of 2010 Gruell and Kent McAdoo observed many mahogany seedlings beneath mahogany stands killed by the high-intensity 2007 Murphy wildfire.

Pronounced changes have also occurred in the structure and distribution of woody plants growing at upper elevations. Common species include aspen, willow, snowberry, wild currant, woods rose, snowbrush ceanothus, serviceberry, and chokecherry. Though these shrubs and aspen are widespread, their local distribution is strongly influenced by aspect, soil texture, precipitation, moisture retention, growth characteristics, and disturbance history. Unlike fire-sensitive sagebrush, juniper, pinyon, and mahogany, these higher-elevation broadleaf woody species are fire-dependent. They regenerate from seeds and sprout from underground stems, dormant buds, and root crowns. In the absence of fire for a prolonged period, they become decadent.

Aspen is recognized for its importance in stabilizing watersheds and for its contribution to wildlife habitat. Undergrowth beneath aspen is often a rich assortment of herbs and shrubs.[28] A large majority of the aspens in Nevada grow in self-perpetuating stands that periodically produce many shoots called "root suckers" that form trees. As the leaves turn gold in the fall, the clumps turn just before or after neighboring groups of trees. Each group is a clone of identical genetic constitution, having been produced by one seedling and reproducing thereafter by vegetative reproduction. The original seedling may have lived during the Pleistocene.

Contemporary photographs suggest that when Euro-Americans reached the region, many aspen groves were in early stages of growth, having been disturbed by periodic fire. During the era of heavy livestock grazing, aspen trees were growing but not reproducing. Concerns over the lack of reproduction in the 1920s led to experimentation within 16-square-foot exclosures placed on Humboldt National Forest summer sheep ranges. Profuse suckering from trees protected within these exclosures indicated that aspen could reproduce if freed from grazing pressure. A reduction in sheep numbers in subsequent years resulted in development of new trees.

By the mid-1960s, Humboldt National Forest sheep allotments were being converted to cattle allotments. This administrative decision had a significant

Figure 10.7. Expansion of an aspen clone from profuse root suckering following wild-fire that killed the parent trees. Photograph by George E. Gruell.

influence on aspen. The replacement of sheep by cattle favored aspen repro-duction. There was a massive release of aspen suckers, which have grown into dense stands. This ingrowth of aspen and an increase of other woody plants have choked off openings that once supported herbaceous plants.

Aspen is replaced over time by conifers in areas where the latter are a part of the plant cover, particularly on cooler north slopes where aspen cannot com-pete. Aspen can also be found as remnants in sagebrush communities. Sage-brush competing for soil moisture and excessive grazing of root suckers have taken a toll in some localities. Where grazing has been curtailed or managed with an eye toward season of use, rotation of use, or especially short duration of use, stands show signs of recovery. Repeated season-long use, allowing live-stock to seek out aspen when it is most palatable and to do so repeatedly, has

FACING PAGE: Figure 10.8. Photograph sequence showing changes in aspen, snowbrush ceanothus, and chokecherry in Copper Basin, Mountain City Ranger District. (a) Summer 1920: Aspen is mostly in early stages of growth. The dark shrubs at center are snowbrush ceanothus. Courtesy U.S. Forest Service. (b) August 31, 1965: Aspen has grown and filled the openings. The ceanothus patch in the midground and others in the distance have been encroached by chokecherry. Subalpine fir is more conspicuous. (c) August 11, 2004: Further thickening of aspen has closed openings, and chokecherry now dominates the ceanothus. Conifers are slowly displacing other woody plants. Photographs (b) and (c) by George E. Gruell.

(a)

(b)

(c)

(a)

(b)

Figure 10.9. (a) 1915: Upper McConnell Creek, Santa Rosa Range. Early succession aspen predominates on the far slope. The open character of the stands reflects heavy sheep grazing. Courtesy U.S. Forest Service, photograph by B. S. Martineau. (b) July 30, 1998: Absence of sheep grazing since the 1970s has resulted in prolific growth of aspen and willow. Photograph by George E. Gruell.

Figure 10.10. This old aspen clone is dying because it lacks a viable root system to produce reproductive suckers. Photograph by George E. Gruell.

been most detrimental. Many small aspen stands were lost when such grazing mismanagement followed the cutting by beavers of mature aspen previously out of the reach of livestock.

Changes in structure and distribution of snowberry, wild currant, and woods rose have been more subtle. These low-growing shrubs, of considerable forage value, were formerly a significant component of the shrub cover. In the absence of fire they have lost vigor and are commonly reduced to remnants within dense stands of sagebrush.

Historical documents and early photographs verify that snowbrush ceanothus, an important nitrogen-fixing shrub, grew profusely at upper elevations in the nineteenth century. The prolific growth reflected fire disturbances that stimulated sprouting and establishment of seedlings. Seeds in the litter can remain viable for a century or longer. They need heat of 140°F to germinate. In the absence of fire, snowbrush ceanothus has undergone widespread stand deterioration, with virtually no successful reproduction. Stands on many sites have been reduced to remnants and have been invaded by chokecherry and aspen. Despite this decline, snowbrush ceanothus can reappear when fire returns where dormant seeds persist. The surge of wildfires in recent years has stimulated abundant seedlings on sites where there was no evidence of this shrub in the preburn plant community.

(a)

(b)

(c)

Figure 10.12. Snowbrush ceanothus seedlings beneath mahoganies killed by a 1994 wildfire. The seedling response indicates the historical dominance of fire-perpetuated ceanothus on many sites now occupied by mountain mahogany. Photograph by George E. Gruell.

Although there has been retrogression in areas that have been heavily grazed, there is considerable evidence that serviceberry and chokecherry grow profusely in localities where grazing has been eliminated or well managed. Increase in the occurrence of serviceberry is evidenced by the presence of sagebrush remnants beneath serviceberry canopies. A hedged growth form within an expanded canopy shows an increase in the size of serviceberry.

The increased density of sagebrush particularly has contributed to widespread deterioration and loss of mountain meadows. Historically, meadows played a critical role in contributing to biodiversity by producing an assortment of sedges, grasses, and forbs. The plant cover on these meadows owed

FACING PAGE: **Figure 10.11.** Photograph sequence showing long-term trend of snowberry near the Gold Creek Ranger Station. (a) August 16, 1919: Snowberry dominates the shrub cover. The lighter-looking mountain sagebrush is limited to widely scattered plants. Courtesy U.S. Forest Service. (b) August 29, 1966: The density of sagebrush has increased, while snowberry is less conspicuous. (c) August 30, 2004: Dense sagebrush dominates the shrub cover, in sharp contrast to snowberry dominance in 1919. Snowberry is of reduced growth form and low vigor. Photographs (b) and (c) by George E. Gruell.

its high productivity to good soil moisture and rejuvenation by fires. In the absence of fire, sagebrush and other evergreen shrubs that use more moisture displaced herbaceous plants. Heavy or poorly managed livestock grazing weakened the protective plant cover; erosion enlarged stream channels and created or enlarged incised gullies. This lowered the water table of meadows, which allowed invasion by sagebrush.

The process of stream channel incision has been discussed from a variety of perspectives. Geomorphologists, who think in terms of geological time, study the changes in climate that drive the availability of water and sediment. Investigations in central Nevada determined that significant alluvial fans developed in mountain valleys during the late Holocene drought, and that these led to valley aggradations (accumulation of sediment) behind the fan toes.[29] Later wet periods began the process of incision, with less sediment available and more water to move it.

Riparian managers tend to think in terms of more recent history, borrowing context from the geomorphologists and integrating it with a focus on the historical effects of land use and management. They often address the rapid changes that have occurred within the lifetimes of land managers or management agencies, focusing on connections between land uses and riparian functions.[30] Studies have shown that the productivity and type of valley-bottom vegetation away from channels was determined by the pattern of floodplain flooding and the elevation of the water table and its capillary fringe relative to the soil surface. Water spreading and maintenance of a high water table are enhanced by riparian vegetation that stabilizes stream banks, slows water movement, and maintains channel form. Riparian vegetation is especially important for keeping water on the land longer in low-gradient, wide valleys such as along Huntington Creek, where it helped maintain a meandering pattern. When riparian vegetation becomes weakened by repeated loss of the leaves needed to turn sunlight and water into living tissue, root systems shrink. Fewer and shorter plants are not effective in slowing the water of high flows, and weakened roots are not effective in stabilizing stream banks. As channels widen they tend to straighten, and straighter streams are steeper and therefore faster. Faster water picks up and carries more sediment. As streams enlarge, they convey more of the water from floods and spread less of it across floodplains. Without the capture of water by infiltration (the aquifer recharge from water spreading), the reduction of velocity with riparian vegetation roughness, and the spread of water in shallow floodplain flows, high waters turn into raging torrents flowing in deepening channels. Roads magnify floods in areas where they have reduced the time needed for upland water to get to the stream; captured the stream when floodwaters followed the road; or diminished the floodplain with side-cast material, elevated berms, or fill.

Across the Great Basin, thousands of miles of streams have been incised since the mid-1800s. In many places stream incision continues to cut toward the headwaters of watersheds. Incision and loss of water that once spread across floodplains have caused major changes to fish and wildlife habitats, have degraded water quality, have reduced summer flows to downstream water users, and have increased the discharge of floods. The volume of soil exported from riparian areas and then deposited as sediment downstream has been tremendous. This soil had been the sponge holding water from wet seasons until it was needed in dry ones. With incision, much of the remaining soil that once served as a sponge rarely gets flooded or has no opportunity to absorb the water, which drains out to the bottom of the gully and flows quickly away.

As time progresses, narrow incised gullies become wider. Eventually the bottom becomes so wide that the wide, shallow flow no longer transports its coarse sediment load, and bars form, further slowing the water flow. As the bars vegetate, the slower water deposits finer sediments. Colonizing species prepare the way for stabilizing species. As bars build into floodplains inside the incision, a new (smaller) aquifer recharges during frequent high flows and the riparian sponge begins to function anew. Reflecting these changes, many valleys, streams, or rivers are steadily improving their riparian functionality. Water flows become more reliable as habitats and water quality improve. Nevertheless, many streams are not improving, some because they are not yet ready; others because vegetation, water, or watersheds are not yet managed properly.

Forest Service and BLM personnel have prepared a technical reference work for land managers documenting many successful riparian and wetland grazing strategies.[31] Determining which strategies to use depends on which attributes or processes are missing or what type of management is causing the problem. For example, some grazing strategies need to target willow growth by restricting access during late summer periods when shrubs are more palatable. In other places, a change in road design or water management is needed. Along the lower Truckee River it became evident that rapid drops in water flow were causing cottonwood seedlings to dehydrate and die.[32] This problem was addressed through the new Truckee River Operating Agreement.

The unprecedented increase in woody vegetation across Nevada's cold desert has had mixed influences on resources. A particularly worrisome consequence has been alteration of the hydrological cycle. Thickening conifer woodlands

Figure 10.13. Improved stream functionality as meander is forming and sedges and young willows grow near the water. Photograph by Sherman Swanson.

create an umbrella effect that can prevent substantial amounts of precipitation from reaching the ground because the dense growth intercepts precipitation while it also increases evapotranspiration, thereby depleting water availability to plants and allowing water tables to sink deeper below ground. Over a watershed, the hydrological effect of trees and shrubs is perhaps most pronounced in the late winter and early spring. Before herbaceous plants begin growth with consistent spring warmth, the soil moisture has been depleted by evergreens (including sagebrush) that can grow during incidental warm days or hours. When such plants repeatedly dehydrate the soil profile, water does not accumulate to saturate soils. Rains and snowmelt thus cannot push water out the bottom of saturated soils, and limited excess water is available for deep percolation to recharge the aquifer. Because precipitation, soils, and vegetation vary across a watershed, the source area for groundwater varies in time and space. As woody evergreen vegetation expands in area and plants grow in size, interception and evapotranspiration increasingly affect the groundwater replenishment process. Springs dry up, late-season stream flows are reduced, and riparian habitats shrink.

These relationships have been substantiated by removal of dense vegetation by wildfire. Following the 1989 Delmue Ranch wildfire in the Wilson Mountain–White Rock area of Lincoln County, springs began flowing and were able to maintain stream flows throughout the summer. Likewise, the intermittent stream in Potato Canyon in the Simpson Park Range flowed continuously in the dry years after the Trail Creek wildfire of 1999 burned the pinyon pine–dominated watershed. These and other examples suggest that during pre-historic times early-succession watersheds yielded much higher flows than the densely covered watersheds of the twentieth and twenty-first centuries. Hydrological research supports these conclusions. Results of a 20-year study of mountain big sagebrush suggested that sagebrush control can increase water yield.[33] This could be translated into increased stream flow in localities where precipitation exceeds water required to rewet soil to field capacity. Cutting of post-European western juniper in a 13-inch yearly precipitation zone resulted in an increase in spring flow, groundwater, and soil moisture the first 2 years following treatment.[34]

Changes in vegetation have had striking influences on wildlife. Some animals have benefited from habitat changes; many others have not. Next we will examine the consequences of habitat change, with particular attention to sage grouse and mule deer—species at the center of growing controversies.

11

Wildlife
Habitat Relationships

The discovery of gold in California brought large numbers of Euro-Americans through Nevada on their way to the gold fields. The discovery of silver and gold on the Comstock a decade later began a century and a half of extensive changes to Nevada's cold desert. The shift in landscape vegetation from a high incidence of grasses to dominance by woody shrubs would bring dramatic changes in wildlife populations. Unregulated hunting would also become a factor. Some species were extirpated, others became scarce or rare, and still others responded favorably to habitat change. Black bear and wolverine had essentially disappeared from northern Nevada by the turn of the century. Rocky Mountain and California bighorn sheep had disappeared north of Nevada Highway 50 by the early 1920s. The last reliable sighting of a sharp-tailed grouse was made in 1960.

The plight of the sage grouse and mule deer has received particular attention in recent years. Both species responded favorably to habitat change in the years immediately following Euro-American settlement, apparently for reasons directly related to livestock grazing and absence of fire.

As their name implies, sage grouse are closely associated with sagebrush. They feed almost exclusively on sagebrush leaves during the fall, winter, and early spring. In late spring their diet shifts to herbaceous plants. After nesting, and after upland forbs dry out, they frequent meadows and moist sites critical to the growth of their young. These environments provide insects and succulent forbs high in the protein essential for chick survival during early stages of development. Sage grouse depend more on wet meadows in the western Great Basin than in the eastern part of their range, where higher summer rainfall makes upland forbs more available and keeps them green later in the summer.

Considerable controversy has developed as sage grouse populations have declined.[1] Historical observations indicate both scarcity and abundance, depending on location. Immigrants' journals report their presence along the Humboldt River. On the other hand, the journals of Hudson's Bay Company leaders make no mention of sage grouse in northern Nevada. In certain western Nevada localities sage grouse were locally abundant. These contrasting accounts have led to differing conclusions about sage grouse populations during presettlement and settlement periods.

Though scientific documentation is lacking, eyewitness accounts from the late 1800s and early 1900s indicate that sage grouse were indeed often abundant. Syd Tremewan reported that sage grouse were so plentiful on the Evans Ranch meadows north of Elko in the 1890s that they clouded the sky when they took to the air. While mowing hay, he "would just reach out and rap them over the head with a stick. Oh, they were thick." He added, "Parties would come out in wagons from Elko. They would camp for weeks at a time just hunting and fishing. When they were ready to go home, they usually had one last shoot. . . . They would just leave them on the ground in big piles to rot. It was a contest to see who could kill the most."[2]

In the 1890s George Nelson was living on a homestead on Gance Creek, to the south of the Evans Ranch, where he saw "lots of sage hens. I would see them when they would fly up from the mountain right in back of the house. An eagle or something would scare them and they sounded like thunder. I'm not exaggerating, there were thousands."[3]

As a young boy in 1907, Walt Wilhelm accompanied his family on an extended wagon trip that took them from Washoe Lake south of Reno to the Quinn River; the Santa Rosa range; and the Bull Run, Independence, and Tuscarora mountains. On the Carson River above Dayton they saw "sage hens at every turn in the road." In the Quinn River country they "found sage hens at every water." In the Santa Rosas "there was fish in the creeks and the meadows were full of sage hens evenings and mornings." While the family was camping on the north fork of the Humboldt River southwest of today's Wildhorse Reservoir, "sage hens were so thick we killed them with rocks." On McCann Creek above the town of Tuscarora "the whole country was alive with sage hens. We had better hunting there than anywhere we'd traveled."[4]

William Kent had the opportunity to observe and hunt sage grouse between 1895 and 1915 on ranches north of Winnemucca, where they "thrived greatly on alfalfa" during the summer. A keen observer, Kent described the anatomy of sage grouse, their habits, eating quality, and the ease with which they could be taken, even on the fly with a rifle. "They are normally in immense flocks," he reported, "and the old cocks, reach a weight of six pounds."[5]

Walter P. Taylor of the University of California, Berkeley identified amphibians, reptiles, birds, and mammals during the summer of 1909 in the Pine Forest Range of Humboldt County. He saw sage grouse "commonly the last of June and thereafter in the mountains above 6000 feet." They were "very numerous on the Leonard Creek flats [above the Leonard Creek Ranch], where the broad expanse of country covered by sagebrush, with streams intersecting it at intervals, furnished the necessary food and shelter for thousands."[6]

Eyewitness accounts from reputable observers indicate that sage grouse were also plentiful in parts of western Nevada. Laddy Furlong, of Carson City, spoke of hunting sage grouse east of town at the head of Brunswick Canyon in the early 1900s. Flocks numbering in the hundreds would fly from the hillsides in the late afternoon and feed in the valley, which looked like "plowed ground" although the area had never been farmed. Laddy, who later owned Meyer's Hardware in Carson, was emphatic that sage grouse in this locality numbered in the thousands.[7] Today the valley bottom is covered by dense brush and the slopes by pinyon pine. The sighting of a sage grouse would be unusual.

Likewise, the late Ira H. (Hami) Kent, a Fallon rancher, spoke of seeing four hundred to five hundred sage grouse during a day's horseback ride as a teenager in the Stillwater Range in the 1920s.[8] Today one is lucky to sight one grouse in this region. Residents of White Pine County described sage grouse in the 1920s as being so numerous that they "got up in waves" and "blotted out the sun."[9]

The above descriptions suggest that sage grouse populations at the turn of the century and into the 1920s were at levels higher than those witnessed by presettlement travelers. This implies exceptionally productive habitat. What brought this about? It seems to have been a result of livestock grazing, which led to an increase in sagebrush that previously had been suppressed by frequent fires. Heavy grazing of grass prevented fire from spreading while favoring the development of sagebrush and other shrubs. This provided cover for grouse, protecting them from avian and terrestrial predators.

Other factors came into play that improved habitat productivity. Contemporary studies have shown that grouse select grazed meadows over ungrazed meadows.[10] Grazing reduces plant height, making meadows more attractive. The regrowth resulting from cropping of the plants improves their quality. Regrowth contains more moisture and protein, making it more nutritious than ungrazed plants and more accessible because new leaves are not elevated beyond reach. Grazing also creates spaces that allow the wide-bodied birds and their young to walk with ease, whereas decadent or ungrazed plants hinder access.

Yet another factor associated with grazing that benefited sage grouse was a transition in the composition of the flora growing on meadows. The hoofs of livestock broke up the sod, allowing the invasion of highly desirable food plants such as common dandelion, yarrow, and other forbs. Acreage of summer sage grouse habitat increased markedly with the development of irrigated meadows and alfalfa fields.

Naturalist Jean Linsdale and colleagues from the Museum of Vertebrate Zoology at the University of California studied the relationship of animals to their habitat in the Toiyabe Range between 1930 and 1933.[11] He reported that the "sage hen is still present in considerable numbers in the Toiyabe Mountains region [but] has become reduced from former numbers in the mountains." Testimony from local residents indicated that the birds nested on the lower slopes and moved into the higher mountains after their eggs hatched. Sage grouse were common on other mountain ranges as well. Linsdale saw "many sage grouse" in the Santa Rosa Range on September 6–9, 1934.

Nevada's sage grouse populations have been declining at least since the 1950s.[12] Populations fluctuate along with annual weather patterns during nesting. During years of favorable precipitation and high nesting success, they increase; in drought years reproduction is minimal. In central and eastern Nevada, where sage grouse habitat is relatively limited, numbers have declined to a greater extent. Many local or regional populations have declined by 40–80 percent, with a mean decline of about 50 percent.[13] Throughout the West, sage grouse populations are showing no sign of recovery on BLM lands despite a 50 percent reduction in livestock numbers since 1950. This reduction has led certain environmental activists to advocate listing the sage grouse as a threatened or endangered species.

In 2002, responding to petitions that sage grouse be listed as a threatened or endangered species, Governor Kenny Guinn appointed a statewide task force comprising representatives of industry, Native Americans, conservation organizations, land management agencies, legislators, and biological professionals. The task force developed an initial strategy that led to the development of six regional planning groups (later seven).[14] The mission of these planning groups was to prepare conservation plans that would conserve and protect Nevada's sage grouse and their habitat within designated population management units.

Population management units vary in both their grouse population levels and their habitat potential. The Lassen-Washoe, North-Central, and Elko planning units have the largest populations. Biologists put considerable effort into monitoring sage grouse during the breeding season. Records of brooding activity monitored by the Nevada Department of Wildlife indicate a substantial reduction in sage grouse populations in recent decades. In White Pine County, for example, seven comparable leks (strutting grounds) that were active in 1971 and 2003 showed a 62 percent drop in attendance. Sage grouse numbers in the Shoshone and Toiyabe planning units, which support the largest sage grouse populations in Lander County, decreased by more than 60 percent between 1998 and 2008. Classification of wings collected from birds harvested by hunters during the 2007 hunting season showed far more adults than chicks. It was the lowest recorded production value since wings have been collected.[15]

Planning area participants identified risk factors to help assess overall population risks, including habitat quality and quantity, climate and weather, predation, wildfire, annual grasses and noxious weeds, mining, livestock grazing, hunting, poaching, and disease. Of these risks, habitat quality and quantity were rated high in all population management units. The evaluators concluded that depleted Wyoming big sagebrush–covered valleys and foothills have lost much of their carrying capacity as wintering and brooding areas. A case in point is Sagehen Valley and Wash lying between the Nightingale and Sahwave ranges of Pershing County, which as the name implies once supported many sage grouse but now has very few.

The carrying capacity of upper-elevation mountain big sagebrush brooding and summer habitat has also declined coincidentally with increased sagebrush density and deterioration of the herbaceous understory. Mountain meadow productivity has been much reduced or lost as a result of lower water tables, invasion of sagebrush, and loss of herbaceous plants. Sagehen Basin in the Clan Alpine Mountains is a good example. Encroaching pinyon and sagebrush in the riparian zone along Sagehen Creek have largely eliminated brooding habitat for sage grouse.

The conclusion that grazed meadows are more attractive to sage grouse than ungrazed meadows was confirmed in the meadows at the headwaters of Cherry Creek in the Clan Alpine Mountains. Sage grouse avoided a part of these meadows that had dense cover because it had been fenced to protect plants from livestock grazing. When a break in the fence allowed cattle to enter, however, the moderately grazed plants became attractive to sage grouse. Heavy grazing can, of course, be detrimental, especially when it leads to faster runoff and incision by erosion draining the water table needed for meadow vegetation to grow.

Other factors also contributed to reduction in sage grouse habitat. Abandonment of homesteads and ranches has led to loss of irrigated meadows and alfalfa fields once utilized by sage grouse. Encroachment of pinyon and juniper into sagebrush-grass areas has eliminated millions acres of habitat that once supported large numbers of sage grouse in central and eastern Nevada. BLM biologist Mike Perkins commented in 2004 that all the leks in the Ely District that had been lost or were in trouble were located where pinyon-juniper was expanding.[16]

Wildfires are detrimental to sage grouse in the drier degraded Wyoming big sagebrush communities because they remove sagebrush and promote domination by cheatgrass. On more productive mountain big sagebrush sites, sagebrush, perennial grass, and forbs have responded well following fires. As these plants become better established, sage grouse habitat will materially improve over prefire conditions in many areas. His investigation of early succession vegetation following fire suggested to sage grouse biologist Gary Back that sagebrush plants growing where they are not crowded by neighbors produce higher-quality forage with less of the problematic volatile oils and more protein.[17]

In retrospect, the dramatic reduction in sage grouse numbers reflects significant habitat changes initiated by livestock grazing and the absence of fire. During the formative years of livestock grazing, sage grouse habitat was enhanced and grouse populations exploded. Population levels declined as sagebrush became dense and decadent and understory plants deteriorated. Erosion and channel incision substantially reduced the productivity of mountain meadows. Many hay meadows are no longer suitable for sage grouse because they are not being irrigated for hay production.

Mule deer were also beneficiaries of the habitat changes that followed Euro-American settlement. Livestock grazing triggered growth of preferred forage plants, particularly fire-sensitive sagebrush, bitterbrush, and curlleaf mountain-mahogany. Removal of grassy fuels allowed shrubs to outcompete grasses, while soil disturbance created optimal conditions for the widespread establishment of shrub seedlings. The closely grazed fuels no longer supported fire, which allowed development of dense, shrub-dominated communities that materially improved the capacity of winter ranges to support deer. After sheep numbers were reduced and shrubs developed, forage and cover approached optimum levels. In the early 1900s, and although deer numbers were low in most areas, the stage was set for their irruption.[18]

During his 1909 survey of the Pine Forest Range Walter Taylor concluded that "deer did not seem to be common in the mountains."[19] At the time, this range was heavily stocked with sheep and cattle. Taylor sighted only six deer and some tracks and other sign during the course of the summer. Two prospectors wounded a large buck the last week of July, and a homesteader told of seeing deer tracks around his garden about the same time. During the winter, deer were reported to frequent meadows to the east at Quinn River Crossing.

Deer numbers were also low in the Ruby Mountains, as suggested in the writings of Lewis Sharp. "The year 1906 was a busy one as I took care of the sheep camps for Ira D. Wines and John Hankins, Sr. in the Ruby Mountains. One day that summer I killed a deer. There was no deer season then as at that time few deer were seen in the Ruby ranges."[20]

The 1917 annual wildlife report for the Humboldt National Forest estimated the deer population in the six-hundred-square-mile Ruby Mountains at fifty animals.[21] Deer numbers were still very low ten years later. The Borell and Ellis 1927–29 mammal-collecting survey reported that mule deer ranged throughout the Ruby Mountains but were "nowhere numerous." Members of the party observed a total of sixteen deer on four occasions during the course of three summers. Their report explained that deer "numbers were undoubtedly kept down by lack of sufficient cover and forage plants of the required type. The area probably never supported ideal vegetation for deer. Heavy grazing by sheep and cattle has reduced the already insufficient forage crop. Improved grazing regulations now in force by the United States Forest Service will help to restore the former conditions and result in an increase in the numbers of deer."[22]

In contrast, deer numbers in central Nevada had increased by 1930. Jean Linsdale reported: "The mule deer was common over most of the Toiyabe Mountains during the time of our work there. Ranger A. R. Torgerson told me in 1930 that he had estimated that there were 559 deer in his district, between Austin and Summit Creek, in 1929. On June 11, 1930, Otto and Albert Daniels told me that they believed that the deer were increasing in the mountains. The latter had counted 56 deer in one day the previous fall in the upper-part of Kingston Canon."[23]

Raymond Hall wrote in 1929 that the eastern Nevada mule deer population had increased significantly and had reached high numbers.[24] A survey of overpopulated deer ranges in the United States concluded that irruptions (sudden and excessive density) in mule deer took place in the Santa Rosa, Toiyabe, Schell Creek, and Snake ranges, peaking between 1942 and 1944.[25]

When mule deer began to heavily utilize forage plants, the Nevada Fish and Game Commission authorized controlled hunts. The first took place in Kingston and Birch canyons in the Toiyabe Range in 1941. Six hundred bucks and 260 does were removed.

The Nevada mule deer population increased markedly in the 1940s and reached an all-time high in the 1950s.[26] During this era browse plants were producing an abundance of annual forage despite being heavily browsed by deer and livestock. Close cropping stimulated regrowth of tender leaders, which in turn enhanced forage quality. Special doe hunts were held in an effort to reduce heavy use of browse, and considerable numbers of does and bucks were harvested during annual deer seasons as well. The hunts had little effect in reducing utilization levels.

In the early 1960s Nevada experienced a general decline in mule deer numbers. A 1974 symposium addressing declining mule deer populations in the West failed to identify a particular reason. Speakers noted probable causes including predation, overharvesting, range deterioration, poor reproduction, and fire suppression. More specific reasons included expansion of pinyon and juniper on winter ranges and attendant deterioration of browse, loss of forbs, and reduced nutrients on summer ranges and reduction of fawns being produced.[27]

Mule deer habitat has continued to decline. Stands of sagebrush—a staple in the winter diet of deer—have reached senescence, and there is little recruitment of new plants. Bitterbrush, a mainstay for deer in fall, early winter, and early spring, is mostly senescent as well, and is likewise not recruiting new plants. Lacking vigor, these plants produce little forage. The treelike growth form of older mountain mahogany provides little for deer to eat. Forage availability on pinyon-juniper winter ranges continues to deteriorate from the adverse effects of canopy closure.

The unprecedented growth of woody vegetation following the removal of domestic sheep from summer ranges has had unforeseen consequences. Growth of aspen, chokecherry, and other woody plants has materially reduced species diversity. Dense, woody growth now chokes former trails and openings. The herbs and palatable shrubs essential for nutritional forage have been substantially reduced by competition and shading, which reduces the sugar content of understory species. This has resulted in reduced landscape diversity and carrying capacity for mule deer, which prefer open brushlands.

Deer habitat has continued to deteriorate as livestock allotments and management techniques have improved. Reductions or removal of livestock and changes in management systems have resulted in considerable quantities of standing grass and forbs at the end of the grazing season. This trend has helped to stabilize watersheds, but it has unfavorably influenced the carrying capacity of deer ranges. Competition from forbs and grasses inhibits recruitment in aging shrub stands.[28] Ironically, grazing disturbance and absence of fire initi-ated the postsettlement enhancement of mule deer habitat. Livestock grazing in moderation and fire will be necessary to rejuvenate deer habitat and main-tain populations.

One might question the logic of further disturbing vegetation with fire when millions of acres have already burned. These fires have largely swept through degraded vegetation in the drier valleys and foothills, however, much of which had a limited capacity to support wildlife. Fire has had a comparatively mini-mal influence on summer ranges, which are badly in need of disturbance.

Following the 1999 wildfires, some media sources claimed that wildfires devastated prime wildlife habitat. The Nevada Department of Wildlife reported that home for approximately four thousand sage grouse was effectively lost for the next thirty to fifty years, conservatively, after being burned in 2006. Another spokesperson for the department said that it can take thirty to forty years for a sagebrush habitat to recover to preburn conditions and that some areas would never return to their original prefire state.[29] Such predictions have left the public with the impression that the future for wildlife is bleak. Unques-tionably, high-intensity fires have had an unprecedented impact on wildlife habitat, but the impact of fire on wildlife habitat is highly variable across the millions of acres that have burned.

The initial loss of sagebrush and bitterbrush and the propagation of cheat-grass following wildfire materially reduced the carrying capacity for mule deer on northern Nevada winter ranges, particularly Hunt Area Six in western Elko County. The likelihood of browse recovery is negligible on sites where cheat-grass predominates. Browse recovers in localities where there was a seed pool and bunchgrass survived fire to keep cheatgrass from dominating.

On higher-elevation transitional ranges between deer summering and wintering areas, the prognosis for recovery of forage plants after fire is more often good. Much of the burned landscape is within this important component of the yearly habitat. The loss of browse was initially acute, but reestablish-ment is taking place on sites of good potential. Expansion of grass and forbs increases the availability of nutrients above their preburn levels. This has been

FACING PAGE: **Figure 11.1.** Concentrated cattle grazing at Warm Creek Trough, Mountain City Ranger District. (a) September 24, 1930: Season-long grazing has reduced grasses and shrubs. Courtesy U.S. Forest Service. (b) August 29, 1966: Heavy grazing continues. The snowberry on the near slope shows the debilitating effects of long-term cattle use. Willow has grown profusely under protection. (c) July 28, 2004: Managed under a rest rotation system, this unit was not grazed in 2004. Photographs (b) and (c) by George E. Gruell.

(a)

(b)

(c)

particularly beneficial for pregnant does migrating toward summer ranges, increasing the likelihood that they will give birth to strong fawns.

Wildfires on summer ranges have had a positive influence by rejuvenating forage. In areas of good potential, herbaceous plants produce abundant forage by the third season, and crown-sprouting shrubs display vigorous growth.

Unlike mule deer, which initially benefited from livestock grazing and absence of fire, bighorn sheep and pronghorn were not benefited. By the turn of the twentieth century, bighorn numbers in the Ruby Mountains were in free fall. William Toyn reported seeing three or four mountain sheep at the head of Lamoille Canyon during the winter of 1904–5. U.S. Forest Service ranger August Rohwer observed one or two mountain sheep on several occasions between 1915 and 1921 but none thereafter. The Borell and Ellis survey reported no evidence of mountain sheep in the Ruby Mountains except a pair of well-preserved horns and a portion of a skull.[30] For all practical purposes, Rocky Mountain and California bighorn sheep had disappeared north of Highway 50 by the mid-1920s, although desert bighorns persisted in some of the roughest and most remote mountain ranges south of the highway.[31]

Disease introduced by domestic sheep or depleted forage resulting from heavy grazing by domestic sheep are thought to be responsible for the extermination of bighorn sheep. Many biologists believe depleted forage was the cause. Bighorn sheep prefer open habitats with a high density of acceptable forage, and they avoid vegetation where visibility is obstructed.[32] This is not surprising, considering the prevalence of open landscapes occupied by mountain sheep historically. They use areas where trees and brush have been removed by fire significantly more than they use unburned sites. The sheep are drawn to these areas by herbaceous plants and young shrubs.

Pronghorn (antelope) populations were at extremely low levels at the beginning of the twentieth century.[33] Rancher F. M. Payne reported that they were still seen from time to time between Quinn River Crossing and the Big Creek Ranch east of the Pine Forest Range. During his 1909 survey Walter Taylor found no evidence of antelope in this region. Ranger Rohwer saw five antelope at the head of Jerry Creek in the Ruby Mountains in the spring of 1924 but none thereafter. Members of the Borell and Ellis survey saw no evidence of antelope in the Ruby Mountains and vicinity in the late 1920s. Several long-term residents reported that antelope were previously numerous in Ruby Valley and along the east base of the Ruby Mountains. Raymond Hall noted that the area occupied by pronghorn and their numbers had been greatly reduced by 1946.[34] In 1953 the statewide pronghorn population was estimated at four thousand animals.

In 2003 the Nevada Department of Wildlife reported that general improvement of land management in some areas, along with numerous wildfires, had increased the overall quantity and quality of pronghorn habitat throughout much of the state. Grasses and forbs, their primary forage in spring, summer, and fall, had largely replaced sagebrush on burned landscapes. Biologists estimated that pronghorn occupied 21,246 square miles in 1983. Twenty years later, suitable pronghorn habitat had increased to approximately 55,952 square miles and the estimated population was placed at twenty thousand.[35] The 2009 population estimate was twenty-five thousand. Evidence of an expanding population is reflected in a steady increase in the number of annual hunting tags issued.

Historical perspective and current research indicate that improvement in habitat quality has indeed had a significant influence on pronghorn population increases. Conversion by wildfire of dense stands of sagebrush to predominance of herbaceous plants produced productive landscapes akin to presettlement conditions when pronghorn were common. Reduced and better-managed livestock grazing and the attendant increased availability of grasses and forbs have further enhanced pronghorn habitat. Considering the expansion of productive pronghorn habitat, it is likely that populations exceed current estimates.

Habitat changes had a particularly noticeable effect on white-tailed jackrabbit and black-tailed jackrabbit populations after the turn of the century. White-tails are creatures of open grasslands; black-tails prefer brushy areas. The depletion of grasses on rangelands led to widespread disappearance of white-tails by the 1930s. The 1927–29 Borell and Ellis study reported that white-tailed jackrabbits, although abundant locally, had a limited distribution in the Ruby Mountains, largely in Ruby Valley from Harrison Pass north to Secret Pass and Pole Canyon. Interviews by Hall in the late 1920s and early 1930s confirmed the presence of white-tails in the Santa Rosa and Desatoya ranges, in the vicinity of Hamilton, and at the top of Mount Magruder in southwestern Nevada.[36] These reports suggest that white-tails were occupying localities where remnants of their grassy habitat still remained. They still persist in some of these regions.

Dayton Hyde described the fate of the white-tailed jackrabbit as follows:

The Indians wove long nets of fiber, staged drives, and netted great quantities of white-tailed jackrabbits. . . . Year by year the white man's cattle, sheep, and horses cover[ed] the land in incredible numbers, cropping the grass into the dirt. . . . While the Indian muttered about the white man's stock, he could not have known the more insidious results of overgrazing. Sagebrush and rabbit brush were always present, but the plants were small and scattered, held in check by competition with the grasses. But with overgrazing, inedible brush took over millions of acres of once productive grassland, and soon grass existed in quantity only on the bottoms too wet for sage. The white-tail jackrabbit . . . preferred grassland to sage, and when the brush took over, the white-tailed jacks lost out to huge populations of the blacktailed jack, a small, scrawny, tough, inferior, and prolific denizen of the desert sage. The blacktails multiplied to incredible numbers.[37]

White-tailed jackrabbits have vanished over wide areas.[38] They now occur largely in remnant populations on and adjacent to hay meadows in northern Nevada. The increased availability of grasses resulting from wildfire and reductions in livestock grazing has been favorable for white-tails. Remnant populations appear to be rebounding in some localities.

The black-tailed jackrabbit, in contrast, thrived under heavy grazing. In the 1930s black-tails were numerous in the valleys adjacent to the Toiyabe Range.[39] Anthropologist Julian Steward reported in the late 1930s that the black-tailed jackrabbit "now occurs in enormous herds, having increased in numbers and range in recent years."[40] Black-tails can be extremely numerous and then suddenly almost disappear. Tularemia, or "rabbit fever," has been identified as the organism responsible for many rabbit deaths. High black-tail populations are often a result of overgrazing.[41] Once habitat deterioration has begun, the rabbits may contribute to the overgrazing and may be the primary cause of depletion in its final stages. Black-tailed jackrabbits have spread widely into areas formerly occupied by white-tailed jackrabbits.

Beaver have been both praised and condemned, depending on the mindset of the speaker.[42] Fishermen like them because the ponds they create provide habitat for trout. Ranchers in northern Nevada considered beaver a valuable asset along the Humboldt River, crediting huge yields of native hay and abundant pasture in the 1930s to their activities. Ranchers near Lovelock, at the lower end of the Humboldt River, had quite the opposite view, favoring extermination of the beavers because their upstream dams retarded the flow of water.

In the years prior to Euro-American settlement the trapping success of the Hudson's Bay Company in the mountains of northern Nevada was generally poor. Following settlement, beaver numbers increased significantly. By the 1940s populations had expanded in response to favorable habitat conditions. The Nevada Fish and Game Commission employed a full-time beaver trapper to handle the numerous complaints involving blocked culverts, flooded campgrounds, and diversion of irrigation water from ranchers' hay meadows. Beaver progressively moved to the headwaters of streams, many of which showed no signs of having been occupied previously. In the Independence Mountains they had outstripped their food supply in less than two decades. Dams were breached during high water, head-cutting ensued, and streambeds were deeply incised. District Ranger Frank Beitia witnessed these events but was powerless to mitigate the damage.[43] Where ponds prevailed at mid-century there is now sediment and, often, dense vegetation.

Long-term buildup and maturation of aspen in the absence of fire favored beaver, and populations in mountainous regions exploded. A precipitous drop in the number of these industrious animals followed as they literally ate themselves out of house and home. Beaver populations will likely continue to increase and then decline with succession and variation in availability of mature aspen and willow.

The ecological changes Euro-American settlement has brought to Nevada sweep across the full spectrum of wildlife. Except for sage grouse, upland game birds suffered the consequences of early postsettlement impacts on their habitats. Destruction of grassy habitats and fruit-bearing shrubs was the undoing of sharp-tailed grouse. Sightings were periodically reported after the turn of the century. University of Nevada professor Ira La Rivers saw a flock of six on July 9, 1939, in the Bull Run Mountains. Reliable reports indicate that sharp-tails were still in Ruby Valley in the 1940s. A dozen were observed on September 14, 1952, in the Capitol Range in Humboldt County. The last authentic sighting was of four birds by Nevada game warden Earl Dudley in the Lamoille Canyon area of the Ruby Mountains in 1960.[44] The Nevada Department of Wildlife has no record of a confirmed sighting since, with the exception of reintroduced birds in northeastern Nevada during the last decade.

Blue grouse and mountain quail currently exist in numbers sufficient to provide hunting opportunities, but populations are restricted in their distribution. Blue grouse are limited to regions supporting conifers, whose needles make up virtually their entire winter diet. Post-1900 reports of this species are few. In the early 1930s Linsdale found them in the higher elevations of the Toiyabe Range, but they were not numerous. During the summer and fall, blue grouse feed on the leaves of herbaceous plants and fruits of shrubs. Nesting takes place on the lower slopes and benches, preferably in a mixture of open herbaceous cover, low shrubs, and mixed deciduous thickets. The widespread increase in pinyon, juniper, and sagebrush with associated loss of food plants in brooding areas of central Nevada has no doubt restricted recruitment.

William Kent's observations of mountain quail north of Winnemucca at the turn of the century offer insight on that species: "Occasionally the mountain country has been full of California mountain Quail, the finest of all the quail family, bigger and heavier than the bobwhite, and superior in juice and fat to any of the tribe. They come and go sporadically, dependent on the severity of the winters. For about ten years after 1895 they furnished wonderful shooting, lying close to a dog."[45]

Walter Taylor reported a scarcity of these birds during his 1909 survey of the Pine Forest Range. He saw or heard single birds and a dozen juveniles on only three occasions over a period of two months. Mountain quail were sighted in small numbers at two locations in the Toiyabes during the course of Linsdale's 1930–33 survey. Local residents reported seeing fewer numbers than formerly. The long-term trend in mountain quail populations is downward. The Nevada Department of Wildlife has made major efforts to reestablish mountain quail in areas where they existed in the 1940s and 1950s.[46] Maturation of woody plants and loss of herbs appear to be the primary reasons for the population decline.

Neotropical songbirds and small mammals constitute a majority of the wildlife species found in cold desert landscapes. With some exceptions these species are adapted to habitats that historically had been disturbed by fire. This infers a preference for open shrubs with a significant grass and forb component.

Shrub-nesting birds, including sage thrashers, sage sparrows, and Brewer's sparrows, prefer sagebrush communities and have been favored by the absence of fire and subsequent increase in density of sagebrush and other shrubs. Removal of sagebrush by fire is initially detrimental to these species and permanently detrimental if sagebrush is replaced by cheatgrass. Following wildfire, one can expect an increase in ground- and grass-nesting birds such as horned larks, meadowlarks, and lark sparrows, especially if bunchgrass thrives.

Studies of avian species diversity and abundance in areas of sagebrush replaced by seeded grasses and in areas that had been seeded and then reoccupied by shrubs showed, as expected, that shrub habitats attracted shrub-nesting birds.[47] These birds were replaced by grassland birds after conversion and seeding. Areas where shrubs returned and grasses persisted had the greatest diversity, with a mixture of shrub and grassland birds.

Changes in songbird populations in more productive riparian, mountain shrub, and aspen communities have been continuing since settlement, although with little scientific documentation. Loss or deterioration of trees and shrubs along riparian corridors resulting from human development has been recognized as detrimental to species that require dense foliage,[48] while the increased size and density of shrubs and trees at upper elevations has benefited foliage-feeding songbirds.

The increased density of sagebrush in the absence of fire seems to have helped pygmy rabbits and certain rodents, primarily least chipmunks. Long-term loss of grass and forbs may depress other populations, however, because most rodents feed on herbs and seeds. The increase in herbs and seeds following fire is favorable for deer mice, pocket gophers, kangaroo rats, and ground squirrels—species that prefer open, grassy sites.

Nevada's carnivores, including coyotes, foxes, badgers, weasels, and bobcats, depend on rodents and rabbits as a primary food source. When this food source is readily available, carnivores thrive. Raptors (eagles, hawks, and owls) also benefit from early stages of succession when rodent populations are at high levels.

In lakes and waterways, changes wrought by increasing settlement have not been kind to Lahontan cutthroat trout. In 1975 the species was reclassified as threatened. Today, cutthroat trout are believed to occupy only 10 percent of the stream habitats where they were historically found. Improper grazing practices altered much of the riparian vegetation along stream banks, diversions dewatered streams, and unregulated fishing in earlier years devastated populations.[49] Nevada Department of Wildlife stream survey records of the 1950s and 1960s showed fifteen hundred miles of trout streams in Elko County. By the latter 1970s there was half that amount.[50]

Pyramid Lake, a remnant of prehistoric Lake Lahontan, became famous as a commercial fishery for Indians and pioneers alike in the latter 1800s. Through the 1920s it continued to produce incredible catches of cutthroat trout. The largest, caught by an Indian named John Skimmerhorn, set a world record of forty-one pounds. A replica of this fish is deposited in the Nevada State Museum in Carson City. By the 1930s the Pyramid Lake fishery had collapsed. Construction of Derby Dam and the Truckee River Canal diverted much of the Truckee's flow into the Newlands Reclamation Project's Lahontan Reservoir on the Carson River. The remainder was largely used for irrigation at the Pyramid Lake Indian Reservation. In August 1937 Pyramid Lake was eighty feet below its highest level, which was recorded in 1869. Receding further, by 1950 it was considered too alkaline to support trout. Improved flow from the Truckee River and a stocking program initiated in the early 1960s have transformed Pyramid Lake into a productive fishery enjoyed by thousands of sports fishers each year.

Government agencies and private organizations have been trying since the 1970s to restore the cutthroat's habitat. Two of the many projects to restore riparian and aquatic health are located at Mahogany Creek in northwestern Nevada and the Marys River in northeastern Nevada. Revised livestock grazing practices and fencing of damaged areas have stabilized streams and resulted in an increase in woody plants, which provide shade.[51] Plant succession at upper elevations has resulted in prolific growth of willow, which forms quality fish habitat but overtops the stream, restricting the presence of open water and access for those who wish to fish.

Beginning in the 1920s, Nevada's wildlife populations were augmented by trapping, importing, or transplanting and releasing big game animals and game birds. These efforts have been mostly successful, particularly the introduction of chukar partridge imported from the Himalaya Mountains.[52] The chukar was a perfect fit for Nevada's drier mountains with cheatgrass and other annual plants. Populations reached extremely high levels in the mid-1960s. Although wildfire has promoted increased growth of cheatgrass—the staple food of the chukar—cheatgrass was not the limiting factor before wildfire swept many areas. Over the short term, habitats are set back by wildfire until shrubs, critical as hiding cover, develop. Production of cheatgrass and other annuals and reestablishment of shrubs will be favorable for chukar over the long term.

Twenty Himalayan snowcocks, large relatives of the chukar (males reach up to six pounds), were released in the Ruby Mountains in January 1963. These birds, which were live-trapped in the Hunza province of Pakistan, were augmented by subsequent releases, and the species became established in remote settings at high elevations of the Rubies. Several of these birds are harvested yearly by hunters fortunate enough to obtain permits. This bird has also drawn the attention of avid birdwatchers, who travel from afar to the Rubies in an attempt to add it to their life lists.

In the 1970s the Nevada Department of Wildlife sportsmen accelerated efforts to transplant and relocate wildlife. Release of elk, a priority, has been highly successful. Able to digest both grass and browse, elk have taken hold in mountainous and hilly terrain, most of which is no longer grazed by domestic sheep and where cattle grazing has been reduced. Herds are on the increase, and hunters are taking trophy bulls and antlerless animals. Releases of pronghorn have augmented depressed populations and formed the nucleus of new populations in previously unoccupied habitat.

British Columbia, Canada, has been generous with surplus California bighorn sheep, and releases have resulted in their reestablishment in areas the species occupied historically. The release of California and Rocky Mountain bighorns into ranges that have long been devoid of domestic sheep is providing hunting and viewing opportunities. Problems have developed, however, in recent years. California bighorns in the Santa Rosa Range and Rocky Mountain bighorns in the east Humboldt ranges have experienced heavy losses from *Pasteurella pneumonia,* a pathogen that debilitates weakened or stressed animals.

Mountain goats, which are not native to Nevada, were introduced into the Ruby Mountains and have become established in several localities. Nonnative moose appear from time to time in northern Nevada, apparently migrating from the areas they occupy in the southern part of the Sawtooth National Forest in Idaho.

Ruffed grouse, a game bird species closely associated with aspen and not indigenous to Nevada, were released in the Ruby Mountains in the 1950s. This population and additional releases on the Humboldt-Toiyabe National Forest to the north have resulted in a buildup of numbers sufficient to support yearly hunting. Hungarian partridge, a nonindigenous game bird slightly smaller than the chukar, is primarily found in scattered populations in the northern tier of counties. The ancestors of these birds were apparently released in the 1920s or earlier.

Because wildlife requires water, management of springs and riparian areas has gained attention in recent decades. Diversion of all water from a spring is no longer allowed. Escape ramps are increasingly placed in water troughs. When chukars were introduced to waterless mountains, guzzlers were built to supply their needs. Soon it became apparent that many species of wildlife used guzzlers and that these water sources could be used to extend habitat into dry or occasionally dry areas in many mountain ranges. Today there are several thousand guzzlers scattered widely across Nevada. Each has an apron or surface collection area, a storage tank, and a drinker—a small surface area that exposes water to many species.

The preceding discussion provides a sense of long-term change in wildlife habitat and the effect of these changes on wildlife populations. Some of these populations are doing well, particularly transplanted and relocated big game animals, but most of the state's wildlife face deteriorating habitat, an outgrowth of advanced plant succession that has resulted in reduced plant and landscape diversity. Increased density of woody plants, reduction of herbaceous perennial plants, and dominance by weedy annuals have created habitats to which few native wildlife species are adapted. Land management agencies recognize the need to rehabilitate wildlife habitat by disturbing vegetation with fire and other means. In recent years, numerous efforts at collaboration and restoration of rangeland habitats have begun. The Nevada Partners in Conservation and Development, facilitated by the Nevada Department of Wildlife, is focused on proactive management of vegetation that needs rehabilitation.

12

Management Choices
We Cannot Do Nothing

The vegetation and wildlife of the Great Basin have changed profoundly since prehistoric times. A major expansion of woody plants accelerated following settlement, largely because of livestock grazing and suppression of wildfires. By the mid-twentieth century an enormous increase in shrubs and trees had occurred. These potential fuels, combined with an invasion of cheatgrass and better management of perennial grasses, have led to recent fires of extreme size and frequency. Today, Nevada has two major fire problems. Too much fire occurs in the low-elevation Wyoming big sagebrush and nearby types that pre-historically burned infrequently, and too little fire has led to too much woody fuel in the mountain shrub zone where fire was once common. Fires in the mountain shrub zone are now increasing in size and intensity, however, with both natural and unnatural consequences.

Changes in vegetation and fuels and a better understanding of the role of fire have caused the U.S. Forest Service and the Bureau of Land Management (BLM) to reconsider the role of fire in management of resources. By the late 1970s Congress' General Accounting Office had confirmed the futility of attempting to eliminate fire in the wildlands of western North America. Federal wildland fire policy shifted from a narrow focus on suppression to a broader program of managing fire and fuels.[1] This policy was reviewed and updated in 1995 as a single cohesive federal fire policy: "Fire, as a critical natural process, will be integrated into land and resource management plans and activities on a landscape scale, and across agency boundaries."[2] Catastrophic fires in southern California in 2002 and intense and large fires across many parts of the United States gelled a growing recognition of the problems created by past policies. The Healthy Forest Restoration Act of 2003 empowered proactive management of fuels and fire in forests and rangelands. In 2009 the USDA and USDI reaffirmed the soundness of the 1995 fire policy and issued guidelines for consistent practices: "Wildland fire will be used to protect, maintain, and enhance resources and, as nearly as possible, be allowed to function in its natural ecological role."[3] Federal agencies are authorized to implement a new, proactive program of vegetative management.

Wildland fires are categorized as two distinct types: wildfire and prescribed fire. Management response to a wildfire on federal land is based on objectives established in the applicable Land and Resource Management Plan and Fire Management Plan. Fire use for resource benefits occurs when wildfire is intentionally allowed to burn because it helps meet management objectives. Prescribed fires are planned ignitions for land management purposes.

On the Humboldt-Toiyabe National Forest, fire use has been confined to certain wilderness areas. The positive results speak for themselves. During July and August 2004 the Troy Canyon lightning fire in the Grant Range thinned approximately 2,800 acres of pinyon and juniper. Within two years it was evident that this fire had greatly enhanced habitat used by mountain sheep. The East Creek lightning fire was allowed to burn over a six-week period at upper elevations on the Schell Creek Range during the summer of 2008, enhancing wildlife habitat by creating openings in the tree canopy. The Phillips Ranch fire of 1996, burning on upper-elevation land of Great Basin National Park, was managed under an interagency fire plan to reduce hazardous fuels and improve wildlife habitat.

One of the more significant beneficial uses of a lightning fire occurred on East Slide Rock Ridge in the Jarbidge Wilderness. Initially declared a potentially beneficial fire on August 8, 2008, it grew to encompass 3,245 acres during the next ten days. Pushed by increasing winds, it spread beyond the wilderness boundary and had burned nearly 10,000 acres by August 21. The next day it was declared a wildfire, and suppression efforts began. The wind persisted, and the fire more than doubled in size during the next four days, ultimately affecting 53,000 acres. Economic damage was restricted to about 300 acres of livestock forage on private lands, for which loss the Forest Service compensated the owner. Whether this fire should have initially been declared a wildfire and immediate suppression action been taken will continue to be vigorously debated. Considering the rugged nature of the terrain and remote location, it is questionable whether firefighters could have kept it from spreading. In either case, the management objective—to benefit natural resources, including wildlife habitat—was achieved. Twelve months after the fire, new aspen stands were developing from viable root systems where subalpine fir had been displacing aspen. As the fire progressed, it cracked the hard coating of snowbrush ceanothus seeds that had lain dormant in the soil for a century or longer. Now able to imbibe moisture, the seeds sprouted into many thousands of snowbrush seed-lings. In some localities dense stands of low-vigor mountain mahogany were opened, clearing the way for new plants to establish. Increased production of native grasses, forbs, and crown-sprouting shrubs has enhanced the habitat for elk, deer, and other wildlife.

Responding to the success of managed lightning fires in designated wilderness, the Humboldt-Toiyabe National Forest managers have decided to manage wildfires for resource benefits outside wilderness areas in eastern and central Nevada.

Prescribed fire has been practiced on a small scale on the Humboldt-Toiyabe National Forest for several decades in productive mountain sagebrush communities. One of the largest of these, the 1,600-acre Buttermilk burn, was carried out on the Santa Rosa Ranger District in the spring of 2006. The Nevada Department of Wildlife opposed the plan, arguing that the fire would remove sagebrush and be detrimental to sage grouse and other wildlife. The fire broke up the dense sagebrush cover, however, providing openings for the herbaceous plants favored by wildlife. Three years after the fire, local wildlife biologists viewed the results as positive.

Although there is widespread precedent for use of prescribed fire in sage-brush communities supporting remnant grasses and forbs, the practice has been challenged. Biologists from the Western Association of Fish and Wildlife Agencies oppose use of prescribed fire in sagebrush communities where annual precipitation is less than twelve inches.[4] Their primary concern is fragmentation and reduction of available sagebrush stands important to sage grouse, as well as risk of cheatgrass invasion. Although the twelve-inch boundary is a bit arbitrary and not always ideal, this position can be seen as ecologically sound for the drier Wyoming big sagebrush habitats—if or where little or no native plants remain in the understory. But the association is also cautioning against prescribed fires in the moister and more productive mountain big sagebrush habitats. Those habitats have been the focal point for prescribed fires because past fires have led to long-term improvement in the habitat of sage grouse and other wildlife.

Fire increases the resilience of native perennials and helps to make them resistant to domination by cheatgrass later. Except for scattered southerly aspects and heavily disturbed sites, cheatgrass is a minor problem in these productive communities because native plants outcompete it. In the Wyoming big sagebrush sites where fire is not a good management choice, ways must be found to stimulate perennial herbaceous understory plants that have been weakened by competition from shrubs and, often, by unsustainable grazing management. Experiments with exclosures have shown that exclusion of livestock alone will not restore the perennials.

The use of prescribed fire on the Humboldt-Toiyabe National Forest has risen from about one thousand acres initially to ten thousand acres per year in the past decade. This increase has been largely in pinyon-juniper woodlands. Before 2004, prescribed fires in pinyon and juniper were small—on the order of one hundred acres or less. The May 2004 Underdown Canyon burn of approximately nine hundred acres over many small patches was the first deliberate large burn. Scientists designed the burn pattern to learn about the effects of fire across a landscape of different tree densities and sizes.[5] It also provided the needed experience to carry out the four-thousand-acre 2008 Elkhorn II fire on the Tonopah Ranger District, which exceeded expectations by burning out of control. Ignited from a helicopter, this fire created a mosaic of openings across a pinyon-juniper canopy. Native plant response has been negligible where the tree cover was dense and understory plants were virtually absent. More productive sites with remnant shrubs and herbs have shown a more positive response. A thirty-two-hundred-acre prescribed fire was carried out in May 2008 on the Bridgeport Ranger District, removing pinyon pine and encouraging growth of shrubs, grass, and forbs. Fire disturbance is improving the long-term habitat potential for sage grouse nesting and brood-rearing, as well as enhancing mule deer habitat by providing some diversity at the landscape scale by restoring plant succession in patches.

Prescribed fire planning has been aided by publication of the *Piñon and Juniper Field Guide,* written by scientists who have studied these woodlands for many years.[6] This guide will help field biologists and land managers identify sites that will benefit from fire or other treatments and avoid sites where treatments might do more harm than good.

Planning, preparing, and executing prescribed fire is a laborious process. The National Environmental Policy Act (NEPA) requires agencies to assess the environmental effects of their proposed actions prior to making decisions. This time-consuming process requires input from specialists who study soils, water, air quality, and wildlife as well as collaboration with local governments, fire protection districts, Native American tribes, grazing permitees, the Nevada Department of Wildlife, and other entities. Cultural and archaeological surveys must be carried out. State historical preservation and smoke abatement requirements must be met, as must Endangered Species Act requirements. Costs escalate during the process, and final approval can be delayed for years because of appeals and litigation. Once the fire is approved, scheduling can be a problem where wildfire suppression needs have priority for manpower, budget, and equipment. Appropriate weather and fuel moisture are critical to meeting the required burning conditions. Windows of opportunity may be narrow, especially where risky conditions or cautious managers require tight prescriptions.

Eastern Nevada has taken the lead in planning for fire use on public lands. In 1997 a technical review team sanctioned by the Coordinated Resource Management (CRM) Steering Committee prepared a fire management plan for the Ely BLM District in White Pine, Lincoln, and Nye counties. As an expression of the National Fire Plan, the team provided for fire to resume a more natural ecological role. This and similar work has been roundly endorsed and supported by the BLM and members of the grant-funded Eastern Nevada Landscape Coalition (ENLC). The ENLC conducts vegetation management projects, monitoring, and tours and other public education events in support of proactive vegetation management to restore resilience to plant communities across eastern Nevada. Building on the CRM fire management plan, a BLM interdisciplinary team prepared a natural and prescribed fire plan that identifies 3.6 million acres where prescribed and natural fire can be utilized.[7]

By the end of the 2009 fire season, considerable progress had been made applying fire under this plan. In the Gleason area near Robinson Summit, application of prescribed fire in four phases over several years resulted in removal of pinyon and juniper, with very good growth response by native grasses and shrubs. An earlier wildfire at Robinson Summit responded very well except in local areas where trees had become too dense. In these limited areas, competition had already removed or weakened the understory plants that normally would survive fire, and the intense heat generated by the accumulated fuels killed them. Then plant succession began anew with rabbit tobacco, silverstems, and other early pioneer species. Such areas are vulnerable to invasive weeds, and managers now realize that planned fire is needed earlier to prevent unwanted fire effects later.

In 2008 a thirty-five-hundred-acre managed natural fire on Mount Grafton removed insect-killed white fir and stimulated aspen regrowth. One year later, native grasses were growing profusely on many sites. BLM fire personnel anticipate that lightning-ignited fire in areas covered by expanded fire plans will become a preferred management tool. This will provide the benefits of prescribed fire to many more acres at far less cost than could be accomplished by many small-scale prescribed burns.

A major effort to improve the health and productivity of western public lands is incorporated into the BLM's *Healthy Lands Initiative*.[8] Targeting lands in Oregon, Idaho, and Nevada, this partnership between state and federal agencies is funded at $1.9 million. Twenty-three thousand acres have been identified for maintenance and restoration of upland and riparian shrub-steppe wildlife habitats. Restoring sage grouse habitat is a crucial issue.

In the 1990s the National Riparian Service Team—with BLM and Forest Service interdisciplinary professionals and the support of many other agencies and citizen's groups—began working cooperatively to restore riparian areas across the West by focusing on the physical functioning of riparian areas.[9] The Nevada Creeks and Communities Team began teaching Riparian Proper Functioning Condition Assessment classes in 1997. These efforts emphasize management of vegetation in the realization that stabilizing water-loving plants, water to sustain them, and land forms to spread water in high flows all help riparian areas to withstand high flows without excess erosion and damage. The importance of functionality is increasingly being recognized as critical to the interests of private landowners (who control the best and biggest waters of Nevada) as well as biologists, environmentalists, and downstream water users.[10] There is a compelling interest in keeping water on the land longer and dampening floods and droughts.

The Sagebrush Steppe Treatment Evaluation Project (SagesTEP) has brought together wildlife agencies, federal land managers, and university researchers to study the suitability of alternative land management treatments in the pinyon- and/or juniper-encroached areas of the Great Basin.[11] Prescribed fire, mowing, chainsaw lop-and-scatter, Bull Hog treatment (grinding brush and trees), and application of herbicides are all being tested. Initiated in 2006, this six-year project now includes fourteen sites in Oregon, California, Nevada, Idaho, and Utah. A companion sage-cheat study is under way in six arid big sagebrush locations including a site in Nevada and two sites in Washington.

The Governor's Sage-Grouse Conservation Plan for Nevada and Eastern California has identified many projects to improve habitat.[12] Treatments in the plan include cutting of encroaching pinyon and juniper near sage grouse leks (strutting grounds) and riparian areas where meadow expansion, by reducing competition from trees, will improve water flow in the vicinity of springs; seeding previously burned sage grouse habitat to hasten establishment of sagebrush and fire-resistant perennial herbaceous plants; and use of prescribed fire and mechanical treatments to reduce wildfire hazard and generally improve habitat. Through 2009, economic conditions largely prevented funding for these projects. A new effort, Nevada Partners in Conservation and Development, is patterned after the Utah PCD, which has been very successful in getting treatment applied for a variety of such benefits over millions of acres.[13] The Pinyon Juniper Partnership, which hosted the Pinyon Juniper Summit, focuses on the need to restore sagebrush ecosystems by augmenting federal funding with funds from commercial enterprises.[14] The partnership has proposed a demonstration area centered on Ely and Caliente where power-generating plants could consume excess biomass and produce revenues to offset the costs of landscape-scale restoration.

The need for treatments to restore mule deer habitat is recognized in *Habitat Guidelines for Mule Deer: Intermountain West Ecoregion* (2009), which among other things suggests use of the Dixie Harrow (pulled behind a crawler tractor) or prescribed fire to regenerate sagebrush and a vigorous herbaceous layer in the mountain big sagebrush type.[15] Fall prescribed fire treatments were recommended to establish new plants in decadent stands of snowbrush ceanothus. Aerial ignitions are being considered to thin curlleaf mountain-mahogany and create openings for seedling establishment and new stands.

Although considerable progress has been made in planning for prescribed fire, the actual accomplishments are unsatisfactory considering the millions of acres in need of treatment. In the meantime, nearly all wildfires are suppressed, regardless of their potential benefits to wildlife habitat.

The threat of loss or damage from wildfires especially where homes and other structures are situated in or adjacent to wildlands remains a major concern. The Carson Range Strategic Planning Area near Carson City has a fuels reduction plan developed cooperatively by several agencies that identifies areas where fuel treatments could be most effective in reducing fire hazard.[16]

Funding under the National Fire Plan allowed hazardous fuels removal on the Humboldt-Toiyabe National Forest adjacent to Lakeview Estates near Carson City. Fuel reduction treatments in this area were instrumental in allowing firefighters to defend homes during the 2004 Waterfall Canyon wildfire. The fire destroyed homes to the south where hazardous fuels had not been removed. Nevada Fire-Safe Councils formed in communities across the state have funded many fuel reduction efforts using grant money made available through the Forest Service and the Nevada Division of Forestry. Fuel reduction projects have been completed on private property adjacent to wildland–urban interfaces and adjacent to federal lands in rural areas in northern and eastern Nevada.

Nationally, the focus of federal funding has been on the wildland–urban interface where fire threatens homes and where firefighting resources are often diverted while wildfires burn undeveloped wildlands.[17] Yet, wildlands far from urban interfaces are badly in need of treatment. They predominate in most of Nevada where wildlife, agriculture, and other land uses and various eco-system services provide important economic value. When considering future wildland wildfire suppression costs, proactive vegetation management or pre-suppression treatments will pay handsome dividends.

Fuel treatment has also been under way in other parts of Nevada. The BLM, in cooperation with the Nevada Department of Transportation, has created fuel breaks along Highways 95, 140, and 147 in northern Nevada. Fuel reduction has stopped wildfires on several occasions and reduced risks to communities and ranches. Fuel breaks or green strips have been placed across large blocks of highly flammable vegetation by planting introduced crested wheatgrass and other species that remain green late into summer. Fuel treatments that limit the size of future fires also reduce fire frequency—two major concerns, especially in low-elevation areas. Improved riparian functionality can also restore green moist areas where fire often stops or slows enough to enable control.

An encouraging trend for increasing the acreage of pinyon and juniper removed involves processing the trees into wood chips. Because wood chips have value, this form of habitat improvement can sometimes pay for itself or at least offset costs. Chips have been used to heat schools and industrial buildings, and, to a limited extent, to produce power.[18] This treatment allows follow-up burning of the fuels left on the ground, resulting in a much less intense fire and better recovery of shrubs and desirable herbaceous plants than would high-intensity fire in untreated fuels. The utility of this treatment over significant areas may materialize as the demand for heating and power generation increases. How-ever, some areas may be too remote for economic marketing of harvested fuels because of the energy needed to transport chips to urban areas or power plants. Chipping fuels and leaving them on the soil surface reduces the onsite fire risk and creates fuel breaks needed for prescribed fire use across the landscape. Plant recovery can be inhibited, however, where chips are spread too deep.

Today we are at a crossroads with respect to management of wildlife habitat and the wildlife populations that depend on enlightened proactive management of vegetation, fuels, and fire. Sagebrush-grass communities continue to decline in too many areas. Pinyon and juniper tree dominance, with its associated dete-rioration of understory plants, is forecast to double in Nevada by 2050.[19] About eighty thousand acres a year cross an ecological threshold preventing natural recovery.[20] Mountain shrub communities decline steadily as plants grow old, and critical forage in annual leader growth progressively decreases.

Restricted use of prescribed fire and managed wildfire will not meet the need for fire treatment on the millions of acres of federal lands that need disturbance.[21] Fire and fuel management plans being prepared for the vast areas administered by the BLM and USFS could greatly expand the opportunity to allow beneficial use of lightning-ignited wildfires. Use of wildland fire for resource benefits at upper elevations could contribute significantly to achieving the level of disturbance necessary for rejuvenating vegetation and creating sustainable mosaics of habitats to meet the needs of various wildlife species. Creation of mosaics would produce fuel breaks that would help alleviate the problem of burning excessively large homogeneous areas. They would also reduce fire suppression costs when wildfires burn during extreme conditions.

Priority for prescribed fire should be focused on mountain meadows heavily encroached by sagebrush. Removal of sagebrush by fire would result in expansion of the sage grouse habitats critical for reproduction. The surrounding brood areas densely covered by sagebrush and other shrubs should also receive fire treatments that create mosaics, with shrubs important for nesting habitat remaining in significant portions of each planning area. Within a few years the development of open sagebrush cover and an increase in native grasses and forbs would result in greatly improved and sustainable habitat.

Land managers and their resource staff typically know what treatments will invigorate plants and improve wildlife habitat. Bureaucratic processes should be streamlined to alleviate delays from politics and burdensome regulations. A program of habitat enhancement on a significant scale will require commitment to refine and expand the advanced use of fire and complementary tools. If we cannot accomplish this, Nevada's wildlife legacy will continue to decline and change as large, severe, and more frequent wildfires become more prevalent, haphazard, risky, and costly.

Progress in treating vegetation will require much more public involvement. People interested in progressive resource management should accompany resource managers into the field and see for themselves the great potential for vegetation treatments by examining examples of what has been accomplished. This would materially strengthen the case being made by some in public agencies and academia for treating vegetation. As a society, we cannot afford to take a passive attitude if we wish to continue to enjoy viable wildlife populations.

It has taken public agencies more than fifty years to overcome the mistaken idea that wildlife habitat should be protected from the natural disturbance of fire. Other disturbances that simulate natural processes are also essential for perpetuating the diversity of productive wildlife habitats. Enlightened management will require a united commitment for planning and sustaining vegetation disturbance. Since all of us have a stake in Nevada's changing wildlands, we should find the courage to voice our opinions at the table of decision makers. We cannot do nothing; failure to act leads to consequences just as significant as acts of management. It is our sincere hope that this book helps you and others find words to express the insight and commitment needed for sound habitat management in the face of continued change.

Appendix 1

Chronology of Changes in Vegetation, Fire, and Wildlife

TIME PERIOD	VEGETATION	FIRE	WILDLIFE
Pleistocene	Vegetation responded to fluctuating intensities of glacial and interglacial cycles of varying frigid and warm periods.	Lightning-caused fires of unknown frequency, intensity, and size may have burned for extended periods creating irregular vegetation mosaics	Numerous large mammals dominated the fauna, including now-extinct herbivores and carnivores.
Holocene–1870	Fluctuating climate resulted in falling and rising lake levels, buildup and melting of glaciers, and elevation and latitudinal shifts in vegetation. New species moved into open niches in the valley bottoms.	Lightning- and human-caused fires varied with changes in climate and vegetation.	Extinction and/or eradication of many large mammals occurred as dry periods restricted habitat.
1826–1870	Grasses dominated vegetation in many areas, especially in mountains; woody shrubs dominated arid valleys with limited fuel. Pinyon and juniper were largely confined to fire-safe sites.	Fire played a major role in promoting the growth of grass, the dominant vegetation. Unhindered fires burned until extinguished by precipitation or lack of fuel.	Mule deer were scarce. Bighorn sheep, pronghorn, sage and sharp-tailed grouse, Lahontan cutthroat trout, and salmon were locally abundant. Black bear and wolverine roamed northeastern Nevada.
1870–1910	Exploitation of forage for livestock and locally of pinyon and juniper trees for fuel was extreme and widespread. Trees began expanding away from fire-safe sites into areas formerly swept by periodic fires.	Grasses dominated owing to heavy livestock grazing and a major reduction in human ignitions, fire was no longer a prominent factor shaping vegetation on the Nevada landscape.	Large game animals were exploited. Livestock grazing favored increases in sage grouse but was detrimental for bighorn sheep and pronghorn.

TIME PERIOD	VEGETATION	FIRE	WILDLIFE
1910–1976	Efforts to manage grazing met some success on national forests and much later on BLM lands.Sagebrush and pinyon-juniper expansion focused attention on range improvement treatments. Cheatgrass became the most abundant livestock forage.	Fire eradication became the accepted national fire policy, and agencies were largely successful at controlling wildland fire. The 1964 firestorm near Elko provided a wake-up call.	Mule deer became abundant, responding to increasing shrubs and developed water. Black-tailed jackrabbits replaced white-tailed jackrabbits in most areas. Many streams were incised, with severe erosion.
1976–1999	Cheatgrass was increasingly recognized as a problem to the establishment of perennial grasses. Pinyon and juniper trees and sagebrush continued to increase in density in most areas. Vegetation treatments were seldom applied. Livestock grazing continued to decline with restrictions.	Growth of highly combustible annual cheatgrass and buildup of woody fuels allowed fires to burn unprecedented acreages. Federal agencies reconsidered the role of fire in management of resources. The federal wildland fire policy shifted from its narrow focus on suppression to a broader program of managing fire and fuel.	Deer and sage grouse populations declined. Bighorn sheep were reestablished in many mountain ranges. Transplanted elk increased and spread from range to range. Concerns for fish and other resources initiated a shift toward better riparian area management.
1999–2010	Emphasis was placed on identifying and restoring upland and riparian shrub-steppe wildlife habitats. Extensive areas in arid valleys, especially in the Wyoming big sagebrush, were reseeded after wildfire to aid their recovery. Invasive weeds became a central focus for local groups and agencies.	Wildfire acreage exponentially increased with several record-breaking fire years. The 1995 National Fire Policy was confirmed and guidelines were issued. Fire will be used to protect, maintain, and enhance resources and, as nearly as possible, be allowed to function in its natural ecological role.	Attempts to list sage grouse united many interests be-hind conservation planning. Sagebrush and pinyon-juniper ecosystem became the focus of proactive vegetation treatments. Improved habitat allowed a marked increase in pronghorn. Deer habitat continued to decline. Collaboration increases for riparian management

Appendix 2

Nevada's Wildland Plants

COMMON NAME	SCIENTIFIC NAME
alkali bulrush (cosmopolitan bulrush)	*Schoenoplectus maritimus*
alkali sacaton	*Sporobolus airoides*
balsamroot (arrowleaf balsamroot)	*Balsamorhiza sagittata*
big sagebrush	*Artemisia tridetata*
black sagebrush	*Artemisia nova*
blazingstar	*Mentzelia*
bluebunch wheatgrass	*Pseudoroegneria spicata*
blue grass	*Poa*
brook grass (mannagrass)	*Glyceria*
buffalo-berry (silver buffaloberry)	*Shepherdia argentea*
cacti (pricklypear)	*Opuntia*
cattail	*Typha*
cheatgrass	*Bromus tectorum*
chenopods	Chenopodiaceae (goosefoot family)
	Chenopodium (goosefoot)
chokecherry (western chokecherry)	*Prunus virginiana* var. *demissa*
clover	*Trifolium*
common threesquare	*Schoenoplectus pungens*
corn	*Zea mays*
cottonwood	*Populus*
creosote bush	*Larrea tridentata*
crested wheatgrass	*Agropyron cristatum desertorum*
curlleaf mountain-mahogany	*Cercocarpus ledifolius*
currant	*Ribes*
desert peach	*Prunus andersonii*
dogwood (redosier dogwood)	*Cornus sericea*
elderberry (blue elderberry)	*Sambucus nigra* ssp. *cerulea*
four-wing saltbush (fourwing saltbush)	*Atriplex canescens*
foxtail pine	*Pinus balfouriana*
greasewood	*Sarcobatus vermiculatus*
Great Basin wildrye grass (basin wildrye)	*Leymus cinereus*
halogeton (saltlover)	*Halogeton glomeratus*
hardstem bulrush	*Schoenoplectus acutus* var. *acutus*
hawthorn	*Crataegus*

COMMON NAME	SCIENTIFIC NAME
herd grass (timothy)	*Phleum pratense*
Idaho fescue	*Festuca idahoensis*
Indian currant (coralberry)	*Symphoricarpos orbiculatus*
Indian ricegrass	*Achnatherum hymenoides*
Jeffrey pine	*Pinus jeffreyi*
Joshua tree	*Yucca brevifolia*
juniper (cedar)	*Juniperus*
knapweeds	*Centaurea*
lambs quarters	*Chenopodium album*
limber pine	*Pinus flexilis*
lodgepole pine (Sierra lodgepole pine)	*Pinus contorta* var. *murrayana*
low or Douglas rabbitbrush (yellow rabbitbrush)	*Chrysothamnus viscidiflorus*
low sagebrush (little sagebrush)	*Artemisia arbuscula* ssp. *arbuscula*
lupine	*Lupinus*
mountain big sagebrush	*Artemisia tridentata* ssp. *vaseyana*
mountain mahogany (curlleaf mountain-mahogany)	*Cercocarpus ledifolius*
narrow-leafed cottonwood (narrowleaf cottonwood)	*Populus angustifolia*
Nebraska sedge	*Carex nebrascensis*
needle and thread grass	*Hesperostipa comata*
Nevada bluegrass	*Poa nevadensis*
perennial pepperweed (tall whitetop)	*Lepidium latifolium*
pinyon pine	*Pinus monophylla*
ponderosa pine	*Pinus ponderosa*
quaking aspen	*Populus tremuloides*
rabbitbrush	*Chrysothamnus* or *Ericameria*
rabbit tobacco (tobacco)	*Nicotiana*
rice grass (Indian ricegrass)	*Achnatherum hymenoides*
rose bushes (Woods' rose)	*Rosa woodsii*
rubber rabbitbrush	*Ericameria nauseosa*
rye grass (Basin wildrye)	*Leymus cinereus*
sagebrush	*Artemisia*
sago pond-weed (sago pondweed)	*Stuckenia pectinata* or *Potamoaeton*
saltbushes	*Atriplex*
salt grass (saltgrass)	*Distichlis spicata*
sandbar willow (narrowleaf willow)	*Salix exigua*
Sandberg bluegrass	*Poa secunda*
serviceberry	*Amelanchier*
shadscale (shadscale saltbush)	*Atriplex confertifolia*
silverstems (whitestem blazingstar)	*Mentzelia albicaulis*
silvery mug-wort	*Artemisia argentea*
snowberry	*Symphoricarpos*
snowbrush ceanothus	*Ceanothus velutinus*
spikefescue	*Leucopoa* or *Leucopoa kingii*

COMMON NAME	SCIENTIFIC NAME
spike rush	*Eleocharis*
squirrel tail	*Elymus elymoides*
subalpine fir	*Abies lasiocarpa*
sunflowers	*Helianthus*
Thurber's needlegrass	*Achnatherum thurberianum*
tobacco	*Nicotiana*
Utah juniper	*Juniperus osteosperma*
western juniper	*Juniperus occidentalis*
Whipple yucca	*Yucca whipplei*
whitebark pine	*Pinus albicaulis*
white bursage (burrowed)	*Ambrosia dumosa*
white fir	*Abies concolor*
white sage (winterfat)	*Krascheninnikovia lanata*
wild currant	*Ribes*
wild peas (pea)	*Lathyrus*
wildrye grass	*Leymus cinereus*
willow	*Salix*
woods rose	*Rosa woodsii*
Wyoming big sagebrush	*Artemisia tridentata* ssp. *wyomingensis*
yarrow	*Achillea millefolium*
yellow pine	*Pinus ponderosa*

Notes

Preface

1. D. Dagget, *Beyond the Rangeland Conflict* (Flagstaff, Ariz.: Gibbs-Smith in cooperation with the Grand Canyon Trust, 1995).

1 | The Pleistocene and Holocene Epochs: Prehuman Context

1. D. Grayson, *The Desert's Past: A Natural Prehistory of the Great Basin* (Washington, D.C.: Smithsonian Institution Press, 1993).

2. P. V. Wells and C. D. Jorgensen, "Pleistocene wood rat middens and climatic change in the Mohave Desert: A record of juniper woodlands," *Science* 143 (1964): 1171–74.

3. V. C. LaMarche, "Paleoclimatic inferences from long tree-ring records," *Science* 183, no. 4129 (1974): 1043–48.

4. Grayson, *The Desert's Past.*

5. P. J. Mehringer, "Late-Quaternary pollen records from the interior Pacific Northwest and northern Great Basin of the United States," in *Pollen Records of the Late-Quaternary North American Sediments,* ed. V. M. Bryant Jr. and R. G. Holloway, pp. 167–89 (Dallas: American Association of Stratigraphic Palynologists, 1985).

6. P. E. Wigand and P. J. Mehringer Jr., "Pollen and seed analysis," in *The Archaeology of Hidden Cave, Nevada,* ed. H. D. Thomas, pp. 108–24, *American Museum of Natural History Anthropological Paper* 61, no. 1 (1985).

7. P. E. Wigand and C. L. Nowak, "Dynamics of Northwest Nevada plant communities during the last 30,000 years," in *The History of Water: Eastern Sierra Nevada, Owens Valley, White-Inyo Mountains,* ed. C. A. Hall Jr., V. D. Jones, and B. Widawski, pp. 40–62, White Mountain Research Station Symposium, vol. 4 (1982).

8. Grayson, *The Desert's Past.*

9. R. S. Thompson, "Late Quaternary environments in Ruby Valley, Nevada," *Quaternary Research* 37 (1992): 1–15.

10. LaMarche, "Paleoclimatic inferences from long tree-ring records."

11. Grayson, *The Desert's Past.*

12. L. V. Bensen, P. A. Meyers, and R. J. Spencer, "Change in the size of Walker Lake during the past 5000 years," *Paleogeography, Paleoclimatology, and Paleoecology* 81, nos. 3–4 (1991): 189–214; R. J. Tausch, C. L. Nowak, and S. A. Mensing, "Climate change and associated vegetation dynamics during the Holocene: the paleoecological record," in *Great Basin Riparian Areas: Ecology, Management, and Restoration,* ed. J. C. Chambers and J. R. Miller, pp. 24–48 (Covelo, Wash.: Island Press, 2004).

13. Grayson, *The Desert's Past.*

14. Tausch and others, "Climate change and associated vegetation dynamics during the Holocene."

15. H. C. Stutz and S. C. Sanderson, "Evolutionary studies of *Atriplex*: Chromosome races of *A. confertifolia* (shadscale)," *American Journal of Botany* 70, no. 10 (1983): 1536–47.

16. Grayson, *The Desert's Past.*

17. Ibid.

18. Ibid.

19. Ibid.

20. D. Grayson, *Danger Cave, Last Supper Cave, and Hanging Rock Shelter: The Faunas,* Anthropological Papers of the American Museum of Natural History 66, pt. 1 (1988).

21. Ibid.

22. A. D. Barnosky, P. L. Koch, R. S. Foranec, S. L. Wing, and A. B. Shobel, "Assessing the causes of Late Pleistocene extinctions on the continents," *Science* 306 (2004): 70–78.

2 | The First People: Hunters and Gatherers

1. J. D. Jennings and E. Norbeck, "Great Basin prehistory: A review," *American Antiquity* 21, no. 1 (1955): 1–11; R. F. Spencer and J. D. Jennings, *The Native Americans* (New York: Harper and Row, 1965).

2. K. T. Harper, "Historical environments," in *Handbook of North American Indians,* vol. 11: *Great Basin,* ed. W. L. d'Azevedo, pp. 51–63 (Washington, D.C.: Smithsonian Institution Press, 1986).

3. D. H. Thomas, "Historic and prehistoric land-use patterns at Reese River," *Nevada Historical Society Quarterly* 14, no. 4 (1971): 2–9.

4. Ibid.

5. T. W. Canaday and S. E. Reutebuch, "Searching for the past: Aerial photography and alpine archeology on the Toiyabe National Forest," in *Remote Sensing and Ecosystem Management,* Proceedings of the Fifth Forest Service Remote Sensing Applications Conference, Portland, Oregon, April 11–15, 1994.

6. J. H. Steward, *Basin-Plateau Aboriginal Sociopolitical Groups,* Smithsonian Institution Bureau of American Ethnology Bulletin 120 (Washington D.C.: Government Printing Office, 1938); J. H. Steward, "Cultural element distributions: XIII. Nevada Shoshone," *University of California Anthropologic Records* 4, no. 2 (1941): 209–59.

7. P. S. Ogden, *Peter Skene Ogden's Snake River Journals, 1824–25 and 1825–26,* ed. E. E. Rich and A. M. Johnson, Hudson's Bay Record Society Publication 13 (London, 1971).

8. J. Work, *John Work's Field Journal: The Snake Country Expedition of 1830–31,* ed. F. D. Haines Jr. (Norman: University of Oklahoma Press, 1971).

9. E. B. Patterson, L. A. Ulph, and V. Goodwin, *Nevada's Northeast Frontier* (Sparks, Nev.: Western Printing and Publishing, 1969).

10. W. L. d'Azevedo, "Washoe," in *Handbook of North American Indians,* vol. 11: *Great Basin,* ed. W. L. d'Azevedo (Washington, D.C.: Smithsonian Institution Press, 1986).

11. C. S. Fowler, *In the Shadow of Fox Peak: An Ethnography of the Cattail-Eater Northern Paiute People of Stillwater Marsh,* Cultural Resource Series 5, U.S. Department of the Interior [USDI], Fish and Wildlife Service, Region 1, Stillwater National Wildlife Refuge, 1992.

12. O. B. Huntington, "A trip to Carson Valley," in *Eventful Narratives*, ed. R. Averson, pp. 77–98, Faith Promoting Series no. 13, *Juvenile Instructor*, Salt Lake City, Utah, 1877.

13. Capt. J. H. Simpson, *Report of the Explorations across the Great Basin of the Territory of Utah for a Direct Wagon-Route from Camp Floyd, Utah, to Genoa in Carson Valley* (Washington, D.C.: Government Printing Office, 1876).

14. D. (William Wright) DeQuille, *The Big Bonanza* (New York: Alfred A. Knopf, 1953).

15. Steward, *Basin-Plateau Aboriginal Sociopolitical Groups.*

16. W. J. Hoffman, "Miscellaneous ethnographic observations on Indians inhabiting Nevada, California, and Arizona," in F. V. Hayden, *10th Annual Report of the U.S. Geological and Geographical Survey of the Territories* (progress report for the year 1876), pt. 3, pp. 461–78, 1878.

17. DeQuille, *The Big Bonanza.*

18. O. C. Stewart, *Anthropological Records 4:3 Cultural Element Distributions: XIV Northern Paiute* (Berkeley and Los Angeles: University of California Press, 1941).

19. H. R. Egan, *Pioneering the West, 1846–1878: Major Howard Egan's Diary* (Salt Lake City, Utah: Skelton Publishing, 1917).

20. Steward, *Basin-Plateau Aboriginal Sociopolitical Groups.*

21. Lt. E. G. Beckwith, *Report of Explorations for a Route for the Pacific Railroad, of the Line of the Forty-first Parallel of North Latitude,* House of Representatives Executive Document 91, 1854, 33rd Congress, 2nd session.

22. D. (William Wright) DeQuille, *Washoe Rambles* (Los Angeles: Westernlore Press, 1963).

23. Simpson, *Report of the Explorations across the Great Basin of the Territory of Utah.*

24. Egan, *Pioneering the West, 1846–1878.*

25. I. T. Kelly, *Ethnography of the Surprise Valley Paiute,* University of California Publications in American Archaeology and Ethnology 31, no. 3 (Berkeley and Los Angeles: University of California Press, 1932).

26. Fowler, *In the Shadow of Fox Peak.*

27. R. H. Lowie, *The Northern Shoshone,* Anthropological Papers of the American Museum of Natural History vol. 2, pt. 2, 1909.

28. E. Bryant, *Rocky Mountain Adventures* (New York: Worthington, 1888).

29. J. C. Frémont, *Memoirs of My Life,* vol. 1: *Relford* (New York and Chicago: Clarke and Company, 1887).

30. Steward, *Basin-Plateau Aboriginal Sociopolitical Groups.*

31. Frémont, *Memoirs of My Life.*

32. J. P. Yager, "The Yager journals: Diary of a journey across the Plains," *Nevada Historical Society Quarterly* 13, no. 3 (1970).

33. Patterson and others, *Nevada's Northeast Frontier.*

34. W. L. d'Azevedo, "Washoe," in *Handbook of North American Indians,* ed. W. L. d'Azevedo, vol. 11: *Great Basin* (Washington, D.C.: Smithsonian Institution Press, 1986).

35. Egan, *Pioneering the West, 1846–1878.*

36. Steward, *Basin-Plateau Aboriginal Sociopolitical Groups.*

37. Ibid.

38. Ibid.

39. Kelly, *Ethnography of the Surprise Valley Paiute*.

40. Steward, *Basin-Plateau Aboriginal Sociopolitical Groups*.

41. C. C. Mann, *1491: New Revelations of the Americas before Columbus* (New York: Alfred A. Knopf, 2005).

42. O. C. Stewart, "Fire as the first great force employed by man," in *International Symposium on Man's Role in Changing the Face of the Earth*, ed. W. L. Thomas, pp. 115–33 (Chicago: University of Chicago Press, 1956).

3 | Fire: A Natural Disturbance and Human Tool

1. Mann, *1491*; S. J. Pyne, *Fire in America: A Cultural History of Wildland and Rural Fire* (Princeton: Princeton University Press, 1982); O. C. Stewart, *Forgotten Fires: Native Americans and the Transient Wilderness*, ed. and intro. H. T. Lewis and M. K. Anderson (Norman: University of Oklahoma Press, 2002).

2. G. E. Gruell, "Fire on the early western landscape: An annotated list of recorded wildfires in pre-settlement times," *Northwest Science* 59 (1985): 97–107.

3. Steward, *Basin-Plateau Aboriginal Sociopolitical Groups*; Stewart, *Anthropological Records 4:3 Cultural Element Distributions: XIV Northern Paiute*.

4. S. F. Arno and K. M. Sneck, *A Method of Determining Fire History in Conifer Forest of the Mountain West*, General Technical Report INT-42, U.S. Department of Agriculture [USDA] Forest Service, Intermountain Forest and Range Experiment Station, Ogden, Utah, 1977.

5. G. E. Gruell, "Indian fires in the interior West: A widespread influence," in *Proceedings 1983 Wilderness Fire Symposium*, ed. J. E. Lotan, B. M. Kilgor, W. C. Fischer, and R. W. Mutch, pp. 68–74, General Technical Report 182, USDA Forest Service, Intermountain Research Station, Ogden, Utah, 1985.

6. Stewart, "Fire as the first great force employed by man."

7. P. S. Ogden, *Peter Skene Ogden's Snake River Journals, 1827–28 and 1828–29*, ed. Glyndwr Williams, Hudson's Bay Record Society Publication 28 (London, 1950).

8. H. Lienhard, *From St. Louis to Sutter's Fort, 1846*, trans. and ed. E. G. Gudde and E. K. Gudde (Norman: University of Oklahoma Press, 1961).

9. E. B. Patterson, "The diary of Joe F. Triplett." *Nevada Historical Society Quarterly* 2, no. 1 (1959).

10. J. C. Frémont, *Geographical Memoir* (1848; reprint, San Francisco: Book Club of California, 1964).

11. J. S. Alter, ed., "Father Escalante and the Utah Indians," *Utah Historical Quarterly* 1, no. 4 (1928): 109–10.

12. Ogden, *Peter Skene Ogden's Snake River Journals, 1824–25 and 1825–26*.

13. A. W. Leonard, *Leonard's Narrative: Adventures of Zenas Leonard, Fur Trapper and Trader, 1831–36*, ed. F. Wagner (Cleveland: Burrows Brothers, 1904).

14. Sir Richard Burton, *The Look of the West in 1860: Across the Plains to California* (Lincoln: University of Nebraska Press, 1963).

15. USDA and Nevada Department of Conservation and Natural Resources, *Water and Related Land Resources: Humboldt River Basin, Nevada*, Report no. 8: *Reese River Sub-Basin*, 1964.

16. T. B. Heller, journal extracts published in the *Reese River Reveille*, Austin, Nevada, January 25, 1864.

17. J. G. Bruff, *Gold Rush: The Journals, Drawings and Other Papers of J. Goldsborough Bruff, Captain, Washington City and California Mining Association, April 2, 1849–July 20, 1851* (New York: Columbia University Press, 1944).

18. Kelly, *Ethnography of the Surprise Valley Paiute*.

19. Cited in C. S. Fowler, "Subsistence," in *Handbook of North American Indians,* vol. 11: *Great Basin,* ed. W. L. d'Azevedo, pp. 64–97 (Washington, D.C.: Smithsonian Institution Press, 1986).

20. Patterson and others, *Nevada's Northeast Frontier*.

21. Egan, *Pioneering the West, 1846–1878*.

22. E. Bryant, *Rocky Mountain Adventures*.

23. A. Delano, *Across the Plains and among the Diggings* (reprint, New York: Wilson-Erickson, 1936); B. J. Reid, *Overland to California with the Pioneer Line,* ed. M. Gordon (Stanford: Stanford University Press, 1983).

24. J. Bidwell, "The first emigrant train to California," *Century,* 41 (November 1890): 106–30.

25. W. H. Kilgore, *The Kilgore Journal of an Overland Journey to California in the 1850s,* ed. Joyce Rockwood Muench from the original manuscript journal of William H. Kilgore (New York: Hastings House, 1949).

26. Yager, *The Yager Journals*.

27. J. F. Downs, "The significance of environmental manipulation in Great Basin cultural development," in *The Current Status of Anthropological Research in the Great Basin: 1964,* ed. W. d'Azevedo, pp. 39–57, Technical Series s-h, Social Science and Humanities Publications 1 (Reno: Desert Research Institute, 1966).

28. Steward, *Basin-Plateau Aboriginal Sociopolitical Groups*.

29. Downs, "The significance of environmental manipulation in Great Basin cultural development."

30. Wayne Hage, personal communication, 1996.

31. C. L. Rice, *Fire History of State Parks of the Sierra District of the California Department of Parks and Recreation,* Department of Forestry and Resource Management, University of California, California Department of Parks and Recreation Contract, 1990; S. L. Stephens, *Fire History of Jeffrey Pine and Upper Montane Forest Types at the University of California Valentine Reserve, Mono County, CA,* University of California Natural Reserves System, 1996; A. H. Taylor, "Pre- and post-Comstock logging forest structure and composition, Carson Range, Nevada," paper presented at the 25th Great Basin Anthropological Conference, October 10–12, Kings Beach, California, 1996.

32. E. K. Heyerdahl, P. M. Brown, S. G. Kitchen, and M. H. Weber, *Multicentury Fire and Forest Histories at Nineteen Sites in Utah and Eastern Nevada,* USDA Forest Service, Rocky Mountain Research Station, Fort Collins, Colorado, 2011, online at http://www.treesearch.fs.fed.us.

33. S. G. Kitchen, "Historic fire regimes of eastern Great Basin (USA) mountains reconstructed from tree rings," Ph.D. diss., Brigham Young University, 2010.

34. G. E. Gruell, L. E. Eddleman, and R. Jaindl, *Fire History of the Pinyon-Juniper Woodlands of Great Basin National Park,* Technical Report NPS/PNROSU/NRTR-94/01, USDI, National Park Service, Pacific Northwest Region, 1994; G. E. Gruell, "Historic and modern roles of fire in pinyon-juniper woodlands," in *Proceedings: Ecology and Management of Pinyon-Juniper Communities within the Interior West,* comp. S. B. Monson and R. Stevens, pp. 24–28, Proceedings RMRS P-9, USDA Forest Service, Rocky Mountain Research Station, Ogden, Utah, 1999.

35. G. E. Gruell, "Historical role of fire in pinyon-juniper woodlands: Walker River watershed project, Bridgeport Ranger District," USDA Forest Service, Contracted Report, Humboldt-Toiyabe National Forest, Reno, Nevada, 1997.

4 | Vegetation: A Sea of Sagebrush or Landscape of Great Variety

1. G. Stewart, "Historic records bearing on agriculture and grazing ecology in Utah," *Journal of Forestry* 39 (1941): 362–75.

2. T. R. Vale, "Presettlement vegetation in the sagebrush-grass area of the Intermountain West," *Journal of Range Management* 28 (1975): 32–36.

3. A. A. Humphreys and G. K. Warren, *Reports of Explorations and Surveys to Ascertain the Most Practicable and Economical Route for a Railroad from the Missouri River to the Pacific Ocean, 1853–54,* 1855, Corps of Topographical Engineers, Senate Executive Document 78, vol. 1, 33rd Congress, 2nd session.

4. Simpson, *Report of the Explorations across the Great Basin of the Territory of Utah.*

5. S. Watson, "Botany," in *Professional Papers of the Engineer Department, U.S. Army,* no. 18, vol. 5, *Report of the Geological Exploration of the Fortieth Parallel* (Washington, D.C.: Government Printing Office, 1871).

6. Beckwith, *Report of Explorations for a Route for the Pacific Railroad.*

7. Simpson, *Report of the Explorations across the Great Basin of the Territory of Utah.*

8. Bryant, *Rocky Mountain Adventures*; Beckwith, *Report of Explorations for a Route for the Pacific Railroad.*

9. Watson, "Botany"; Simpson, *Report of the Explorations across the Great Basin of the Territory of Utah.*

10. Yager, *The Yager Journals*; Bryant, *Rocky Mountain Adventures.*

11. *Reese River Reveille,* September 9, 1865.

12. Kilgore, *Journal of an Overland Journey to California in the 1850s.*

13. Yager, *The Yager Journals.*

14. R. Ridgway, "Ornithology," in *Professional Papers of the Engineer Department, U.S. Army,* no. 18, vol. 4, pt. 3, *Report of the Geological Explorations of the Fortieth Parallel* (Washington, D.C.: Government Printing Office, 1877).

15. Kilgore, *Journal of an Overland Journey to California in the 1850s*; Bryant, *Rocky Mountain Adventures.*

16. Ridgway, "Ornithology."

17. Yager, *The Yager Journals.*

18. Beckwith, *Report of Explorations for a Route for the Pacific Railroad.*

19. Burton, *The Look of the West in 1860.*

20. E. M. Kern, "Journal of Mr. Edward Kern of an exploration of the Mary's River, Carson Lake, and Owens River and Lake in 1845," appendix Q in Simpson, *Report of Explorations across the Great Basin of the Territory of Utah.*

21. E. M. Hattori and A. R. McLane, "Preliminary report of archaeological and historical studies at Cornucopia, Elko County, Nevada," submitted by Desert Research Institute and Board of Regents, University of Nevada System, to Minetek Group, Inc., 1983.

22. Simpson, *Report of Explorations across the Great Basin of the Territory of Utah.*

23. Ridgway, "Ornithology."

24. Simpson, *Report of Explorations across the Great Basin of the Territory of Utah.*

25. Beckwith, *Report of Explorations for a Route for the Pacific Railroad.*

26. Ibid.

27. I. C. Russell, "Sketch of the geologic history of Lake Lahontan," in *Third Annual Report of the United States Geological Survey to the Secretary of the Interior, 1881–82,* pp. 195–235 (Washington, D.C.: Government Printing Office, 1883).

28. J. Muir, *Steep Trails,* ed. William F. Bade (Boston: Houghton Mifflin, 1918).

29. F. I. Bender, "Memoranda of a journey across the plains, from Bell Creek, Washington Co., Nebraska, to Virginia City, Nevada, Territory, May 7 to August 4, 1863," *Nevada Historical Society Quarterly* 1, no. 4 (1958): 166–70.

30. Simpson, *Report of the Explorations across the Great Basin of the Territory of Utah.*

31. Bender, "Memoranda of a journey across the plains."

32. Simpson, *Report of Explorations across the Great Basin of the Territory of Utah.*

33. Watson, "Botany."

34. Ridgway, "Ornithology."

35. Ibid.

36. C. S. Sargent, "Forests of central Nevada," *American Journal of Science* 17 (1879): 417–26.

5 | Wildlife: Abundance and Scarcity

1. Work, *John Work's Field Journal: The Snake Country Expedition of 1830–31.*

2. Frémont, *Memoirs of My Life.*

3. A. E. Borell and R. Ellis, "Mammals of the Ruby Mountains region of northeastern Nevada," *Journal of Mammalogy* 15 (1934): 12–34.

4. G. E. Gruell, "Northern Elko County: The way it was," *Northeastern Nevada Historical Society Quarterly* 98, no. 4 (1998): 105–26; D. Mathis, "Fish and Game Commission's history commences 1877—continues to the present," *Nevada Wildlife* Centennial Issue, vol. 5, nos. 4–7, Nevada Fish and Game Commission, 1965–66.

5. Work, *John Work's Field Journal: The Snake Country Expedition of 1830–31.*

6. Ogden, *Peter Skene Ogden's Snake River Journals, 1827–28 and 1828–29.*

7. Bryant, *Rocky Mountain Adventures.*

8. Ogden, *Peter Skene Ogden's Snake River Journals, 1827–28 and 1828–29.*

9. Ibid.

10. R. S. Bliss, "The journal of Robert S. Bliss, with the Mormon Battalion," *Utah Historical Quarterly* 4, no. 3 (1931): 110–24.

11. Egan, *Pioneering the West, 1846–1878*.

12. Simpson, *Report of Explorations across the Great Basin of the Territory of Utah*.

13. Ogden, *Peter Skene Ogden's Snake River Journals, 1827–28 and 1828–29*.

14. Work, *John Work's Field Journal: The Snake Country Expedition of 1830–31*.

15. Simpson, *Report of Explorations across the Great Basin of the Territory of Utah*.

16. H. Eno, *Twenty Years on the Pacific Slope: Letters of Henry Eno from California and Nevada, 1848–1871* (New Haven: Yale University Press, 1965).

17. T. L. Oddie, *Letters from the Nevada Frontier: Correspondence of Tasker L. Oddie, 1898–1902*, ed. W. A. Douglass and R. A. Nylen (Norman: University of Oklahoma Press, 1992).

18. Frémont, *Memoirs of My Life*.

19. Muir, *Steep Trails*.

20. Simpson, *Report of Explorations across the Great Basin of the Territory of Utah*.

21. Work, *John Work's Field Journal: The Snake Country Expedition of 1830–31*.

22. Gruell, "Northern Elko County: The way it was."

23. Ibid.

24. Ogden, *Peter Skene Ogden's Snake River Journals, 1824–25 and 1825–26*.

25. Work, *John Work's Field Journal: The Snake Country Expedition of 1830–31*.

26. Beaver numbers calculated from daily journal entries in Ogden, *Peter Skene Ogden's Snake River Journals, 1827–28 and 1828–29*.

27. Ibid.

28. Ibid.

29. Ibid.

30. G. E. Gruell, personal observations made in northern Nevada during the period 1953–67.

31. Ridgway, "Ornithology."

32. Simpson, *Report of Explorations across the Great Basin of the Territory of Utah*.

33. H. W. Henshaw, "Ornithological report from observations and collections made in portions of California, Nevada, and Oregon," appendix L in G. W. Wheeler, Appendix OO, *Annual Report upon the Geographical Surveys West of the 100th Meridian . . . for 1879* (Washington, D.C.: Government Printing Office, 1880); J. Le Conte, *Journal of Ramblings through the High Sierras of California by the University Excursion Party in 1870* (San Francisco: Sierra Club, 1960).

34. Ridgway, "Ornithology."

35. W. J. Hoffman, "Miscellaneous ethnographic observations on Indians inhabiting Nevada, California, and Arizona."

36. Henshaw, "Ornithological report from observations and collections made in portions of California, Nevada, and Oregon."

37. Eno, *Twenty Years on the Pacific Slope*.

38. Henshaw, "Ornithological report from observations and collections made in portions of California, Nevada, and Oregon."

39. Ibid.

40. Simpson, *Report of Explorations across the Great Basin of the Territory of Utah*.

41. A. B. Hulbert, *Forty-niners: The Chronicle of the California Trail* (Boston: Little, Brown, 1931).

42. I. La Rivers, *Fishes and Fisheries of Nevada* (Reno: Nevada Fish and Game Commission, 1962).

43. E. J. Laudenslager and G. A. E. Gall, "Geographic patterns of protein vatiation and subspeciation of cutthroat trout, *Salmon clarki*," *Systematic Zoology* 1, no. 1 (1980): 27–42; R. J. Behnke, *Native Trout of Western North America*, American Fisheries Society Monograph, 1992.

44. R. W. Ellison, *First Impressions: The Trail through Carson Valley, 1848–1852* (Minden, Nev.: Hot Springs Mountain Press, 2001).

45. DeQuille, *Washoe Rambles*.

46. Simpson, *Report of Explorations across the Great Basin of the Territory of Utah*.

47. L. A. Scott, unpublished diary, 1859, excerpted in *Central Overland Route and Transcontinental Telegraph through Nevada, 1858–1868* (Oakland, Calif.: TRASH, 1985).

48. H. W. Bigler, "Journal extracts of Henry W. Bigler," *Utah Historical Quarterly* 5, no. 4 (1932): 159.

49. R. S. Bliss, "The journal of Robert S. Bliss, with the Mormon Battalion."

50. Yager, *The Yager Journals*.

51. E. R. Smith oral interview, October 31, 1945, manuscript at Nevada Historical Society, Reno.

52. Gruell, "Northern Elko County: The way it was."

53. Ibid.

54. Ibid.

6 | Climate: Averages and Extremes

1. J. C. Chambers, "Climate change and the Great Basin," in *Collaborative Management and Research in the Great Basin: Examining the Issues and Developing a Framework for Action,* ed. J. C. Chambers, N. Devoe, and A. Evenden, pp. 29–32, General Technical Report RMRS-GTR-204, USDA Forest Service, Rocky Mountain Research Station, 2008.

2. R. W. Katz and B. G. Brown, "Extreme events in a changing climate: Variability is more important than averages," *Climatic Change* 21 (1992): 289–302.

3. S. R. Reice, *The Silver Lining: The Benefits of Natural Disasters* (Princeton: Princeton University Press, 2001); C. F. Cooper, "Hydrology, ecology, and the 'balance of nature,'" paper presented at the American Geophysical Union Annual Meeting Special Session: Extreme Events and Western U.S. Water Resources, San Francisco, December 11, 1991.

4. K. T. Harper, "Historical environments," in *Handbook of North American Indians,* vol. 11: *Great Basin,* ed. W. L. d'Azevedo, pp. 51–63 (Washington, D.C.: Smithsonian Institution Press, 1986).

5. S. Archer, "Woody plant encroachment into southwestern grasslands and savannas: Rates, patterns and proximate causes," in *Ecological Implications of Livestock Herbivory in the West,* ed. M. Vavra, W. A. Laycock, and R. D. Pieper, pp. 13–68 (Denver: Society for Range Management, 1994); R. F. Miller, T. J. Svejear, and N. E. West, "Implica-

tions of livestock grazing in the intermountain sagebrush region: Plant composition," in *Ecological Implications of Livestock Herbivory in the West,* ed. M. Vavra, W. A. Laycock, and R. D. Pieper, pp. 101–46 (Denver: Society of Range Management, 1994).

6. E. Anteves, *Rainfall and Tree Growth in the Great Basin,* American Geological Society Special Publication 21 (Washington, D.C.: Carnegie Institution; New York: American Geographic Society, 1938).

7. J. Clyman, *Journal of a Mountain Man,* ed. L. M. Hasselstrom (Missoula, Mont.: Mountain Press, 1984).

8. Anteves, *Rainfall and Tree Growth in the Great Basin.*

9. Russell, "Sketch of the geologic history of Lake Lahontan."

10. Anteves, *Rainfall and Tree Growth in the Great Basin.*

11. Ibid.

12. Ibid.

13. Data at Western Regional Climate Center, online at www.wrcc.dri.edu.

14. The Earth Institute, Columbia University, "Carbon dioxide higher today than the last 2.1 million years," *Science Daily,* 2009, online at http://www.sciencedaily.com/releases/2009/06/090618143950.htm, accessed April 25, 2011.

7 | Woodcutting: Boomtowns before Fossil Fuels

1. E. Lord, *Comstock Mining and Miners* (1883; reprint, Berkeley: Howell-North, 1959).

2. J. R. Browne, *Reports on the Mineral Resources of the United States* (Washington, D.C.: Government Printing Office, 1868).

3. S. W. Paher, *Nevada Ghost Towns and Mining Camps* (Berkeley: Howell-North Books, 1970).

4. J. A. Young and J. D. Budy, "Nevada's pinyon-juniper woodlands," *Journal of Forestry* 23 (1979): 113–23.

5. Muir, *Steep Trails.*

6. Ibid.

8 | Livestock Grazing: Herbivory and Range Depletion

1. B. Hazeltine, S. Saulisbery, and H. A. Taylor, "A range history of Nevada," pt. 1: "Stockmen wrote Silver State's range history," pt. 2: "They came for the native grass," pt. 3: "They came for the native range . . . and left a heritage," Nevada Section, American Society of Range Management, 1965.

2. B. D. Sawyer, *Nevada Nomads: A Story of the Sheep Industry* (San Jose, Calif.: Harlan-Young Press, 1971); C. Georgette, *Golden Fleece in Nevada* (Reno: Venture Publishing, 1972).

3. Hazeltine and others, "A range history of Nevada."

4. H. C. Greeley, *An Overland Journey from New York to San Francisco in the Summer of 1859,* ed. T. Duncan (New York: Alfred A. Knopf, 1969).

5. *Reese River Reveille,* 1863.

6. Hazeltine and others, "A range history of Nevada."

7. Ibid.

8. J. A. Young and A. B. Sparks, *Cattle on the Cold Desert* (Logan: Utah State University Press, 1985).

9. Hazeltine and others, "A range history of Nevada."

10. Ibid.

11. F. W. Reed, "The proposed Ruby Mountains Forest Reserve, Nevada," 1905, 18 pp. with photos, Humboldt-Toiyabe National Forest files, Elko.

12. G. C. Thompson, Favorable report on proposed Bruneau addition to the Humboldt National Forest, 1908, 17 pp., Humboldt-Toiyabe National Forest files, Elko, Nevada.

13. C. N. Woods, "Grazing inspection, 1915, memorandum for the district forester," Humboldt-Toiyabe National Forest files, Elko, Nevada.

14. U.S. Bureau of Land Management, *An Overview of the Battle Mountain District,* Cultural Series Monograph 4 (Reno: Nevada Office of the Bureau of Land Management, 1982).

15. Gruell, "Northern Elko County: The way it was."

16. U.S. Bureau of Land Management, *Overview of the Battle Mountain District.*

17. Reed, "The proposed Ruby Mountains Forest Reserve, Nevada"; R. B. Wilson, "Favorable report on the proposed Bruneau addition to the Independence National Forest, Nevada," 1906, 34 pp., Humboldt-Toiyabe National Forest files; Thompson, Favorable report on the Bruneau addition to the Humboldt National Forest.

18. H. E. Woolley, Favorable report on the proposed Santa Rosa National Forest, Nevada, 1910, 13 pp., Humboldt-Toiyabe National Forest files, Elko.

19. Gruell, "Northern Elko County: The way it was."

20. Ibid.

21. D. Griffiths, *Forage Conditions on the Northern Border of the Great Basin,* U.S. Bureau of Plant Industry Bulletin 15 (Washington, D.C.: Government Printing Office, 1902).

22. W. P. Taylor, "Mammals of the Alexander Nevada expedition of 1909," *University of California Publications in Zoology 7,* no. 7 (1911): 205–307.

23. P. B. Kennedy, *Summer Ranges of the Eastern Nevada Sheep,* Nevada Agricultural Experiment Station Bulletin 55 (1903).

24. E. H. Clapp, "The major range problems and their solution: A resume," in *The Western Range,* pp. 1–68, 1936, Senate Document 199, 74th Congress, 2nd session.

25. P. Herndon, "The history of grazing on the public lands," in *Your Public Lands,* 32, no. 2, pp. 19–22 (Washington, D.C.: USDI, Bureau of Land Management, 1982).

26. S. T. Dana and S. K. Fairfax, *Forest and Range Policy* (New York: McGraw-Hill, 1980).

27. Ibid.

28. Ibid.

29. W. S. Platts, "Livestock grazing," in *Influence of Forest and Rangeland Management on Salmonid Fishes and Their Habitats,* chap. 11, American Fisheries Society Special Publication 19 (1991).

30. University of Idaho Stubble Height Review Team, "University of Idaho Stubble Height Study report," University of Idaho Forest, Wildlife and Range Experiment

Station Contribution 986, 2004, online at http://www.cnrhome.uidaho.edu/documents/Stubble_Height_Report.pdf&pid=74895&doc=1; C. Evans, "Monitoring summary and evaluation of biological standards," Maggie Creek Watershed Restoration Project, Elko District Bureau of Land Management, Nevada, 2006.

31. G. Simmons, M. Ritchie, and E. Sant, "Evaluating riparian condition and trend in three large watersheds," project report to the U.S. Fish and Wildlife Service for agreement 4240-7-H009, 2009.

32. K. N. Schmidt, "Riparian response to the interactive effects of livestock grazing and wildfire in northern Nevada," master's thesis, University of Nevada, Reno, 2009; D. Kozlowski, S. Swanson, and K. Schmidt, "Channel changes in burned streams of northern Nevada," *Journal of Arid Environments* 74, no. 11 (2010): 1494–1506.

33. J. A. Young and C. D. Clements, *Cheatgrass* (Reno: University of Nevada Press, 2009).

34. R. N. Mack, "Invasion of *Bromus tectorum* into western North America: An ecological chronicle," *Agro-Ecosystems* 7 (1981): 145–65.

35. Nevada Weed Action Committee, "Nevada's coordinated invasive weed strategy," Nevada Department of Agriculture, 2006, online at http://agri.nv.gov/nwac/PLANT_NoxWeedPlan.

9 | Fire: A Changing Force on the Landscape

1. Harper, "Historical environments"; G. E. Gruell, "Influence of fire on Great Basin wildlife habitats," *Transactions of the Western Section of the Wildlife Society* 32 (1996): 55–61.

2. Gruell, "Historic and modern roles of fire in pinyon-juniper woodlands."

3. Griffiths, *Forage Conditions on the Northern Border of the Great Basin.*

4. Wilson, "Favorable report on the proposed Bruneau addition to the Independence National Forest, Nevada."

5. Thompson, Favorable report on proposed Bruneau addition to the Humboldt National Forest.

6. Woolley, "Favorable report on the proposed Santa Rosa National Forest, Nevada."

7. Humboldt National Forest records stored at National Archives–Pacific Region, San Bruno, California.

8. Gruell and others, *Fire History of the Pinyon-Juniper Woodlands of Great Basin National Park.*

9. *Humboldt River Basin Nevada, Water and Related Land Resources,* report 1: *Little Humboldt Sub-Basin* (Reno: Nevada Department of Conservation and Natural Resources and USDA, 1962).

10. *Humboldt River Basin Nevada, Water and Related Land Resources,* report 8: *Reese River Sub-Basin*; and report 9: *Battle Mountain Sub-Basin* (Nevada Department of Conservation and Natural Resources and USDA, 1964).

11. J. A. Young, R. E. Eckert Jr., and R. A. Evans, "Historical perspective regarding the sagebrush ecosystem," in *Proceedings: The Sagebrush Ecosystem,* pp. 1–13 (Logan: Utah State University Press, 1979).

12. *Humboldt River Basin Nevada, Water and Related Land Resources,* report 12: *Basin-wide Report* (Nevada Department of Conservation and Natural Resources and USDA, 1966).

13. USDI, USDA, and Nevada Department of Forestry, Western Great Basin Coordination Center, Incident Activity Reports, 1999–2009.

14. Ibid.

15. Ibid.

16. Ibid.

17. Ibid.

18. Interpretation of data at interagency incident support website, http://gacc.nifc.gov/wgbc/predictive/intelligence/statistics.htm.

19. J. W. Burkart, "Scientist contributions," in *Great Basin Wildlife Forum: The Search for Solutions,* ed. E. Miller and R. Narayanan, pp. 26–27 (Reno: Nevada Agricultural Experiment Station, University of Nevada, 2008).

20. Robin Tausch, personal communication, 2011; A. Stebleton and S. Bunting, *Guide for Quantifying Fuels in the Sagebrush Steppe and Juniper Woodlands of the Great Basin,* Technical Note 430, Bureau of Land Management, Denver, Colorado, BLM/ID/002+2824, 2009.

21. J. K. McAdoo, B. Schultz, S. Swanson, and G. Back, "Northeastern Nevada wildfires 2006, pt. 1: Fire and land use history," University of Nevada Cooperative Extension, Fact Sheet 07-20, 2007.

22. Schmidt, "Riparian response to the interactive effects of livestock grazing and wildfire in northern Nevada"; Kozlowski, Swanson, and Schmidt, "Channel changes in burned streams of northern Nevada."

10 | Vegetation: Resilience and Succession Meet Abuse and Decadence

1. Hazeltine and others, "A range history of Nevada."

2. A. H. Winward, "A renewed commitment to management of sagebrush grasslands," in *Management of the Sagebrush Steppe,* Special Report 880, pp. 2–7, Agricultural Experiment Station, Oregon State University, Corvallis, 1991.

3. Hazeltine and others, "A range history of Nevada."

4. DeQuille, *Washoe Rambles.*

5. H. O. Smeathman, "Notes of a prospecting trip in Humboldt County, N.T.," *San Francisco Evening Bulletin,* February 18, 1864.

6. J. H. Robertson and P. B. Kennedy, "Half-century changes on northern Nevada ranges," *Journal of Range Management* 7, no. 3 (1954): 117–21.

7. *Humboldt River Basin Nevada, Water and Related Land Resources,* report 12: *Basin-wide Report.*

8. Ibid., p. 83.

9. Gruell, "Northern Elko County: The way it was."

10. *Humboldt River Basin Nevada, Water and Related Land Resources,* report 12: *Basinwide Report.*

11. *Humboldt River Basin Nevada, Water and Related Land Resources,* report 9: *Battle Mountain Sub-Basin.*

12. *Humboldt River Basin Nevada, Water and Related Land Resources,* report 8, *Reese River Sub-Basin.*

13. D. H. Thomas, "Historic and prehistoric land-use patterns at Reese River," *Nevada Historical Society Quarterly* 14, no. 4 (1971): 2–9.

14. *Humboldt River Basin Nevada, Water and Related Land Resources,* report 12: *Basinwide Report.*

15. Ibid., 81.

16. M. B. Moorman, *The Journal of Madison Berryman Moorman, 1850–51,* ed. and intro. I. D. Paden (San Francisco: California Historical Society, 1948).

17. *Humboldt River Basin Nevada, Water and Related Land Resources,* report 12: *Basin-wide Report,* 82.

18. Ridgway, "Ornithology."

19. R. F. Miller, R. J. Tausch, E. D. McArthur, D. D. Johnson, and S. C. Sanderson, "Age structure and expansion of piñon-juniper woodlands: A regional perspective in the Intermountain West," Research Paper Report RMRS-RP-69, USDA Forest Service, Rocky Mountain Research Station, 2008.

20. R. F. Miller and R. J. Tausch, "The role of fire in juniper and pinyon woodlands: A descriptive analysis," in *Proceedings of the Invasive Species Work-Shop: The Role of Fire in the Control and Spread of Invasive Species,* ed. K. E. M. Gulley and T. P. Wilson, pp. 15–30, Tall Timbers Research Station Miscellaneous Publications 11, 2001.

21. Miller and others, "Age structure and expansion of piñon-juniper woodlands."

22. Ridgway, "Ornithology."

23. G. E. Gruell, S. C. Bunting, and L. F. Neuenschwander, "Influence of fire on curlleaf mountain-mahogany in the Intermountain West," in *Fire's Effects on Wildlife Habitat—Symposium Proceedings,* ed. J. E. Lotan and J. K. Brown, pp. 58–72, General Technical Report INT-186, USDA Forest Service, Ogden, Utah, 1984.

24. Ibid.

25. B. B. Schultz, "Ecology of curlleaf mahogany in western and central Nevada: Community and population structure," *Journal of Range Management* 43, no. 1 (1990): 13–20.

26. Gruell, onsite interpretations in 1996 and 2006.

27. Gruell and others, "Influence of fire on curlleaf mountain-mahogany in the Intermountain West."

28. W. F. Muggler, "Vegetation associations," in *Aspen: Ecology and Management in the Western United States,* ed. N. V. DeByle and R. P. Winokur, pp. 45–55, General Technical Report RM-119, USDA Forest Service, Rocky Mountain Forest and Range Experiment Station, Fort Collins, Colorado, 1985.

29. J. R. Miller, K. House, K. Germanoski, R. J. Tausch, and J. C. Chambers, "Fluvial geomorphic response to Holocene climate change," in *Great Basin Riparian Areas: Ecology, Management and Restoration,* ed. J. C. Chambers and J. R. Miller, pp. 49–87 (Covelo, Wash.: Island Press, 2004).

30. D. Prichard, J. Anderson, C. Correll, J. Fogg, K. Gebhart, R. Kraft, L. Leonard, B. Mitchell, and J. Statts, *Riparian Area Management: A User Guide to Accessing Proper*

Functioning Condition and the Supporting Science for Lotic Areas, TR-1737-15, Bureau of Land Management, National Applied Resource Sciences Center, Denver, Colorado, 1998.

31. S. Wyman, D. W. Bailey, M. Borman, S. Cote, J. Eisner, W. Elmore, B. Leinard, S. Leonard, F. Reed, S. Swanson, L. Van Riper, T. Westfall, R. Wiley, and A. Winward, *Riparian Area Management: Grazing Management Processes and Strategies for Riparian-Wetland Areas,* Technical Reference 737-20, USDI, Bureau of Land Management, and USDA Forest Service, 2006.

32. S. B. Rood, C. R. Gourley, E. M. Ammon, L. G. Heki, J. R. Klotz, S. Swanson, M. L. Morrison, D. Mosley, G. G. Scoppettone, and P. L. Wagner, "Flows for floodplain forests: A successful riparian restoration," *BioScience* 53, no. 7 (2003): 647–56.

33. D. L. Sturges, "Soil-water and vegetation dynamics through 20 years after big sagebrush control," *Journal of Range Management* 46 (1993): 161–69.

34. T. L. Deboodt, M. P. Fisher, J. C. Buckhouse, and J. Swanson, *Monitoring Hydrologic Changes Related to Western Juniper Removal, a Paired Watershed Approach, The Grazier,* no. 336 (Oregon State University, 2009).

11 | Wildlife: Habitat Relationships

1. J. W. Burkart, "Sage grouse myths," *Range* (Summer 2008): 56–57.

2. Gruell, "Northern Elko County: The way it was."

3. Ibid.

4. W. Wilhelm, *Last Rig to Battle Mountain* (New York: William Morrow, 1970).

5. W. Kent, *Reminiscences of Outdoor Life* (San Francisco: A. M. Robertson, 1929).

6. W. P. Taylor, "Field notes of amphibians, reptiles and birds of northern Humboldt County, Nevada," *University of California Publications in Zoology* 7, no. 10 (1912): 319–436.

7. Personal communication, 1998.

8. Personal communication, 1998.

9. D. Mathis, "Fish and Game Commission's history commences."

10. D. A. Klebenow, "Livestock interactions with sage grouse," in *Wildlife-Livestock Relations Symposium Proceedings* 10, ed. J. M. Peek and P. D. Dalke, pp. 113–23 (Moscow: University of Idaho Forest, Wildlife and Range Experiment Station, 1982); C. C. Evans, "The relationship of cattle grazing to sage grouse use of meadow habitat on the Sheldon National Refuge (master's thesis, University of Nevada, Reno, 1986).

11. J. M. Linsdale, "Environmental responses of vertebrates in the Great Basin," *American Midland Naturalist* 18, no. 1 (1938): 1–206.

12. Klebenow, *Enhancing Sage Grouse Habitat . . . a Nevada Landowner's Guide,* Northwest Nevada Sage Grouse Working Group Publication, 2002.

13. Ibid.

14. Nevada Department of Wildlife Governor's Sage Grouse Conservation Team, *The Nevada Sage Grouse Conservation Strategy,* ed. Larry A. Neel, 2001.

15. Nevada Department of Wildlife, "Nevada Sage-Grouse Conservation Project W-64-R-8," Annual Progress Report, September 2008.

16. Mike Perkins, personal communication, 2004.

17. Gary Back, Elko County Sagebrush Ecosystem Conservation Strategy, p. 67, Northeastern Nevada Stewardship Group, Elko, 2004.

18. O. Julander, "Range management in relation to mule deer management and herd productivity," *Journal of Range Management* 15, no. 5 (1962): 278–81; G. E. Gruell, "Post-1900 mule deer irruptions in the Intermountain West: Principal cause and influences," General Technical Report 206, USDA Forest Service, Intermountain Research Station, Ogden, Utah, 1986.

19. Taylor, "Mammals of the Alexander Nevada Expedition of 1909."

20. L. Sharp, "Life of Lewis Sharp," manuscript in Lewis and Florence Beatrice Wines Sharp Collection, Nevada Historical Society, Reno, 1986.

21. Gruell, "Post-1900 mule deer irruptions in the Intermountain West."

22. A. E. Borell and R. Ellis, "Mammals of the Ruby Mountains region of northeastern Nevada," *Journal of Mammalogy* 15 (1934): 12–34.

23. Linsdale, "Environmental responses of vertebrates in the Great Basin."

24. E. R. Hall, *Mammals of Nevada* (Berkeley and Los Angeles: University of California Press, 1946).

25. A. Leopold, L. K. Sowls, and D. L. Spencer, "A survey of over-populated deer ranges in the United States," *Journal of Wildlife Management* 11, no. 2 (1947): 1–10.

26. Mathis, "Fish and Game Commission's history commences 1877—continues to the present."

27. G. W. Workman and J. B. Low, eds., *Mule Deer Decline in the West: A Symposium*, Utah State University College of Natural Resources, Utah Agricultural Experiment Station, Logan, 1976.

28. P. J. Urness, "Livestock as manipulators of mule deer winter habitats in northern Utah," in *Can Livestock Be Used as a Tool to Enhance Wildlife Habitat?*, pp. 25–40, GTR Report RM-194, USDA Forest Service, Rocky Mountain Forest and Range Experiment Station, Fort Collins, Colorado, 1990.

29. *Wildfire '99*, special edition newsletter from Nevada Bighorns Unlimited, Reno; "Fires are an environmental disaster for wildlife," Nevada Bighorns Unlimited newsletter, 2006; "Wildlife: Wildfires' lesser-known victims," *Reno Gazette-Journal*, June 30, 2006.

30. Borell and Ellis, "Mammals of the Ruby Mountains region of northeastern Nevada."

31. D. Mathis, *Following the Nevada Wildlife Trail: A History of Nevada Wildlife and Wildlife Management* (Nevada Agricultural Foundation, Nevada Heritage Series, 1997).

32. K. L. Risenhoover and J. A. Bailey, "Foraging ecology of mountain sheep: Implications for habitat management," *Journal of Wildlife Management* 49, no. 3 (1985): 797–804.

33. Mathis, *Following the Nevada Wildlife Trail*.

34. Taylor, "Mammals of the Alexander Nevada expedition of 1909;" Borell and Ellis, "Mammals of the Ruby Mountains region of northeastern Nevada"; Hall, *Mammals of Nevada*.

35. Nevada Department of Wildlife, *Nevada's Pronghorn Antelope: Ecology, Management and Conservation*, Biological Bulletin 13 (Reno: Nevada Department of Wildlife, 2003).

36. Borell and Ellis, "Mammals of the Ruby Mountains region of northeastern Nevada"; Hall, *Mammals of Nevada.*

37. D. O. Hyde, *The Last Free Man: The Story behind the Massacre of Shoshone Mike and His Band of Indians in 1909* (New York: Dial Press, 1973).

38. J. K. McAdoo and J. A. Young, "Jackrabbits," *Rangelands* 2, no. 4 (1980): 135–38.

39. Linsdale, "Environmental responses of vertebrates in the Great Basin."

40. Steward, *Basin-Plateau Aboriginal Sociopolitical Groups.*

41. J. K. McAdoo and D. A. Klebenow, "Native faunal relationships in sagebrush ecosystems," in *The Sagebrush Ecosystem: A Symposium* (Logan: Utah State University College of Natural Resources, 1979).

42. Hall, *Mammals of Nevada.*

43. Beitia, personal communication, 1957.

44. J. R. Alcorn, *The Birds of Nevada* (Fallon, Nev.: Fairview West Publishing, 1988).

45. Kent, *Reminiscences of Outdoor Life.*

46. Nevada Department of Wildlife website, http://www.edow.org/wild/animals/facts/birds_mountain_quail.shtm, 2009.

47. J. K. McAdoo, S. R. Swanson, B. W. Schultz, and P. F. Brussard, *Vegetation Management for Sagebrush-Associated Wildlife Species,* USDA Forest Service, Proceedings RMRS-P-31 (2004): 189–93.

48. D. A. Klebenow and R. J. Oakleaf, *Historical Avifaunal Changes in the Riparian Zone of the Truckee River, Nevada,* Nevada Agricultural Experiment Station Journal Series 36, and Nevada Department of Wildlife Federal Aid, Project W-53-R, 1981.

49. Nevada Department of Conservation and Natural Resources, Division of Water Resources, *Humboldt River Chronology: A Chronological History of the Humboldt River, the Humboldt River Basin, and Related Water Issues,* 2000; U.S. Fish and Wildlife Service, U.S. Bureau of Land Management, U.S. Forest Service, Nevada Division of Wildlife, and Trout Unlimited, *Bring Back the Lahontan Cutthroat: A Native Trout Makes a Comeback,* circular, no date.

50. Pat Coffin, personal communication, October 2010.

51. U.S. Fish and Wildlife Service and others, *Bring Back the Lahontan Cutthroat: A Native Trout Makes a Comeback.*

52. G. C. Christensen, "The chukar partridge in Nevada," *Nevada Fish and Game Commission Biological Bulletin* 1 (1954): 1–77.

12 | Management Choices: We Cannot Do Nothing

1. T. C. Nelson, "Fire management policy in the national forests—a new era," *Journal of Forestry* 77 (1979): 723–25.

2. USDI and USDA, *Federal Wildland Fire Management Policy and Program Review,* final report, Washington, D.C., 1995.

3. USDA and USDI, *Guidance for Implementation of Federal Fire Management Policy,* Washington, D.C., 2009.

4. Western Association of Fish and Game Agencies, "Prescribed fire as a management tool in xeric sagebrush ecosystems: Is it worth the risk to sage grouse?," white

paper prepared by the Sage and Columbia Sharp-tailed Grouse Committee for the Western Association of Fish and Wildlife Agencies, 2009.

5. B. M. Rau, J. C. Chambers, R. R. Blank, and D. W. Johnson, "Fire, soil and plants: Burn effects and interactions in the central Great Basin," *Rangeland Ecology and Management* 61 (2008): 169–81.

6. R. J. Tausch, R. F. Miller, B. A. Roundy, and J. C. Chambers, *Piñon and Juniper Field Guide: Asking the Right Questions to Select Appropriate Management Actions*, USGS Circular 1335, USDI, U.S. Geological Survey, 2009.

7. Bureau of Land Management, "Managed natural and prescribed fire plan—Ely Field Office," 2009, online at http://www.blm.gov/ely/managed_fires.htm, 2009.

8. Bureau of Land Management, *Healthy Lands Initiative—Oregon, Idaho, Nevada*, USDI, Washington, D.C., 2007.

9. Prichard and others, *Riparian Area Management.*

10. National Riparian Service Team, "A progress report on the creeks and communities strategy," USDI, Bureau of Land Management, National Operations Center, Denver, Colorado, 2008.

11. Online at http://www.sagestep.org.

12. Nevada Department of Wildlife, Governor's Sage Grouse Conservation Team, *The Nevada Sage Grouse Conservation Strategy*, ed. L. A. Neel, Nevada Department of Wildlife, 2008; Nevada Sage-Grouse Conservation Project W-64-R-8, annual progress report, 2001.

13. Nevada Partners in Conservation and Development, http://www.ndow.org/nevped/index.shtm.

14. Pinyon-Juniper Partnership, http://www.nvpjpartnership.org/pinyon_summit .htm.

15. Western Association of Fish and Wildlife Agencies, Mule Deer Working Group, *Habitat Guidelines for Mule Deer: Intermountain West Ecoregion*, 2009.

16. Western Great Basin Coordination Center, "Living with fire," Sierra Front Interagency Dispatch Center, 2009, online at Sierra Front.net/SierraFrontCoop/sierra_coop_index.htm.

17. K. Rollins, M. Kobayashi, and M. Taylor, "Measuring the economic value of fire and fire surrogate treatments to maintain healthy ecosystems in the sagebrush steppe," *SageSTEP News—Sagebrush Steppe Treatment Evaluation Project Newsletter* no. 12 (Spring 2010).

18. Economic Action Biomass Utilization Program, "Success: State and private forestry accomplishment," U.S. Forest Service, Northern and Intermountain regions and Nevada Division of Forestry, 2007.

19. Miller and others, "Age structure and expansion of piñon-juniper woodlands."

20. Robin Tausch, personal communication, 2010.

21. S. Swanson, "Scientist contributions," in *Great Basin Wildfire Forum: The Search for Solutions*, ed. E. Miller and R. Narayanan, pp. 28–29 (Reno: Nevada Agricultural Experiment Station, University of Nevada, 2008).

Bibliography

Alcorn, J. R. *The Birds of Nevada*. Fallon, Nev.: Fairview West Publishing, 1988.

Alter, J. S., ed. "Father Escalante and the Utah Indians." *Utah Historical Quarterly* 1, no. 4 (1928): 109–10.

Anteves, E. "Climatic changes and pre-white man." In *The Great Basin with Emphasis on Glacial and Postglacial Times. Bulletin of the University of Utah* 38, no. 20, Biological Series 10, no. 7 (1948).

———. *Rainfall and Tree Growth in the Great Basin*. American Geological Society Special Publication 21. Washington, D.C.: Carnegie Institution; New York: American Geographic Society, 1938.

Archer, S. "Woody plant encroachment into southwestern grasslands and savannas: Rates, patterns and proximate causes." In *Ecological Implications of Livestock Herbivory in the West*, ed. M. Vavra, W. A. Laycock, and R. D. Pieper. Denver: Society for Range Management, 1994.

Arno, S. F., and K. M. Sneck. "A method of determining fire history in conifer forest of the mountain West." General Technical Report INT-42. USDA Forest Service, Intermountain Forest and Range Experiment Station, Ogden, Utah, 1977.

Barnosky, A. D., P. L. Koch, R. S. Foranec, S. L. Wing, and A. B. Shobel. "Assessing the causes of Late Pleistocene extinctions on the continents." *Science* 306 (2004): 70–78.

Beckwith, Lt. E. G. *Report of Explorations for a Route for the Pacific Railroad, of the Line of the Forty-first Parallel of North Latitude*. 1854. House of Representatives, Executive Document 91, 33rd Congress, 2nd session.

Behnke, R. J. *Native Trout of Western North America*. American Fisheries Society Monograph no. 6, 1992.

Bender, F. I. "Memoranda of a journey across the plains, from Bell Creek, Washington Co., Nebraska, to Virginia City, Nevada, Territory, May 7 to August 4, 1863." *Nevada Historical Society Quarterly* 1, no. 4 (1958): 166–70.

Bensen, L. V., P. A. Meyers, and R. J. Spencer. "Change in the size of Walker Lake during the past 5000 years." *Paleogeography, Paleoclimatology, and Paleoecology* 81, nos. 3–4 (1991): 189–214.

Bidwell, J. "The first emigrant train to California." *Century* 41 (1890): 106–30.

Bigler, H. W. "Journal extracts of Henry W. Bigler." *Utah Historical Quarterly* 5, no. 4 (1932): 159.

Billings, W. D. "Ecological impacts of cheatgrass and resultant fire on ecosystems of the western Great Basin." In *Proceedings: Ecology and Management of Annual Rangelands,* ed. S. B. Monson and S. G. Kitchen, pp. 22–30. General Technical Report 313. USDA Forest Service, Intermountain Research Station, Ogden, Utah, 1994.

Bliss, R. S. "The journal of Robert S. Bliss, with the Mormon Battalion." *Utah Historical Quarterly* 4, no. 3 (1931): 110–12.

Borell, A. E., and R. Ellis. "Mammals of the Ruby Mountains region of northeastern Nevada." *Journal of Mammalogy* 15 (1934): 12–34.

Branson, F. A. *Vegetation Changes on Western Rangelands.* Range Monograph 2. Denver: Society for Range Management, 1985.

Browne, J. R. *Reports on the Mineral Resources of the United States.* Washington, D.C.: Government Printing Office, 1868.

Bruff, J. G. 1849–51. *Gold Rush: The Journals, Drawings and Other Papers of J. Goldsborough Bruff, Captain, Washington City and California Mining Association, April 2, 1849–July 20, 1851.* New York: Columbia University Press, 1944.

Bryant, E. *Rocky Mountain Adventures.* New York: Worthington, 1888.

Burkart, J. W. "Sage grouse myths." *Range* (Summer 2008): 56–57.

———. "Scientist contributions." In *Great Basin Wildlife Forum: The Search for Solutions,* ed. E. Miller and R. Narayanan, pp. 26–27. Nevada Agricultural Experiment Station, University of Nevada, Reno, 2008.

Burton, Sir Richard. *The Look of the West in 1860: Across the Plains to California.* Lincoln: University of Nebraska Press, 1963.

Canaday, T. W., and S. E. Reutebuch. "Searching for the past: Aerial photography and alpine archeology on the Toiyabe National Forest." In *Remote Sensing and Ecosystem Management.* Proceedings of the Fifth Forest Service Remote Sensing Applications Conference, Portland, Oregon, April 11–15, 1994.

Chabot, B. F., and A. Harold, eds. *Physiological Ecology of North American Plant Communities.* New York: Chapman and Hall, 1985.

Chambers, J. C. "Climate change and the Great Basin." In *Collaborative Management and Research in the Great Basin: Examining the Issues and Developing a Framework for Action,* ed. J. C. Chambers, N. Devoe, and A. Evenden, pp. 29–32. General Technical Report RMRS-GTR-204. USDA Forest Service, Rocky Mountain Research Station, 2008.

———. "Fire and the Great Basin." In *Collaborative Management and Research in the Great Basin: Examining the Issues and Developing a Framework for Action,* ed. J. C. Chambers, N. Devoe, and A. Evenden, pp. 33–37. General Technical Report RMRS-GTR-204. USDA Forest Service, Rocky Mountain Research Station, 2008.

Chambers, J. C., and J. R. Miller. "Restoring and maintaining sustainable riparian ecosystems: The Great Basin Ecosystem Management Project." In *Great Basin Riparian Ecosystems,* ed. J. C. Chambers and J. R. Miller, pp. 1–23. Covelo, Wash.: Island Press, 2004.

Christensen, G. C. "The chukar partridge in Nevada." *Nevada Fish and Game Commission Biological Bulletin* 1 (1954): 1–77.

Clapp, C. H. "The major range problems and their solution: A resume." In *The Western Range.* Senate Document 199. Washington, D.C.: Government Printing Office, 1936.

Clements, C. D., and J. A. Young. "A viewpoint: Rangeland health and mule deer habitat." *Journal of Range Management* 50, no. 2 (1997): 129–38.

Clyman, J. *Journal of a Mountain Man.* Ed. L. M. Hasselstrom. Missoula, Mont.: Mountain Press, 1984.

Creech, E., L. Singletary, J. Davison, L. Blecker, and B. Shultz. *Nevada's 2008 Weed Management Extension Program Needs Assessment: A Survey of Agricultural Producers and Public Land Managers.* University of Nevada Cooperative Extension Special Publication SP-10-03, 2010.

Dagget, D. *Beyond the Rangeland Conflict.* Flagstaff, Ariz.: Gibbs-Smith in cooperation with the Grand Canyon Trust, 1995.

Dana, S. T., and S. K. Fairfax. *Forest and Range Policy.* New York: McGraw-Hill, 1980.

d'Azevedo, W. L. "Washoe." In *Handbook of North American Indians.* Vol. 11: *Great Basin,* ed. W. L. d'Azevedo, pp. 466–99. Washington, D.C.: Smithsonian Institution Press, 1986.

Dealy, J. E. "Ecology of curlleaf mountain mahogany (*Cercocarpus ledifolius* Nutt.) in eastern Oregon and adjacent areas." Ph.D. diss., Oregon State University, Corvallis, 1975.

Deboodt, T. L., M. P. Fisher, J. C. Buckhouse, and J. Swanson. *Monitoring Hydrologic Changes Related to Western Juniper Removal, a Paired Watershed Approach. The Grazier,* no. 336. Oregon State University, 2009.

Delano, A. *Across the Plains and among the Diggings.* Reprint. New York: Wilson-Erickson, 1936.

DeQuille, D. (William Wright). *The Big Bonanza.* New York: Alfred A. Knopf, 1953.

———. *Washoe Rambles.* Los Angeles: Westernlore Press, 1963.

Downs, J. F. "The significance of environmental manipulation in Great Basin cultural development." In *The Current Status of Anthropological Research in the Great Basin: 1964,* ed. W. d'Azevedo, pp. 39–56. Technical Series S-H, Social Science and Humanities Publications 1. Reno: Desert Research Institute, 1966.

Earth Institute, Columbia University. "Carbon dioxide higher today than the last 2.1 million years." *Science Daily,* 2009.

Economic Action Biomass Utilization Program. *Success: State and Private Forestry Accomplishment.* U.S. Forest Service, Northern and Intermountain Regions, and Nevada Division of Forestry, 2007.

Egan, H. R. *Pioneering the West, 1846–1878. Major Howard Egan's Diary.* Salt Lake City: Skelton Publishing, 1917.

Ellison, R. W. *First Impressions: The Trail through Carson Valley, 1848–1852.* Minden, Nev.: Hot Springs Mountain Press, 2001.

Eno, H. *Twenty Years on the Pacific Slope: Letters of Henry Eno from California and Nevada, 1848–1871.* New Haven: Yale University Press, 1965.

Evans, C. "Monitoring summary and evaluation of biological standards." Maggie Creek Watershed Restoration Project. Elko District Bureau of Land Management, Nevada, 2006.

———. "The relationship of cattle grazing to sage grouse use of meadow habitat on the Sheldon National Refuge." Master's thesis, University of Nevada, Reno, 1986.

Fowler, C. S. *In the Shadow of Fox Peak: An Ethnography of the Cattail-Eater Northern Paiute People of Stillwater Marsh.* Cultural Resource Series 5. U.S. Department of the Interior, Fish and Wildlife Service, Region 1, Stillwater National Wildlife Refuge, 1992.

———. "Subsistence." In *Handbook of North American Indians.* Vol. 11: *Great Basin,* ed. W. L. d'Azevedo, pp. 64–97. Washington, D.C.: Smithsonian Institution Press, 1986.

Frémont, J. C. *Geographical Memoir*. 1848. Reprint, San Francisco: Book Club of California, 1964.

——. *Memoirs of My Life*. Vol. 1: *Relford*. Chicago and New York: Clarke and Company, 1887.

Georgette, C. *Golden Fleece in Nevada*. Reno: Venture, 1972.

Gilbert, G. H. *Lake Bonneville*. U.S. Geological Survey Monograph 1, 1890.

Grayson, D. *Danger Cave, Last Supper Cave, and Hanging Rock Shelter: The Faunas*. Anthropological Papers of the American Museum of Natural History, New York, vol. 66, pt. 1, 1988.

——. *The Desert's Past: A Natural Prehistory of the Great Basin*. Washington, D.C.: Smithsonian Institution Press, 1993.

Greeley, H. *An Overland Journey, from New York to San Francisco in the Summer of 1859*. Ed. C. T. Duncan. New York: Alfred A. Knopf, 1969.

Griffiths, D. *Forage Conditions on the Northern Border of the Great Basin: Being a Report upon Investigations Made during July and August 1901 in the Region between Winnemucca, Nevada, and Ontario, Oregon*. U.S. Bureau of Plant Industry Bulletin 15. Washington, D.C.: Government Printing Office, 1902.

Gruell, G. E. "Fire on the early western landscape: An annotated list of recorded wildfires, 1776–1900." *Northwest Science* 59 (1985): 97–107.

——. "Historical perspective: A prerequisite for better public understanding of fire management challenges." In *High Intensity Fire in Wildlands: Management Challenges and Options*. Fire Ecology Conference, Tall Timbers Research Station, Tallahassee, Florida, 1991.

——. "Historical role of fire in pinyon-juniper woodlands: Walker River watershed project, Bridgeport Ranger District." Report contracted by USDA Forest Service, Humboldt-Toiyabe National Forest, Reno, Nevada, 1997.

——. "Historic and modern roles of fire in pinyon-juniper woodlands." In *Proceedings: Ecology and Management of Pinyon-Juniper Communities within the Interior West*, comp. S. B. Monson and R. Stevens, pp. 24–28. RMRS P-9, USDA Forest Service, Rocky Mountain Research Station, Ogden, Utah, 1999.

——. "Indian fires in the interior West: A widespread influence." In *Proceedings of the 1983 Wilderness Fire Symposium*, ed. J. E. Lotan, B. M. Kilgor, W. C. Fischer, and R. W. Mutch, pp. 68–74. General Technical Report 182. USDA Forest Service, Intermountain Research Station, Ogden, Utah, 1985.

——. "Influence of fire on Great Basin wildlife habitats." *Transactions of the Western Section of the Wildlife Society* 32 (1996): 55–61.

——. "Northern Elko County: The way it was." *Northeastern Nevada Historical Society Quarterly* 98, no. 4, (1998).

——. *Post-1900 Mule Deer Irruptions in the Intermountain West: Principal Cause and Influences*. General Technical Report 206. USDA Forest Service, Intermountain Research Station, Ogden, Utah, 1986.

Gruell, G. E., S. C. Bunting, and L. F. Neuenschwander. "Influence of fire on curl-leaf mountain-mahogany in the Intermountain West." In *Fire's Effects on Wildlife*

Habitat—Symposium Proceedings, ed. J. E. Lotan and J. K. Brown, pp. 58–72. General Technical Report INT-186. USDA Forest Service, Ogden, Utah, 1984.

Gruell, G. E., L. E. Eddleman, and R. Jaindl. *Fire History of the Pinyon-Juniper Woodlands of Great Basin National Park.* Technical Report NPS/PNROSU/NRTR-94/01. U.S. Department of the Interior, National Park Service, Pacific Northwest Region, 1994.

Hall, E. R. *Mammals of Nevada.* Berkeley and Los Angeles: University of California Press, 1946.

Harper, K. T. "Historical environments." In *Handbook of North American Indians.* Vol. 11: *Great Basin,* ed. W. L. d'Azevedo, pp. 51–63. Washington, D.C.: Smithsonian Institution Press, 1986.

Hattori, E. M., and A. R. McLane. "Preliminary report of archaeological and historical studies at Cornucopia, Elko County, Nevada." Submitted by Desert Research Institute and Board of Regents, University of Nevada System to Minetek Group, Inc., 1983.

Hazeltine, B., S. Saulisbery, and H. Taylor. "A range history of Nevada." Pt. 1: "Stockmen wrote Silver State's range history"; pt. 2: "They came for the native grass"; pt. 3: "They came for the native range . . . and left a heritage." Nevada Section, Society for Range Management, 1965.

Heller, T. B. Extracts of a journal kept by Heller published in the January 25, 1864, edition of the *Reese River Reveille,* Austin, Nevada, 1864.

Henshaw, H. W. "Ornithological report from observations and collections made in portions of California, Nevada, and Oregon." Appendix L in G. W. Wheeler, Appendix OO, *Annual Report upon the Geographical Surveys West of the 100th Meridian . . . for 1879.* Washington, D.C.: Government Printing Office, 1880.

Herndon, P. "The history of grazing on the public lands." In *Your Public Lands* 32, no. 2 (1982).

Heyerdahl, E. K., P. M. Brown, S. G. Kitchen, and M. H. Weber. *Multicentury Fire and Forest Histories at Nineteen Sites in Utah and Eastern Nevada.* USDA Forest Service, Rocky Mountain Research Station, Fort Collins, Colorado, 2011.

Hoffman, W. J. "Miscellaneous ethnographic observations on Indians inhabiting Nevada, California, and Arizona." In F. V. Hayden, *Tenth Annual Report of the U.S. Geological and Geographical Survey of the Territories,* pt. 3, pp. 461–78. Progress report for 1876. 1878.

Hulbert, A. B. *Forty-niners: The Chronicle of the California Trail* (Boston: Little, Brown, 1931).

Humboldt River Basin Nevada, Water and Related Land Resources. Report 1: *Little Humboldt Sub-Basin.* Nevada Department of Conservation and Natural Resources and USDA, March 1962.

Humboldt River Basin Nevada, Water and Related Land Resources. Report 8: *Reese River Sub-Basin.* Nevada Department of Conservation and Natural Resources and USDA, June 1964.

Humboldt River Basin Nevada, Water and Related Land Resources. Report 9: *Battle Mountain Sub-Basin.* Nevada Department of Conservation and Natural Resources and USDA, October 1964.

Humboldt River Basin Nevada, Water and Related Land Resources. Report 12: *Basin-wide Report.* Nevada Department of Conservation and Natural Resources and USDA, November 1966.

Humphreys, A. A., and G. K. Warren. *Reports of Explorations and Surveys to Ascertain the Most Practicable and Economical Route for a Railroad from the Missouri River to the Pacific Ocean, 1853–54.* Corps of Topographical Engineers. Senate Executive Document 78, vol. 1, 1855, 33rd Congress, 2nd session.

Huntington, O. B. "A trip to Carson Valley." In *Eventful Narratives,* ed. Robert Averson, pp. 77–98. Faith-Promoting Series 13. Salt Lake City, Utah, 1877.

Hyde, D. O. *The Last Free Man: The Story behind the Massacre of Shoshone Mike and His Band of Indians in 1909.* New York: Dial Press, 1973.

James, S. R., J. C. Janetski, and J. A. Vlasich. *Prehistory, Ethnohistory, and History of Eastern Nevada: A Cultural Resources Summary of the Elko and Ely Districts,* ed. Steven R. James. Contract no. YA-533-CTO-1025 between the Bureau of Land Management and the University of Utah Archeological Center. Reports of Investigations 81-5, 1981.

Jennings, J. D., and E. Norbeck. "Great Basin prehistory: A review." *American Antiquity* 21, no. 1 (1955): 1–11.

Julander, O. "Range management in relation to mule deer management and herd productivity." *Journal of Range Management* 15, no. 5 (1962): 278–81.

Julander, O., and J. B. Low. "A historical account and present status of the mule deer in the West." In *Mule Deer Decline in the West: A Symposium,* ed. G. W. Workman and J. B. Low, pp. 3–19. Logan: Utah State University College of Natural Resources, Utah Agricultural Experiment Station, 1976.

Keane, R. E., K. C. Ryan, T. T. Veblen, C. D. Allen, J. Logan, and B. Hawkes. *Cascading Effects of Fire Exclusion in Rocky Mountain Ecosystems: A Literature Review.* RMRS-GTR-91, USDA Forest Service, Rocky Mountain Research Station, 2002.

Kelly, I. T. *Ethnography of the Surprise Valley Paiute.* University of California Publications in American Archaeology and Ethnology 31, no. 3, 1932.

Kennedy, P. B. *Summer Ranges of the Eastern Nevada Sheep.* Nevada Agricultural Experiment Station Bulletin 55, 1903.

Kent, W. *Reminiscences of Outdoor Life.* San Francisco: A. M. Robertson, 1929.

Kern, E. M. "Journal of Mr. Edward Kern of an exploration of the Mary's River, Carson Lake, and Owens River and Lake in 1845." Appendix Q in *Report of Explorations across the Great Basin of the Territory of Utah in 1859 by Captain J. H. Simpson.* U.S. Army Engineer's Department. Washington, D.C.: Government Printing Office, 1876.

Kilgore, W. H. 1850. *The Kilgore Journal of an Overland Journey to California in the 1850s.* Ed. J. R. Muench. New York: Hastings House, 1949.

Kitchen, S. G. "Historic fire regimes of eastern Great Basin (USA) mountains reconstructed from tree rings." Ph.D. diss., Brigham Young University, 2009.

Klebenow, D. A. *Enhancing Sagegrouse Habitat . . . a Nevada Landowners Guide.* Northwest Nevada Sage Grouse Working Group Publication, 2002.

———. "Livestock interactions with sage grouse." In *Wildlife-Livestock Relations Symposium Proceedings* 10, ed. J. M. Peek and P. D. Dalke, pp. 113–23. Moscow: University of Idaho Forest, Wildlife, and Range Experiment Station, 1982.

Klebenow, D. A., and R. J. Oakleaf. *Historical Avifaunal Changes in the Riparian Zone of the Truckee River, Nevada.* Nevada Agricultural Experiment Station Journal Series Contribution 356, and Nevada Department of Wildlife Federal Aid Project w-53-r, 1981.

Kozlowski, D., S. Swanson, and K. Schmidt. "Channel changes in burned streams of northern Nevada." *Journal of Arid Environments* 74, no. 11 (2010): 1494–1506.

LaMarche, V. C. "Paleoclimatic inferences from long tree-ring records." *Science* 183, no. 4129 (1974): 1043–48.

La Rivers, I. *Fishes and Fisheries of Nevada.* Reno: Nevada Fish and Game Commission, 1962.

Laudenslager, E. J., and G. A. E. Gall. "Geographic patterns of protein variation and subspeciation of cutthroat trout *Salmon clarki.*" *Systematic Zoology* 1, no. 1 (1980): 27–42.

Le Conte, J. *Journal of Ramblings through the High Sierras of California by the University Excursion Party in 1870.* San Francisco: Sierra Club, 1960.

Leonard, A. W. *Leonard's Narrative, Adventures of Zenas Leonard, Fur Trapper and Trader, 1831–36.* Ed. F. Wagner. Cleveland: Burrows Brothers, 1904.

Leopold, A., L. K. Sowls, and D. L. Spencer. "A survey of over-populated deer ranges in the United States." *Journal of Wildlife Management* 11, no. 2 (1947): 1–10.

Leopold, A. S. "Deer in relation to plant successions." *Journal of Forestry* 48, no. 10 (1950): 675–78.

Lienhard, H. *From St. Louis to Sutter's Fort, 1846.* Trans. and ed. E. G. Gudde and E. K. Gudde. Norman: University of Oklahoma Press, 1961.

Linsdale, J. M. *The Birds of Nevada.* Cooper Ornithological Club, Pacific Coast Avifauna 2. Berkeley, California, 1936.

———. "Environmental responses of vertebrates in the Great Basin." *American Midland Naturalist* 18, no. 1 (1938): 1–206.

Lord, E. *Comstock Mining and Miners.* 1838. Reprint, Berkeley, Calif.: Howell-North, 1959.

Lowie, R. H. *The Northern Shoshone.* Anthropological Papers of the American Museum of Natural History 2, pt. 2 (1909).

Mack, R. N. "Invasion of *Bromus tectorum* into western North America: An ecological chronicle." *Agro-Ecosystems* 7 (1981): 145–65.

Mann, C. C. *1491: New Revelations of the Americas before Columbus.* New York: Alfred A. Knopf, 2005.

Mathis, D. "Fish and Game Commission's history commences 1877—continues to the present." *Nevada Wildlife* Centennial Issue, vol. 5, nos. 4–7 (1965–66), Nevada Fish and Game Commission.

———. *Following the Nevada Wildlife Trail: A History of Nevada Wildlife and Wildlife Management.* Nevada Agricultural Foundation, Nevada Heritage Series, 1997.

McAdoo, J. K., and D. A. Klebenow. "Native faunal relationships in sagebrush ecosystems." In *The Sagebrush Ecosystem: A Symposium.* Utah State University College of Natural Resources, Logan, 1979.

McAdoo, J. K., B. Schultz, S. Swanson, and G. Back. "Northeastern Nevada wildfires 2006: Part 1, Fire and land use history." University of Nevada Cooperative Extension Fact Sheet 07-20, 2007.

McAdoo, J. K., and J. A. Young. "Jackrabbits." *Rangelands* 2, no. 4 (1980): 135–38.

McArdle, R. E., and D. F. Costello. "The virgin range." In *The Western Range*. Senate Document 199, 74th Congress, 2nd session. Washington, D.C.: Government Printing Office, 1936.

Mehringer, P. J. "Late-Quaternary pollen records from the interior Pacific Northwest and northern Great Basin of the United States." In *Pollen Records of the Late-Quaternary North American Sediments*, ed. V. M. Bryant Jr. and R. G. Holloway, pp. 167–89. Dallas: American Association of Stratigraphic Palynologists, 1985.

Miller, J. R., K. House, K. Germanoski, R. J. Tausch, and J. C. Chambers. "Fluvial geomorphic response to Holocene climate change." In *Great Basin Riparian Areas: Ecology, Management and Restoration*, ed. J. C. Chambers and J. R. Miller, pp. 49–87. Covelo, Wash.: Island Press, 2004.

Miller, R. F., and L. L. Eddleman. *Spatial and Temporal Changes of Sage Grouse Habitat in the Sagebrush Biome*. Oregon State University Agricultural Experiment Station Technical Bulletin 151, 2001.

Miller, R. F., T. J. Svejcar, and N. E. West. "Implications of livestock grazing in the intermountain sagebrush region: Plant composition." In *Ecological Implications of Livestock Herbivory in the West*, ed. M. Vavra, W. A. Laycock, and R. D. Pieper, pp. 101–46. Denver: Society for Range Management, 1994.

Miller, R. F., and R. J. Tausch. "The role of fire in juniper and pinyon woodlands: A descriptive analysis." In *Proceedings of the Invasive Species Work-Shop: The Role of Fire in the Control and Spread of Invasive Species*, ed. K. E. M. Gulley and T. P. Wilson, pp. 15–30. Tall Timbers Research Station Miscellaneous Publication 11, 2001.

Miller, R. F., R. J. Tausch, E. D. McArthur, D. D. Johnson, and S. C. Sanderson. "Age structure and expansion of piñon-juniper woodlands: A regional perspective in the Intermountain West." Research Paper Report RMRS-RP-69, USDA Forest Service, Rocky Mountain Research Station, 2008. Tall Timbers Research Station Miscellaneous Publications 11 (2001).

Miller, R. F., and P. E. Wigand. "Holocene changes in semiarid pinyon-juniper woodlands: Response to climate, fire, and human activities in the U.S. Great Basin." *BioScience* 44, no. 7 (1994): 465–74.

Moorman, M. B. *The Journal of Madison Berryman Moorman, 1850–51*. Ed. and intro. I. D. Paden. San Francisco: California Historical Society, 1948.

Muggler, W. F. "Vegetation associations." In *Aspen: Ecology and Management in the Western United States*, ed. N. V. DeByle and R. P. Winokur, pp. 45–55. General Technical Report RM-119. USDA Forest Service, Rocky Mountain Forest and Range Experiment Station, Fort Collins, Colorado, 1985.

Muir, J. *Steep Trails*. Ed. W. F. Bade. Boston and New York: Houghton Mifflin, 1918.

National Riparian Service Team. "Progress report on the creeks and communities strategy." Bureau of Land Management, National Operations Center, Denver, Colorado, 2008.

Nelson, T. C. "Fire management policy in the national forests—a new era." *Journal of Forestry* 77 (1979): 723–25.

Nevada Department of Conservation and Natural Resources, Division of Water Resources. *Humboldt River Chronology: A Chronological History of the Humboldt River, the Humboldt River Basin, and Related Water Issues.* 2000.

Nevada Department of Wildlife. Governor's Sage Grouse Conservation Team. *Nevada Sage-Grouse Conservation Project W-64-R-8.* Annual progress report, September 2008.

———. *The Nevada Sage Grouse Conservation Strategy.* Ed. L. A. Neel. 2001.

———. "Nevada's pronghorn antelope: Ecology, management and conservation." *Biological Bulletin* 13 (2003).

Nevada Weed Action Committee. *Nevada's Coordinated Invasive Weed Strategy.* Nevada Department of Agriculture, 2006. Online at http://agri.nv.gov/nwac/PLANT_NoxWeedPlan.

Oddie, T. L. *Letters from the Nevada Frontier: Correspondence of Tasker L. Oddie, 1898–1902.* Ed. W. A. Douglass and R. A. Nylen. Norman: University of Oklahoma Press, 1992.

Ogden, P. S. *Peter Skene Ogden's Snake River Journals, 1824–25 and 1825–26.* Ed. E. E. Rich and A. M. Johnson. Publication 13, Hudson's Bay Record Society, London, 1971.

———. *Peter Skene Ogden's Snake River Journals, 1827–28 and 1828–29.* Ed. Glyndwr Williams. Publication 28, Hudson's Bay Record Society, London, 1950.

Paher, S. W. *Nevada Ghost Towns and Mining Camps.* Berkeley, Calif.: Howell-North Books, 1970.

Parry, M. L., and T. R. Carter. "The effects of climate variations on agriculture risk." *Climatic Changes* 7 (1985): 98–110.

Patterson, E. B. "The diary of Joe F. Triplett." *Nevada Historical Society Quarterly* 2, no. 1 (1959).

———. "Early cattle in Elko County." *Nevada Historical Quarterly* 8, no. 2 (1965).

Patterson, E. B., L. A. Ulph, and V. Goodwin. *Nevada's Northeast Frontier.* Sparks, Nev.: Western Printing and Publishing, 1969.

Platts, W. S. "Livestock grazing." In *Influence of Forest and Rangeland Management on Salmonid Fishes and Their Habitats,* chap. 11. American Fisheries Society Special Publication 19 (1991).

Prichard, D., J. C. Anderson, C. Correll, J. Fogg, K. Gebhardt, R. Kraft, S. Leonard, B. Mitchell, and J. Staats. *Riparian Area Management: A User Guide to Accessing Proper Functioning Condition and Supporting Science for Lotic Areas.* Technical Reference 1737-15. U.S. Department of the Interior, Bureau of Land Management, U.S. Department of Agriculture, Forest Service, and National Resource Conservation Service, 1998.

Pyne, S. J. *Fire in America: A Cultural History of Wildland and Rural Fire.* Princeton: Princeton University Press, 1982.

Reed, F. W. 1905. "The proposed Ruby Mountains Forest Reserve, Nevada." Typed manuscript in Humboldt-Toiyabe National Forest files.

Reid, B. J. *Overland to California with the Pioneer Line*. Ed. M. M. Gordon. Stanford: Stanford University Press, 1983.

Rice, C. L. *Fire History of Emerald Bay State Park*. Department of Forestry and Resource Management, University of California, under contract to California Department of Parks and Recreation, 1988.

———. *Fire History of State Parks of the Sierra District of the California Department of Parks and Recreation*. Department of Forestry and Resource Management, University of California, under contract to California Department of Parks and Recreation, 1990.

Ridgway, R. "Ornithology." In *Report of the Geological Explorations of the Fortieth Parallel*. Professional Papers of the U.S. Army Engineer's Department, vol. 3, pt. 3. Washington, D.C.: Government Printing Office, 1876.

Risenhoover, K. L., and J. A. Bailey. "Foraging ecology of mountain sheep: Implications for habitat management." *Journal of Wildlife Management* 49, no. 3 (1985): 797–804.

Robertson, J. H., and P. B. Kennedy. "Half-century changes on northern Nevada ranges." *Journal of Range Management* 7, no. 3 (1954).

Robinette, W. L. "Mule deer mortality from various causes." In *Proceedings of a Symposium on Mule Deer Decline in the West*, pp. 125–27. Utah State University College of Natural Resources, Utah Agricultural Experiment Station, Logan, 1976.

Rollins, K., M. Kobayashi, and M. Taylor. "Measuring the economic value of fire and fire surrogate treatments to maintain healthy ecosystems in the sagebrush steppe." *SageSTEP News—Sagebrush Steppe Treatment Evaluation Project Newsletter*, no. 12 (Spring 2010).

Rood, S. B., C. R. Gourley, E. M. Ammon, L. G. Heki, J. R. Klotz, S. Swanson, M. L. Morrison, D. Mosley, G. G. Scoppettone, and P. L. Wagner. "Flows for floodplain forests: A successful riparian restoration." *BioScience* 53, no. 7 (2003): 647–56.

Russell, I. C. "Sketch of the geologic history of Lake Lahontan." In *Third Annual Report of the United States Geological Survey to the Secretary of the Interior, 1881–82*. Washington, D.C.: Government Printing Office, 1885.

Salwasser, H. "Man, deer and time on the Devil's Garden." *Proceedings of the Western States Game and Fish Commissioners* (1976): 295–318.

Sargent, C. S. "Forests of central Nevada." *American Journal of Science* 17 (1879): 417–26.

Sawyer, B. D. *Nevada Nomads: A Story of the Sheep Industry*. San Jose, Calif.: Harlan-Young Press, 1971.

Schaefer, R. J., D. J. Thayer, and T. Burton. "Forty-one years of vegetation change on permanent transects in northwestern California: Implications for wildlife." *California Fish and Game* 89, no. 2 (2003): 55–71.

Scheldt, R. S. "Ecology and utilization of curl-leaf mountain mahogany in Idaho." Master's thesis, University of Idaho, Moscow, 1969.

Schmidt, K. N. "Riparian response to the interactive effects of livestock grazing and wildfire in northern Nevada." Master's thesis, University of Nevada, Reno, 2009.

Schultz, B. B. "Ecology of curlleaf mahogany in western and central Nevada: Community and population structure." *Journal of Range Management* 43, no. 1 (1990): 13–20.

Scott, L. A. Unpublished diary, 1859. Excerpted in *Central Overland Route and Transcontinental Telegraph through Nevada, 1858–1868*. Oakland, Calif.: TRASH, 1985.

Sharp, L. L. "Life of Lewis Sharp." Manuscript in Lewis and Florence Beatrice Wines Sharp Collection, Nevada Historical Society, Reno, 1986.

Shinn, D. A. "Historical perspective on range burning in the inland Northwest." *Journal of Range Management* 33 (1980): 415–22.

Simmons, G., M. Ritchie, and E. Sant. "Evaluating riparian condition and trend in three large watersheds." Project report to the U.S. Fish and Wildlife Service for agreement 4240-7-H009, 2009.

Simpson, Capt. J. H. *Report of the Explorations across the Great Basin of the Territory of Utah for a Direct Wagon-Route from Camp Floyd, Utah, to Genoa in Carson Valley.* U.S. Army Engineer's Department. Washington, D.C.: Government Printing Office, 1876.

Smeathman, H. O. "Notes of a prospecting trip in Humboldt County, N.T." *San Francisco Bulletin,* February 18, 1864.

Smith, C. W. *Journal of a Trip to California across the Continent from Western Missouri to Weber Creek, California, in the Summer of 1850.* Ed. and intro. R. W. G. Vail. New York: Cadmas Book Shop, 1920.

Spencer, R. F., and J. D. Jennings. *The Native Americans.* New York: Harper and Row, 1965.

Starrs, P. F. *Let the Cowboy Ride: Cattle Ranching in the Interior American West.* Baltimore: Johns Hopkins University Press, 1998.

Stebleton, A., and S. Bunting. *Guide for Quantifying Fuels in the Sagebrush Steppe and Juniper Woodlands of the Great Basin.* Technical Note 430, Bureau of Land Management, Denver, Colorado, BLM/ID/002+2824, 2009. Online at http://www.sagesteppe.org/pubs/fuelsguide.htm.

Stephens, S. L. *Fire History of Jeffrey Pine and Upper Montane Forest Types at the University of California Valentine Reserve, Mono County, CA.* University of California Natural Reserves System, 1996.

Steward, J. H. *Basin-Plateau Aboriginal Sociopolitical Groups.* Smithsonian Institution Bureau of American Ethnology Bulletin 120. Washington, D.C.: Government Printing Office, 1938.

———. "Cultural element distributions: XIII. Nevada Shoshone." *University of California Anthropologic Records* 4, no. 2 (1941): 209–59.

Stewart, G. "Historic records bearing on agriculture and grazing ecology in Utah." *Journal of Forestry* 39 (1941): 362–75.

Stewart, O. C. *Anthropological Records 4:3 Cultural Element Distributions: XIV Northern Paiute.* Berkeley and Los Angeles: University of California Press, 1941.

———. "Fire as the first great force employed by man." In *International Symposium on Man's Role in Changing the Face of the Earth,* ed. W. L. Thomas, pp. 115–33. Chicago: University of Chicago Press, 1956.

———. *Forgotten Fires: Native Americans and the Transient Wilderness.* Ed. and intro. H. T. Lewis and M. K. Anderson. Norman: University of Oklahoma Press, 2002.

Sturges, D. L. "Soil-water and vegetation dynamics through 20 years after big sagebrush control." *Journal of Range Management* 46 (1993): 161–69.

Stutz, H. C., and S. C. Sanderson. "Evolutionary studies of *Atriplex*: Chromosome races of *A. confertifolia* (shadscale)." *American Journal of Botany* 70, no. 10 (1983): 1536–47.

Swanson, S. "Scientist contributions." In *Great Basin Wildfire Forum: The Search for Solutions*, ed. E. Miller and R. Narayanan, pp. 28–29. Nevada Agricultural Experiment Station, University of Nevada, Reno, 2008.

Tausch, R. J., R. F. Miller, B. A. Roundy, and J. C. Chambers. *Piñon and Juniper Field Guide: Asking the Right Questions to Select Appropriate Management Actions.* Circular 1335. U.S. Department of the Interior, U.S. Geological Survey, 2009.

Tausch, R. J., C. L. Nowak, and S. A. Mensing. "Climate change and associated vegetation dynamics during the Holocene: The paleoecological record." In *Great Basin Riparian Areas: Ecology, Management, and Restoration*, ed. J. C. Chambers and J. R. Miller, pp. 24–48. Covelo, Wash.: Island Press, 2004.

Taylor, A. H. "Pre- and post-Comstock logging forest structure and composition, Carson Range, Nevada." Paper presented at the 25th Great Basin Anthropological Conference, Kings Beach, California, October 10–12, 1996.

Taylor, W. P. "Field notes of amphibians, reptiles and birds of northern Humboldt County, Nevada." *University of California Publications in Zoology* 7, no. 10 (1912): 319–436.

———. "Mammals of the Alexander Nevada expedition of 1909." *University of California Publications in Zoology* 7, no. 7 (1911): 205–307.

Thomas, D. H. "The archaeology of Monitor Valley: 1. Epistemology." Contributions by R. R. Kautz, W. N. Melhorn, R. S. Thompson, and D. T. Trexler. *Anthropological Papers of the American Museum of Natural History* 58, pt. 1 (1983): 1–194.

———. "Historic and prehistoric land-use patterns at Reese River." *Nevada Historical Society Quarterly* 14, no. 4 (1971): 2–9.

Thomas, D. H., S. A. Pendleton, and S. C. Capp. "Western Shoshone." In *Handbook of North American Indians.* Vol. 11: *Great Basin,* ed. W. L. d'Azevedo, pp. 262–307. Washington, D.C.: Smithsonian Institution Press, 1986.

Thomas, W. L., Jr. *Man's Role in Changing the Face of the Earth.* Chicago: University of Chicago Press, 1955.

Thompson, G. C. 1908. "Favorable report upon proposed Bruneau addition to the Humboldt National Forest." Typed report, 17 pp., Humboldt-Toiyabe National Forest files.

Thompson, R. S. "Late Quaternary environments in Ruby Valley, Nevada." *Quaternary Research* 37 (1992): 1–15.

Thompson, R. S., and J. I. Mead. "Late Quaternary environments and biogeography in the Great Basin." *Quaternary Research* 17 (1982): 39–55.

University of Idaho Stubble Height Review Team. "University of Idaho Stubble Height Study Report." University of Idaho Forest, Wildlife and Range Experiment Station Contribution 986, 2004. Online at http://www.cnrhome.uidaho.edu/documents /Stubble_Height_Report.pdf&pid=74895&doc=1.

Urness, P. J. "Livestock as manipulators of mule deer winter habitats in northern Utah." In *Can Livestock Be Used as a Tool to Enhance Wildlife Habitat?*, pp. 25–40. Technical Report RM-194. USDA Forest Service, Rocky Mountain Forest and Range Experiment Station, Fort Collins, Colorado, 1990.

———. "Mule deer habitat changes resulting from livestock grazing practices." In *Proceedings of a Symposium on Mule Deer Decline and the West*, pp. 21–35. Logan: Utah State University, 1976.

U.S. Bureau of Land Management. *Healthy Lands Initiative—Oregon, Idaho, Nevada.* Washington, D.C.: Department of the Interior, 2007.

———. "Managed natural and prescribed fire plan." Ely Field Office, 2009.

———. *An Overview of the Battle Mountain District.* Cultural Series Monograph 4. Nevada State Office of the Bureau of Land Management, Reno, 1982.

U.S. Department of Agriculture and U.S. Department of the Interior. *Guidance for Implementation of Federal Fire Management Policy.* Washington, D.C., 2009.

U.S. Department of the Interior, U.S. Department of Agriculture, and Nevada Department of Forestry. Western Great Basin Coordination Center. Incident Activity Reports, 1999–2010.

U.S. Department of the Interior and U.S. Department of Agriculture. *Federal Wildland Fire Management Policy and Program Review.* Final report. Washington, D.C., 1995.

U.S. Fish and Wildlife Service, U.S. Bureau of Land Management, U.S. Forest Service, Nevada Division of Wildlife, and Trout Unlimited. *Bring Back the Lahontan Cutthroat: A Native Trout Makes a Comeback.* Brochure, no date.

Vale, T. R. "Presettlement vegetation in the sagebrush-grass area of the Intermountain West." *Journal of Range Management* 28 (1975): 32–36.

Watson, S. "Botany." In *Report of the Geological Explorations of the Fortieth Parallel.* Professional Papers of the U.S. Army Engineer's Department, no. 18, vol. 3, pt. 3. Washington, D.C.: Government Printing Office, 1876.

Wells, P. V. "Paleobiogeography of montane islands in the Great Basin since the last glaciopluvial." *Ecological Monographs* 53, no. 4 (1983): 341–48.

Wells, P. V., and C. D. Jorgensen. "Pleistocene wood rat middens and climatic change in the Mohave Desert: A record of juniper woodlands." *Science* 143 (1964): 1171–74.

West, N. E. "Intermountain deserts, shrub steppes and woodlands." In *North American Vegetation,* ed. M. B. Barbour and W. D. Bill, pp. 209–30. Cambridge: Cambridge University Press, 1988.

Western Association of Fish and Game Agencies. "Prescribed fire as a management tool in xeric sagebrush ecosystems: Is it worth the risk to sage grouse?" White paper prepared by the Sage and Columbia Sharp-tailed Grouse Committee for the Western Association of Fish and Wildlife Agencies, 2009.

Western Association of Fish and Wildlife Agencies. *Habitat Guidelines for Mule Deer: Intermountain West Ecoregion.* Mule Deer Working Group, 2009.

Western Great Basin Coordination Center. *Living with Fire.* Sierra Front Interagency Dispatch Center, 2009. Online at Sierra Front.net/SierraFrontCoop/sierra_coop_index.htm.

Wigand, P. E., and P. J. Mehringer Jr. "Pollen and seed analysis." In *The Archaeology of Hidden Cave, Nevada,* ed. H. D. Thomas. *Anthropological Papers of the American Museum of Natural History* 61, no. 1 (1985).

Wigand, P. E., and C. L. Nowak. "Dynamics of Northwest Nevada plant communities during the last 30,000 years." In *The History of Water: Eastern Sierra Nevada, Owens Valley, White-Inyo Mountains,* ed. C. A. Hall Jr., V. D. Jones, and B. Widawski, pp. 40–62. White Mountain Research Station Symposium 4, 1982.

Wilhelm, Walt. *Last Rig to Battle Mountain.* New York: William Morrow, 1970.

Wilson, R. B. "Favorable report on the proposed Bruneau addition to Independence National Forest, Nevada." Typed report, 34 pp., in Humboldt-Toiyabe National Forest files, 1906.

Winward, A. H. "Fire in sagebrush ecosystems: The ecological setting." In *Rangeland Fire Effects, a Symposium, 1983,* ed. K. Sanders and J. Durham, pp. 2–6. USDI, Bureau of Land Management, Boise, Idaho, 1985.

———. "A renewed commitment to management of sagebrush grasslands." In *Management of the Sagebrush Steppe,* pp. 2–7. Special Report 880. Agricultural Experiment Station, Oregon State University, Corvallis, 1991.

Woods, C. N. "Memorandum for the district forester: Grazing inspection, Humboldt, Reports, 1915." Humboldt-Toiyabe National Forest files.

Woolley, H. E. "Favorable report on the proposed Santa Rosa National Forest, Nevada." Typed report, 13 pp., 1910, in Humboldt-Toiyabe National Forest files.

Work, J. *John Work's Field Journal: The Snake Country Expedition of 1830–31.* Ed. Francis D. Haines Jr. Norman: University of Oklahoma Press, 1971.

Workman, G. W., and J. B. Low, eds. *Mule Deer Decline in the West: A Symposium.* Utah State University College of Natural Resources, Utah Agricultural Experiment Station, Logan, 1976.

Wyman, S., D. W. Bailey, M. Borman, S. Cote, J. Eisner, W. Elmore, B. Leinard, S. Leonard, F. Reed, S. Swanson, L. Van Riper, T. Westfall, R. Wiley, and A. Winward. *Riparian Area Management: Grazing Management Processes and Strategies for Riparian-Wetland Areas.* Technical Reference 737-20, USDI, Bureau of Land Management, and USDA Forest Service, 2006.

Yager, J. P. "The Yager journals: Diary of a journey across the Plains." *Nevada Historical Society Quarterly* 13, no. 3 (1970).

Yoakum, J. D. "Influences of vegetation on pronghorn in the Intermountain West." *Pronghorn Workshop Proceedings* 22 (2006): 53–68.

———. "Relationships of pronghorn and livestock in the Great Basin: A review." In *Sustaining Rangeland Ecosystems Symposium,* pp. 170–75, 2006.

Young, J. A., and J. D. Budy. "Historical use of Nevada's pinyon-juniper woodlands." *Journal of Forest History* 23 (1979): 113–23.

Young, J. A., and C. D. Clements. *Cheatgrass.* Reno: University of Nevada Press, 2009.

———. "Nevada rangelands." In *Rangelands,* pp. 10–15. Denver: Society for Range Management, 2006.

Young, J. A., R. E. Eckert Jr., and R. A. Evans. "Historical perspective regarding the sagebrush ecosystem." In *Proceedings: The Sagebrush Ecosystem,* pp. 1–13. Logan: Utah State University Press, 1979.

Young, J. A., R. A. Evans, and P. T. Tueller. "Great Basin plant communities—pristine and grazed." In *Proceedings: Holocene Environmental Change in the Great Basin,* ed. R. Halston, 187–215. Nevada Archaeology Society Research Paper 3, Carson City, 1976.

Young, J. A., and A. B. Sparks. *Cattle on the Cold Desert.* Logan: Utah State University Press, 1985.

Index

Italic page numbers refer to illustrations